MUTINY

By the same author:

CRIMEA: THE WAR WITH RUSSIA
THE SAVAGE WARS: THE BRITISH
CONQUEST OF AFRICA

MUTINY

In the British and Commonwealth Forces,
1797–1956

LAWRENCE JAMES

BUCHAN & ENRIGHT, PUBLISHERS
LONDON

First published in 1987 by
Buchan & Enright, Publishers, Limited,
53 Fleet Street, London EC4Y 1BE

British Library Cataloguing in Publication Data

James, Lawrence, *1943-*
    Mutiny : in the British and Commonwealth forces 1797-1956
    1. Mutiny – History   2. Commonwealth of Nations –
    Armed Forces – History   3. Great Britain –
    Armed Forces – History
    I. Title
    355.1′334   UB787

    ISBN 0-907675-70-0

Photoset in 11/12pt Baskerville by
Derek Doyle & Associates, Mold, Clwyd
Printed and bound in Great Britain by
Biddles Ltd, Guildford

TO EDWARD AND HENRY

CONTENTS

ILLUSTRATIONS

Following page 148

The Nore Delegates (*British Museum*)
HMS *Sandwich* (*National Maritime Museum, Greenwich*)
Richard Parker (*BM*)
Flogging (*The Mansell Collection*)
HMS *Hermione* (*NMM*)
Viscount Bridport (*NMM*)
Recruiting poster, 1914 (*IWM*)
Military Police, 1917 (*IWM*)
Etaples Base Camp (*IWM*)
Looking for trouble (*IWM*)
Demob men from the RAF and Army (*Dr Charles Kightly*)
RAMC men setting off for demobilisation (*IWM*)
Slavo-British Legion camp (*IWM*)
Volunteers for the North Russian Rifles and Slavo-British Legion (*IWM*)
Bolshevik prisoners (*IWM*)
Notification of sentence of death (*S. Pollock/Leo Cooper*)
Private Jim Daly (*S. Pollock/Leo Cooper*)
Execution of Indian mutineers, Singapore, 1915 (*IWM*)
Chinese Labour Corps dockers, Boulogne, 1917 (*IWM*)
West Indian soldiers, France, 1918 (*IWM*)

MAPS (*Neil Hyslop*)

Main sites of mutinies: pp. x-xi
Mutinies in North Russia: p. 125

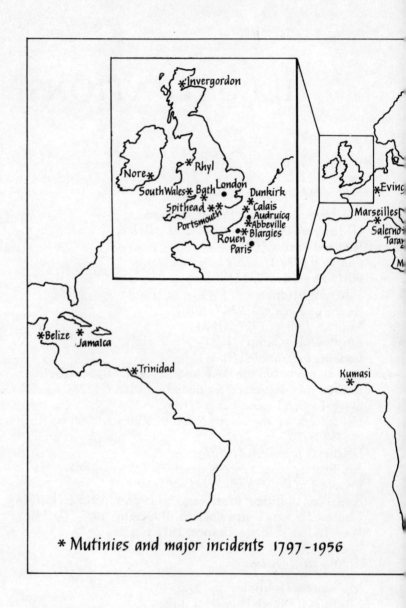

*Invergordon

Rhyl

Nore*

SouthWales* *Bath London   Dunkirk
Spithead* **   *Calais
Portsmouth   Audruicq
            *Abbeville
        Rouen *Blargies
        Paris

*Eving

Marseilles
Salerno
Tara

*Belize *
    Jamaica

*Trinidad   Kumasi
                            *

* Mutinies and major incidents 1797-1956

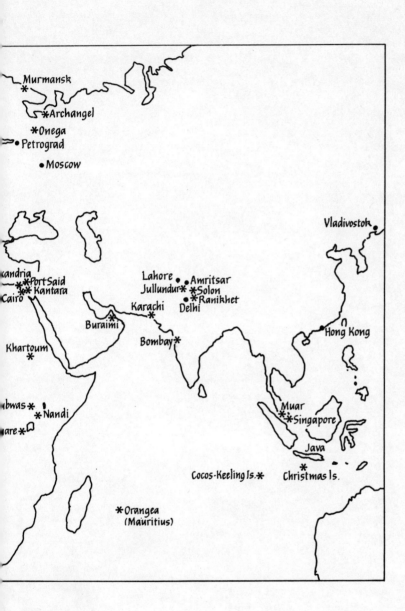

Murmansk
*Archangel
*Onega
• Petrograd
• Moscow

Vladivostok•

 andria
*Port Said
*Kantara
Cairo

Lahore
• Amritsar
Jullundur* *Solon
*Ranikhet
Karachi *
Delhi

Hong Kong•

Buraimi*

Bombay*

Khartoum
*

bwas *
*Nandi

are *

Muar
**Singapore

Java

Christmas Is.
*

Cocos-Keeling Is.*

*Orangea
(Mauritius)

ACKNOWLEDGEMENTS

I would like to thank Major Ewan Campbell, Martin Edmonds, Michael Ffinch, Lieutenant-Commander Carl Hallam, Mr Maurice Lumb, Captain John Metcalfe, RN, Mr A. Roberts, Mr Harry Roberts, Matthew Rogers, Reverend Richard Willcox, Andrew Williams, Vivian Williams, Percy Wood, Mr and Mrs David Vigar and Commander Rex Young RN for their advice, suggestions and criticisms, which have been invaluable in the writing this book. I would also like to extend special thanks to Mr Elwyn Edwards of the *Rhyl Journal*, Mr Sam Milligan, Mr G.J. Parry and Mr F. Wilkins for their assistance and information about the Rhyl Mutiny of 1919. I am also indebted to the kindness of the late General Sir Ouvry Roberts for answering many questions and making available records of his long and distinguished career. I would like to thank, too, those who gave me information privately.

I would also like to express my thanks to the staff of Harrogate Library, the British Museum, the National Army Museum, the Public Record Office and the Imperial War Museum for their kindness and help with my investigations.

Extracts from Crown Copyright material in the Public Record Office, London, appear by permission of the Controller of HM Stationery Office.

Above all, the understanding and support of my wife and family have been an invaluable element in this enterprise, together with the encouragement of Toby Buchan.

1

INTRODUCTION

The Indian Mutiny of 1857 and the great naval mutinies at Spithead and Invergordon are well known. Other mutinies are not widely heard of and a few remain all but unknown. Those which occurred during the recent World Wars were deliberately hushed up for the good reason that news of them would dishearten both civilians and fighting men as well as cheer the enemy. Peacetime mutinies could not be swept under the carpet and so they were often presented in ways which would contain or reduce public alarm. This was understandable, since at home and abroad symptoms of discontent and displays of disloyalty by British servicemen could be interpreted as indications of some deep national malaise. An ability to maintain public order, in the widest sense of the phrase, has become a yardstick by which a nation can be measured, and so recent disturbances in Britain have come to be interpreted as milestones along a road of national decline. This is strange since the period of British economic paramountcy during the last century was one marked by much, often grave, disorder in towns and cities.

Mutiny is, of course, a crime, and still one of the few which can be punished by death if committed in wartime and in circumstances likely to imperil the success of a campaign or operation. Over the past forty years mutiny has become an unfashionable crime, for, unlike others, its causes have been removed. The British armed services, whilst often unwilling to admit their mistakes, have always learned from them. There are some who would not consider mutiny a crime at all, either on the grounds of an ethical rejection of all military values, or because most mutineers merely exercised rights of protest and the withdrawal of labour which are permitted to civilians.

I have, at the beginning of this book, looked into the paradox by

3

which democratic and open societies, which offer a wide range of personal freedoms to their subjects, have been forced by practical necessity to withhold them from their servicemen. The debate over the irreconcilability of martial and naval efficiency with the extension of full civil rights to servicemen has raged for over a century and, in its time, has centred on flogging and the right of soldiers and sailors to write to their MPs. It broke out again recently, after revelations about the interrogation methods the RAF applied to a number of men serving in Cyprus and suspected of trafficking secrets with the Russians. Servicemen in the past have found the different standards of behaviour puzzling, and one feature of mutiny in the twentieth century has been the insistence, by some mutineers, that they were strikers and immune from punishment. After all, civilians who went on strike were not breaking the law.

'Mutiny', unlike 'strike', is an emotive word. In a sense it was an affront to the established social order which, whilst it prides itself on its liberties, still expects obedience from its servicemen. During this century, mutiny has acquired an added dimension since Britain has enjoyed a justifiable confidence and pride in its fighting services, so that mutiny amongst them, like cowardice, can be interpreted as a moral weakness. It is therefore a crime which is not much talked about, either by civilians or servicemen. For what I imagine is this reason, one private archive, held in Sunderland, refused me access to material concerning mutinies which occurred over sixty years ago. By contrast, other public and private archives have been generous and co-operative.

In practical terms, I have divided this book into two parts. In the first, I have examined mutinies amongst British forces, beginning with those in the Navy during the late eighteenth and early nineteenth centuries and passing on to those in the Army during the First World War, and later in Russia. I have concluded this section with accounts of naval and military mutinies between 1919 and 1946, and those by Irishmen who served in the Army and Navy, whose mutinies were inspired by the nationalist cause. In the second part of the book, I have looked at the mutinies by Indian and black soldiers, but have not dwelt on the Indian Mutiny which has been extensively covered elsewhere. In my investigation of all these mutinies, I have given special consideration to the military, social and political background, not so much to discover a pattern, but in an attempt to reveal the extent to which external factors not

4

only contributed to the uprisings but shaped them. In brief, I have tried to place mutinies in their rightful historical rather than military context.

Given that mutinies are an emotional subject, and have been extensively examined for evidence of class war, I have, where possible, made an effort to avoid taking sides. Human folly and mendacity can safely be left to speak for themselves, but, at times, I have endeavoured to draw some attention to the position of those who wielded authority and the problems they faced. They too require understanding as much as the underdog who more easily commands sympathy, since his ideas have often become today's orthodoxy.

Harrogate, February 1987

ORDERS ARE ORDERS

He had no warning of what was to come, and was
already well among the hospitals and dumps that
extended for miles beside the railway, when a military
policeman held up a warning hand.
   'What's the matter, Corporal?'
   'I should not go into Etapps this morning, if I were
you, sir.'
   'Why not?'
   The man shifted his glance. He did not like the job
evidently.
   'Funny goings-on, there, sir.'
   'Goings-on, what does that mean?'
   Dormer was capable of quite a good rasp of the throat,
when required. He had learned it as a Corporal.
   'The men are out of 'and, sir!'
R.H. Mottram, The Spanish Farm Trilogy

'Funny goings-on' and 'The men are out of 'and' added up to one
thing – mutiny. The fictional military policeman describing what
actually happened at Etaples in September 1917 clearly found it
hard to say the word. Mutiny was an emotive and frightening word,
especially for a soldier whose duty it was to uphold discipline and
obedience to authority. Along with cowardice in the face of the
enemy, mutiny was the most shameful military crime. It had
always been so. When, in May 1797, nine ships of Admiral
Duncan's squadron mutinied and refused to sail with him to their
station off the Dutch coast, their commander wrote in despair, 'To
be deserted by my fleet in the face of the enemy is a disgrace which,
I believe, never before happened to a British admiral, nor could I
have supposed it possible'.[1] Men tainted with mutiny also felt
shame. After two companies of his battalion had mutinied in
Singapore, the Subahdar-Major of the Fifth Light Infantry claimed

that the loyal men were determined 'to wipe out the past and prove to the King Emperor that they were worthy of the confidence that had been placed in them'. The sepoys hoped that they would soon get the chance to prove their worth by 'deeds of daring against the enemy'.[2] Four years later, in 1919, all mention of the deeds of the 6th Battalion of the Royal Marine Light Infantry was excised from the official despatches of the North Russian campaign because it had mutinied and refused to go into action against the Bolsheviks.[3]

All this was, in a sense, official odium, since it emanated from officers and war ministries. The view from below was often quite different, particularly in recent times. During August and September 1946, 258 men from the 13th Battalion, the Parachute Regiment faced a court martial for mutiny. On the morning of 14 May they had congregated on a sea-wall at the edge of their camp in Malaya and refused to budge, claiming that they were demonstrating against the wretchedness of their accommodation. At 3.30 in the afternoon, a divisional general addressed them and warned them that they were committing the very serious offence of mutiny. He commanded them to fall in, which they refused to do; then their colonel repeated the caution about mutiny. The response was some shuffling and a few derisive whistles. Another officer wondered whether any of them had really understood what had been said to them that afternoon. 'These men whose education for the most part finished at fourteen years of age,' he argued, were ill-equipped to appreciate that their protest was a mutiny. If they had any ideas of what a mutiny was, they would surely have been based on newspaper reports of the recent disturbances by sailors of the Royal Indian Navy at Calcutta, Bombay and Madras, which ended in bloodshed, or else the bloodily suppressed prison 'mutiny' which had just occurred on Alcatraz Island, off the Californian coast. Both were far removed in tenor and consequences from the good-natured demonstration of the paratroopers, who saw nothing wrong in what they were doing. They were standing up for their rights and this view was upheld by the public and by the Labour government which quashed all their sentences.[4] Soon after, in November 1946, a newly elected Labour MP, James Callaghan, assured an audience of members of the National Council for Civil Liberties, that 'there is no reason why service men who have a collective grievance or a collective request should not represent it collectively'.[5]

A similar kind of civilian attitude to mutiny was widely expressed in the United States during the late 1960s, when drafted men were demanding to be allowed all their rights as American citizens whilst they were in the services. These included unions to negotiate over conditions, freedom to attend anti-Vietnam war rallies and to produce news-sheets crammed full of material hostile to the government and its military authorities. Much to their astonishment, convicts at the army prison stockade at Presidio near San Francisco found themselves charged with mutiny, and facing the death sentence, after they had demonstrated against conditions in the camp and the government's policies in Vietnam.[6] Black Muslims, the editors of underground newspapers, men who refused to train troops for Vietnam and others who openly voiced opinions against the war all found themselves prosecuted – much to their indignation and that of their supporters outside the barracks. The hubbub was so great that in 1969 the Adjutant-General advised a relaxation of discipline over 'dissent', a suggestion which enraged the Senate Armed Forces Committee.[7] For once, civilians demanded the astringent enforcement of military law.

The paratroopers who mutinied in Malaya in 1946, like the American draftees of the late 1960s, were civilians who had been conscripted into the services and, once there, continued to think that in some ways they could continue to behave as if they were still civilians. Walking out from a factory where conditions had become intolerable and demonstrating against government policies were permissible in civilian life, but in the services they were mutiny, a grave and dishonourable crime. Even regular servicemen, who were in theory possessed of a greater understanding of discipline, could become confused. After the 1931 Invergordon mutiny, an officer observed that 'The average sailor thinks of a mutiny as action against his officers, of riots in which officers are murdered and thrown overboard.' To support this contention, he quoted a sailor who had claimed, 'We were not disloyal or mutinying but fighting for our rights.' Another seaman was less reticent about the word mutiny but interpreted his behaviour in civilian terms: 'The mutiny was a spontaneous, commonsense form of strike action.'[8]

The embarrassed Admiralty was uneasy about the word 'mutiny', and official statements about what was taking place at Invergordon referred to 'unrest', 'disaffection' and 'collective action', words designed to calm the public which were repeated in some newspapers and by the BBC. The ultra-conservative *Morning Post* rejected this pussy-footing and announced: 'To use plain

9

language, which is not fashionable nowadays, they committed a mutiny.' The public tended to agree. Twelve thousand sailors refusing to do what their officers told them to do was a mutiny and the incident was known then and after as the Invergordon mutiny.

The public was correct, for all the codes of naval and military law left no doubt as to the fact that men who collectively disobeyed orders committed mutiny. 'Collective insubordination, or a combination of two or more persons to resist or to induce others to resist lawful military authority' defined mutiny in the 1879 Army Discipline and Regulation Act. Its terms were much the same as those of the naval disciplinary legislation of the 1860s and would have been recognisable to soldiers and sailors in earlier periods. The letter of the law remains the same today. Mutiny was a serious crime and the worst offenders were liable to the death penalty. This was passed for the last time on five Sikhs who had mutinied and murdered their officers when the Japanese invaded Christmas Island.[9] They were taken prisoner after the war, but their death sentences were commuted to penal servitude for life in December 1946. The last mutineers to be executed were three Sinhalese artillerymen who were hanged at Colombo in August 1942 for a mutiny in which one man died.

The legal regulations of the Royal Navy and the Army were not drawn up to safeguard the rights of men in the services; they were designed to define and enhance discipline. To function efficiently, units of the Army and Navy required cohesion, and this could only be obtained through a chain of command. Fighting efficiency depended upon immediate and unquestioning obedience to orders. Collective loyalty was to ship, battalion or squadron, and complaint always had to be made by an individual to his superior and could only be handled within the structure of the service.

The serviceman was a different creature from the civilian, for he existed within a complex and rigid hierarchy, had to obey orders and, for these reasons, could not expect to enjoy fully the rights possessed by civilians. He could not demand trial by his peers. Many of his misdemeanours were summarily tried by his superior officers, and his major crimes were judged by a court martial in which a handful of officers heard the evidence, assessed it and passed sentence. Serious cases could be passed to higher authorities, even the Secretary for War or the Board of Admiralty. Complaints about service life had to be made to an immediate superior, or, if they concerned that officer, to his senior.

Anonymous complaints were illegal as was 'any other method of obtaining redress for grievance real or imaginary', which ruled out combinations and petitions. A private of a Lancashire regiment who wrote an anonymous letter to a newspaper in which he criticised his officers was sentenced to six months by a court martial in South Africa in 1901. When, in 1929, a rating from HMS *Repulse* wrote to his MP and complained about arrangements for his leave, he was traced and given 28 days' detention.[10]

Conversations among servicemen in which they commented on their superiors' conduct were forbidden, and they were banned from holding meetings for any political cause in or close to barracks and camps. Any who attended such gatherings had to do so in mufti, and sailors who used the facilities of Speakers' Corner during the 1920s were liable to arrest by a naval patrol which stood by in Hyde Park for the purpose. Disloyal or insulting words about the royal family, a serviceman's ship or regiment or his officers were punishable. A private of the Seaforths who spoke abusively about his regiment was given twelve months in 1901, but the coarse nature of an Irish soldier's remarks about Queen Victoria in 1900 were thought to be too much for Her Majesty so his sentence was not passed to her for confirmation.[11] In the United States' forces the same prohibition obtained. In 1925 a soldier was convicted for expressing the view that President Coolidge 'may be all right as an individual but as an institution he is a disgrace to the whole Goddam country', and in 1945 an officer was given two years for remarking that Roosevelt was 'a son-of-a-bitch'.[12] However ill-informed and offensive, civilians both in Britain and the United States were allowed such outbursts.

Naval and military necessity alone dictated such rules. Questioning and backbiting, whether collective or individual, damaged the morale and effectiveness of a unit if they remained unchecked. The argument is timeless. In the late 1960s Chief Justice Warren of the United States Supreme Court vindicated military necessity as the justification for enforcing absolute conformity, good order and discipline amongst all American servicemen. They could never expect the civil rights and legal privileges of United States citizenship whilst they were in uniform. The same was largely true in Britain where, even in the 1960s, many men serving with a Highland regiment were convinced that whilst in the Army they possessed no rights.[13] The everyday expression 'You're in the Army now' was both answer and

11

explanation for those who wanted to speak out against what they considered mistreatment. It had always been the same. In 1911 a sailor father advised his son, 'You mustn't even speak up for yourself when you're put upon and in the right. Just you mind that. You'll be a marked man if you do. The way to get on in the Navy is to lie low, whatever happens, and jog along quiet, and take what comes, glad that it isn't no worse.' During the Second World War an American serviceman soon learned the value of quietism. 'My first month down here I was allowed to give my opinion on one occasion. I was then told to shut up by our top kick. I try to keep suggestions to myself now and just take orders.'[14] That, in essence, was what military and naval law was about.

Like all forms of human nonconformity, mutinies were eccentric. They do not fall very neatly into categories but certain patterns can be discerned as to timing, objectives and organisation. Since the adjustment to a world of compliance and quietism was never easy for the masses of civilians unwillingly conscripted during periods of national crisis, mutinies became more frequent during world wars. The rash of naval mutinies between 1797 and 1801 coincided with a vast influx of men drafted as part of the war effort against Revolutionary France. The flickering unrest and mutinies in the Navy and Army between 1917 and 1920 were likewise a reflection of the disgruntlement felt by many of the men dragooned into the services by the Conscription Acts of 1916 and 1918. The Second World War was an exception to this rule, for unrest was less marked; this was thanks to the willingness of the services to pay more attention to keeping up morale and to seek and use the suggestions of psychiatrists in order to discover men who were mentally unfitted for soldiering. Once detected, such men were removed from the forces and with them sources of discontent and inefficiency.

In the minds of the public, which included the anonymous sailor from Invergordon, mutiny was always associated with the *Bounty*. The overthrow of officers and seizure of ships was in fact mass desertion and it was a form of mutiny which was alarmingly frequent in the late eighteenth and early nineteenth centuries. The vogue for this kind of mutiny was started in 1778 when the crew of the cutter *Jackal*, who were for the most part former Irish smugglers for whom naval service was an alternative to prison, took over their vessel and sailed it across the Channel to Calais, where they offered themselves as volunteers to the French navy.[15] Their example was copied by the *Bounty*'s crew in 1787, who, after the expulsion of their overbearing Captain Bligh, sought anonymity in the remote islands of the South Pacific. In this case and those of the *Hermione* (1797) and *Ferret* (1806) the strict regime of the vessels' captains served as the provocation for mutiny. These were more or less spontaneous uprisings in which a small knot of desperate men took reprisals for the wrongs they had suffered. Having secured the satisfaction of revenge, the mutineers had no choice but to seek sanctuary with either the French or the Spaniards, as, since the *Bounty* incident, the Royal Navy had been painstaking in tracking down such mutineers and bringing them to trial. Similar enterprises were planned by some of the crews of larger ships, but they met with no success.

Most mutinies were, by contrast, more humdrum affairs. They were protests by servicemen who felt that their sufferings had become so unbearable that only the last resort of collective action could achieve relief. Such mutineers believed that they were justified by natural justice and that this, coupled with the seriousness of their complaints, outweighed all the forms of naval and military law which they were breaking. Complaints were invariably confined to injuries which had their causes in the everyday routine of service life. Overwork, unpalatable or inadequate rations, the removal of privileges, the imposition of new burdens, uncomfortable accommodation, heartless officers and NCOs, vindictive and excessive punishments, low wages and, in earlier periods, slowness in their payment, were the commonest sources of discontent and mutiny. Behind mutinies for such causes was the implication that officers had broken their word or else had been indifferent towards their men's well-being. The apparent triviality of a mutiny's cause often bore little relation to its scale or seriousness. One party of men voicing their grudges about some petty matter often stimulated others to join in and call attention to other sources of annoyance. The first challenge to authority, if successful, opened the way to others. In modern times the possibility that mutineers and their grievances would receive attention in the press and Parliament made mutinous demonstrations a means to publicise a cause.

The stage for this kind of mutiny was a public place where servicemen normally gathered. Parade grounds, other ranks' messes, canteens and even hospital wards where men could

13

assemble legally were the natural starting places for mutiny. Here, the affront to authority by a few could be seen by many, some or all of whom might be encouraged to follow suit. The mutiny aboard the submarine depot ship, *Lucia*, in January 1931 began when men refused to leave the mess deck (where presumably they had talked about their grievances and possible action), and impromptu meetings in canteens were the prelude to the stokers' mutiny at Portsmouth in 1906, the Invergordon mutiny, and that of the paratroopers in 1946.[16] Barrack-hut discussions must have led to the refusal to parade of C Company of the 2nd Battalion of the Machine Gun Corps at Evinghoven in Germany as a protest against extended working hours in June 1919.[17] Conversations about conditions between VD patients confined in 51 General Hospital in northern France in August 1918 may have sparked off the disturbances there. Certainly, the Commander-in-Chief of the British Expeditionary Force, Lord Haig, was anxious that British servicemen in hospitals were not to be exposed to the mutinous grousings of Australian fellow patients.[18]

The development and outcome of this kind of mutiny depended upon the immediate reactions of the mutineers' commanders. If misinterpreted or mishandled, small protests about minor matters could grow alarmingly, and culminate in uncontrollable and even violent demonstrations. Responses which fell back on an arid interpretation of military and naval law, or were over-zealous, inflamed tempers and created fresh sources of discontent. In May 1810 the local volunteers serving with the West Mendip Militia refused to obey their officers after they had discovered that a guinea was to be deducted from their pay to meet the costs of their trousers. The spokesmen were immediately arrested and locked up in Bath gaol, which so incensed the militiamen that they stormed the prison. West Country solidarity provoked another mutiny in 1810 which grew out of a minor incident. An insubordinate sergeant of the Wiltshire Militia had been confined in the guardhouse, and efforts to rescue him were frustrated by the arrival of the local Yeoman cavalry, summoned by an alarmed colonel. Challenged, the militiamen primed their muskets and an exchange of fire was only prevented by the good sense of the sergeant who called on his brothers-in-arms to lay down their weapons, which they did. In much the same way, soldiers at the Etaples base camp tried to retake a comrade who had been detained by the Military Police in September 1917. A military policeman panicked and shot dead a man and so triggered a formidable mutiny by thousands of men which lasted for a week.

West Country volunteers, and servicemen on the Western Front, were mainly civilians in arms and, in so far as they gave any thought to the matter, may well have believed that they were fighting or training to preserve their rights as British subjects. In uniform, they thought that they could behave as if they still possessed these rights and could therefore speak up for themselves. This assumption was most apparent during 1919 when men whom their officers deemed to be mutineers thought of themselves as strikers and demanded to bargain with their generals as if they had been peacetime employers. In 1944 there was another spillage from the world of civilian protest when Canadian soldiers started a 'hunger strike' to secure the removal of an officer whose discipline they found too strict.[19]

There was always a close relationship between the form taken by a mutiny and the methods of protest then current in civilian life. The attacks on officers and seizures of men-o'-war during the French wars were a part of a wider form of underdog resistance. Sailors were adapting the tradition of purblind insurrection which flourished from the 1760s to the 1840s. In these years urban mobs broke the windows of unpopular politicians and pelted their carriages; in the new industrial districts Luddites assailed mills and factories and broke the machines which were edging them out of their livelihoods, and in the countryside farm labourers menaced Poor Law functionaries, destroyed newfangled machinery and burned the hayricks of hard-fisted farmers. The protesters were always angry and, having sated their ire, they dispersed, fearful of detection and punishment. Like the sailors who murdered their officers and handed their ships over to their country's enemies, the mobs could only hurt but not alter the system which ill-used them.

Those servicemen who tried to rescue comrades who had been singled out for punishment after collective action also had their civilian counterparts. In 1819 Bradford-upon-Avon weavers tore the thatched roof from the local lock-up to save colleagues who had been arrested after a riot, and in 1831 a small army of Denbigh miners threatened to march on Shrewsbury and break open the gaol where some of their colleagues were being held.

Just as the methods of contemporary political protest influenced the form taken by mutinies, so did political ideas. The soldier and sailor were expected to be publicly apolitical. Military and naval

15

law discouraged servicemen from taking part in political agitation, and the expression of political views was circumscribed. Yet soldiers were expected to take a part in political life as part of their duty, for successive late eighteenth- and early ninteenth-century governments relied heavily upon regular and part-time forces to prevent and, if necessary, overcome popular disturbances. This meant that infantrymen might be commanded to fire on mobs and cavalrymen charge them. Habits of discipline were expected to carry more weight than any private feelings and there were occasionally times when the struggle was almost unbearable. Benjamin Miller, a gunner with the Gibraltar garrison, was ordered in December 1802 to turn his cannon on mutineers who had recently been his brothers-in-arms during the recent Egyptian campaign. It was a melancholy duty.[20]

> This was a horrid Christmas, for the night after Christmas, we were formed up against another regiment who broke out in rebellion, and killed many of them. I was at a gun that was formed up close in front of them and expected every man of us would have been put to death, our guns were loaded and matches lighted. They frequently cried out 'Charge the Bugars', 'Fire a volley at the Bugars'. I was more afraid than ever I was fighting against the French and we found it more dangerous to fight against exasperated British soldiers standing for their rights.

No such heart-searching troubled soldiers called on to handle civil disorders between the 1790s and 1840s. Whatever political sympathies the soldiers had were put on one side, although in 1795 some militiamen refused to suppress bread riots. Their reaction was perhaps borne of the knowledge that, once they had completed their stint of service, they would have to share the civilians' plight of high prices and shortages. A similar sense of a common cause lay behind the mutiny of the 2nd Battalion, Royal Fleet Reserve, in April 1921.[21] They refused to fall in and undertake duties guarding South Wales pits during the coal strike on the grounds that they were nearly all trade-unionists themselves. They also insisted that they would throw down their rifles if called upon to use them against the miners, and some bold spirits hauled down the White Ensign and replaced it by a Red Flag.

A mutiny of this kind had always been the dream of radical and socialist politicians and the nightmare of governments. During the

1797 Nore mutiny, when Parliament feared an alliance between the mutineers and political extremists, the Incitement to Mutiny Act was passed. It aimed to punish severely civilian agitators found guilty of subverting the loyalty of servicemen and was strengthened in 1934 by the Incitement to Disaffection Act, which was designed to frustrate efforts by the Communist Party to procure members in the armed services. On the whole, such safeguards against political agitators fomenting mutiny were not needed. Joseph Hume's belief that the troops would not fire on crowds agitating for Parliamentary reform between 1830 and 1832 was exposed as naive by the events at Bristol, Nottingham and Exeter. Likewise, the insistence by some Chartists that many soldiers sympathised with their cause and would not fire on their demonstrations was shown to be groundless by the 93rd Highlanders, who had no qualms about shooting the insurgents at Newport in 1839. Indeed, the men had to be restrained from firing before their officer had given the order. The villagers of Sussex had no such illusions, for it was noticed how they shrank from soldiers in the years after the suppression of the Swing riots.

Still, officers were alarmed about the prospects of political mutiny, and in 1832 severe measures were taken after troopers of the Royal Scots Greys had become infected with popular radicalism. The regiment had been drafted to Birmingham, where forceful public protests were expected once the Reform Bill had been scotched by the Lords. Alexander Somerville and a handful of better-educated men discussed the business and contrived a handbill and letters to newspapers in which they claimed that the Greys 'were not to be depended upon to put down public meetings or preventing the people of Birmingham from journeying to London to present their petitions'. They insisted that their duties as soldiers could never embrace the frustration of the will of the public which clearly favoured reform. This was wormwood to the Greys' officers, who made investigations about the authorship of the anonymous threats. When Somerville was examined by Major Wyndham, the adjutant, the latter's suspicions were aroused by the trooper's assertion that his oath of loyalty was first to the people and then to William IV. Wyndham, who considered all political unions a form of treason, may well have been behind Somerville's subsequent flogging for another military offence. Somerville and the radicals sensed victimisation and made a great fuss; yet, Somerville later admitted that most of his fellow cavalrymen were

17

'brutish and intellectually blank', which arouses speculation as to what, if anything, they made of his opinions and behaviour.[22]

Political radicalism which questioned subordination in civil society was naturally anathema to men concerned with the maintenance of military discipline. Socialism too was seen as containing the seeds of mutinous conduct, and its spread amongst sailors during the 1900s caused much anger and alarm. According to one Sea Lord, the mutiny on board the *Leviathan* in 1910 had little to do with grievances over conditions, but was the result of 'mischievous socialistic literature', which showed men 'how to be insubordinate without breaking the law'.[23] What the admiral had in mind was the growth of lower-deck societies – which, like their equivalents in civilian life, were conceived to offer mutual benefits to their members – and the appearance of magazines like *The Fleet*, which were written for men on the lower decks, and often printed their grievances or exposed the injustices which they suffered.

The literature which dismayed naval officers at the beginning of the century was not so much converting sailors to socialism, but encouraging them to think of themselves as workers and to behave like them in respect of their rights. It seemed to be extending the boundaries of trade unionism into the armed services, a movement which if unchecked would make the mutinous sailor think of himself as a striker and of mutiny merely as the collective pursuit of what passed for justice. This was an alarming development which seemed to undermine the basis of traditional discipline, and it was fiercely resisted.

There were other political dimensions to mutinies. Since the eighteenth century the Army and the Navy had recruited men from Ireland, and it was inevitable that many Irishmen came to the forces with a commitment to the nationalist cause. Their value to this cause had been soon recognised by Wolfe Tone and other United Irishmen exiled in Paris in 1793 and they made the most of the opportunity. Between 1798 and 1800 Irishmen serving with the Navy mutinied in the hope that they could take control of their ships and sail them to French ports or else employ them to help their fellow rebels in Ireland. None of these often harebrained schemes had any success, and efforts to subvert the loyalty of Irish soldiers stationed in Ireland during the Fenian troubles of 1865-6 also met with disappointing results. Equally fruitless were the clumsy efforts of Roger Casement to canvass Irish POWs in German camps in 1914-5, although in 1916 there was an outburst of spontaneous unrest amongst Irishmen serving with the small Royal Navy armoured car squadron in North Russia after they heard of the Easter Rising in Dublin. More formidable in its seriousness and dedication to the nationalist cause was the mutiny of the Connaught Rangers in Northern India in 1920. The mutineers demanded the end of British occupation of Ireland, but they were isolated and soon suppressed by loyal troops from British regiments.

Only once did British soldiers refuse to obey orders in protest against the war in which they were fighting. The mutinies amongst soldiers and sailors serving in the Baltic and North Russia during 1919 were largely political, in that the men involved doubted the rightness of their cause and the attitude of the government which had committed them to campaign in an undeclared war. Russian troops, enlisted to fight with the British, were even less sure and at least 4,000 mutinied or deserted to the enemy, sometimes murdering their officers. Many of those involved were soldiers and sailors who were anxious for demobilisation and feared that delays might jeopardise their chances of getting work in an overcrowded labour market. There was much grumbling, obstruction, and even strikes amongst the men from garrisons in Mesopotamia and India who found that their demobilisation was held back in 1919 on the outbreak of the Third Afghan War. None had any objection to frontier defence, but they thought it of secondary importance to the obtainment of jobs in Britain.

Mutinies were not entirely confined to other ranks. During the spring of 1914 officers serving with cavalry units in southern Ireland made it publicly clear that they would resign their commissions rather than obey orders to proceed north and engage the Ulster volunteers. For some time the Ulstermen had been arming and drilling to resist the imposition of Home Rule, which was due to become law in the autumn of 1914. This resistance was publicly encouraged by various Tory politicians and their arguments were endorsed by army officers and some naval officers serving with warships which were stationed off Lamlash, on the Isle of Arran.[24] This ripple of unease which had started amongst Tory cavalrymen at the Curragh camp was given the mistaken name of the Curragh mutiny, although it was nothing of the kind. Officers were merely giving notice that they would use their right to resign rather than be placed in a position where they might have to obey commands which they considered morally wrong. There were

19

rumours that something of this kind may have occurred in 1964, just after Rhodesia declared independence. Soon after there were tales that senior officers preferred resignation to having to command any forces which might have been sent to suppress what Harold Wilson's government considered a rebellion. They have never been confirmed or strenuously denied.

No anatomy of mutiny would be complete without reference to the mutinies amongst the native forces raised by Britain to defend and extend the frontiers of Empire and police Imperial subjects in Africa and Asia. Like British troops, Indians and Africans were also sometimes the victims of unfairness, broken promises and inconveniences, and they mutinied in the same way. The mutinies of Sudanese askari in Uganda in 1898 and West Africans at Kumasi in 1900 were much like those of British forces faced with mistreatment. In microcosm, both had features in common with the Indian Mutiny of 1857-8 which was the largest and most devastating by troops of the Crown. In essence, this mutiny was a negative movement in which objectives were confined to the restoration of former conditions. The re-enthronement of the Mughal emperor, a lacklustre figurehead, and the reinstatement of dispossessed native princes, was a sterile political programme which offered little to the mass of Indians who remained aloof from what was, in the end, a localised revolt. Even the usually volatile and fanatically Muslim Pathans of the North-West Frontier refused to have any part in the Mutiny and a few actually joined the Anglo-Indian forces which suppressed it.

In terms of other mutinies, the Indian created a nervous awareness by many commanders that native troops had to be carefully supervised and any signs of trouble had to be dealt with swiftly and firmly. On campaign, native troops had to be supported by a smaller proportion of British regulars so that even in the late 1930s and 1940s forces on the North-West Frontier had to have their more or less regulation percentage of British battalions. There have been a few attempts to represent the Indian Mutiny as a nationalist movement but they have floundered for lack of evidence. The rebellious sepoys in 1857 were united more by what they disliked rather than any clear idea of what they wanted in its place.

Nationalism as an ingredient in mutiny has been a twentieth-century phenomenon, a side product of modern movements whose leadership has been civilian. The mutineers of the 5th Light Infantry in Singapore in 1915 were influenced by Pan-Islamic propaganda put out by Turco-German sources, and the Sudanese who mutinied in Khartoum in 1924 were convinced that the Sudan should stay under Egyptian control. Hostility to Europeans and rather vague nationalist and pro-Japanese feelings agitated the leader of the Sinhalese mutineers on the Cocos-Keeling Islands in 1942, but he had no other nationalist connections.[25] The mutiny by ratings of the Royal Indian Navy in February 1946 was something which the Indian nationalist leadership could have done without. They were just about to get all that they wanted and did not want the embarrassment and distraction of bloody battles on the quaysides of naval bases. Indian socialists and communists looked on the matter differently and thought that they might have an embryonic revolution on their doorstep. Their exploitation of the sailors' grievances, which had hitherto been confined to service matters, yielded nothing, for the British authorities were determined to break the mutiny.[26]

Just as the form of mutinies and the methods of mutineers varied, so did the official reaction. Before 1914 the Royal Navy passed off mutinies as 'regrettable incidents' since the hint of mutiny would tarnish the national and international reputation of the world's greatest navy. It was usually considered wise to underplay any political dimension in a mutiny since the suggestion that the defenders of the state were hostile to it, or aimed at its overthrow, was bound to generate public alarm. The 1797 Nore mutiny and the Invergordon mutiny had a detrimental effect on the prices of government stocks and the value of the pound. Where the cause of unrest had to be spelled out, it was done so in terms of purely service grievances, which was not always the case. The 1915 Singapore mutiny, and the refusal to perform crowd-control duties by a detachment of Garwhalis in Peshawar in 1930, were publicly explained as the consequence of regimental problems. Yet the Garwhali ringleader on his release from gaol became an active Indian nationalist and the Singapore men's trials had revealed that they were infected with pro-Turkish sentiments.[27]

If an explanation for mutiny had to be made, it was best not to ascribe to soldiers and sailors any thoughts about matters beyond their barracks or ships. They were not, after all, expected to have too many. The agitator, either infiltrated into the Army or Navy, or working on their fringes, was a convenient creature to take the blame for unrest and mutiny. The 1797 mutinies were blamed by Pitt's government on home-grown Jacobin sympathisers and their

21

allies, French agents. Between 1900 and 1939 the Navy looked to socialist and Communist agitators and their printed propaganda as the reason for lower-deck insubordination, and from 1917 the Intelligence Services did what they could to seek out agitators who were disturbing soldiers and sailors. Such men were not always imaginary spectres haunting the minds of commanders and war ministers; they did exist and so did the material they produced to encourage mutiny, both in the 1790s and in 1919. Yet the official mind in its obsession with hidden hands behind mutinies always assumed that the ordinary soldiers and sailors were somehow incapable of making up their own minds or thinking for themselves about matters which affected their daily lives.

For the men who ruled armies and navies, mutinies represented disgrace and failure. The military and naval virtues of quietism, submission and devotion to duty had not been properly instilled into fighting men, and their officers had therefore been remiss or incompetent. Such shortcomings had to be punished and measures put in hand to stop further trouble. There had to be scapegoats, both amongst those who had defied authority and those whose duty it had been to exercise that authority. For most mutineers the consequence of his crime was punishment, for, if he and his activities were ignored, discipline would wither away and command would become impossible. Officers could be censured or dismissed and, where actual responsibility was hard to pin down precisely, black marks would appear on files and promotion would be delayed. Above all, public faith in the armed forces had to be restored.

From the eighteenth century onwards, the British public was proud of its soldiers and sailors, at least in the abstract. They were the guarantee 'That Britons never, never shall be slaves' and 'That Britons shall conquer again and again'. Patriot lyricists also likened soldiers to the warrior heroes of the classical past, they were 'Hectors' and 'Alexanders' on the battlefields of Europe, the New World and India. In the more prosaic language of the newspapers, standard expressions such as 'brave fellows' and 'steadiness and gallantry' spelled out the special courage of Britain's fighting men. In 1801 Nelson wrote warmly of the 'zeal and ardent desire to distinguish themselves by an attack on the enemy' which inflamed his captains and men. Much the same was written about soldiers and sailors in the Crimea, during the many colonial wars of the nineteenth century and both World Wars. Everyone was aware that the everyday existence of the serviceman was often wretched, even degrading, but what Dr Johnson called 'the dignity of danger' gave honour to the profession of arms and its followers. As he subsequently remarked, those men who had not served in arms on land or sea felt themselves the less for this omission.

These were not empty phrases or bogus sentiments. Many men who served in the ranks during the Napoleonic Wars and later were moved by a genuine love of their country and pride in a calling which offered them adventure and honour. Tales of glory from the lips of a crippled veteran of Abercromby's Egyptian campaign stirred Rifleman Costello to enlist in 1806, and the exhortation to 'Young fellows whose hearts beat high to tread the paths of Glory' was presumably written on the recruiting poster for the 7th Hussars in the knowledge that it would excite some positive response. The over-exposed commonplace that the Army and the Navy were crowded with Dr Johnson's scoundrels whom nature and circumstance made incapable of earning an honest penny is untrue. Able, intelligent men, out of fortune or bored with a humdrum life, were drawn into the forces where they were convinced that they could find adventure and advancement. 'The determination ... to be a meritorious soldier, and, by good conduct, rise above the ranks' inspired Alexander Somerville in 1831, and many others, before and after.[28]

In daily life, the public was aware of another kind of serviceman whose habits were all too conspicuous. He was a disorderly fellow who drank too much, as did most of the class he came from, and his antics were often a source of annoyance to the respectable. In November 1804 Trooper Cartwright of the 7th Hussars walked out from his billet at the Three Tuns in Winchester at three in the afternoon and returned eight hours later with a 'woman of the town' whom he took to his room. He climbed the stairs noisily, being, at his own admission, 'in liquor', and woke the landlord, who, on seeing the girl on the stairs ordered her out. This was not what Cartwright had in mind and so he cursed the landlord and set about him with his fists.[29] A court martial gave him 200 lashes.

Given that the armed services took many men who were feckless, living on the margins of crimes, under a burden of debts or were unable to make a regular living, military punishments often exceeded in ferocity those handed out by the civil justices. Men of what was termed unsound character were accepted by the services for want of better and because they could, if disciplined, be of benefit to their ship or regiment and therefore the country. They were not in uniform to be regenerated or reformed, but to serve, and this meant that they had to be trained in habits of unquestioning obedience to their officers and NCOs and to understand the value of corporate loyalty. Such behaviour did not come easily, and since insubordination and desertion remained the commonest military and naval crimes during the nineteenth century, resistance to training must have been frequent. Coercive rules and stiff punishments were therefore considered essential for the Army and Navy, for success on the battlefield depended upon discipline and cohesion.

Men who served with the forces expected such treatment. They had withdrawn from civilian life and accepted another with different customs and values. The right attitude was one of quietist compliance in the face of misfortune and inconvenience. Alexander Wood of the 42nd Highlanders, serving in the Crimea in 1855, summed up what was the correct state of mind for the serviceman. 'I can see that some soldiers send home false statements or at least gross exaggerations of the life we live, he is no true soldier who tries to makes things look worse than they really are ... but there are discontented men in all classes of men, and the army is no exception to the rule.'[30] By contrast many of his officers were expressing open disaffection, and many malcontents were writing to the newspapers with accounts of suffering and implied criticism of their superiors.

Stoic patience in the face of adversity was not universal. One soldier, who volunteered in 1847, refused to succumb to a sheeplike passivity when faced with orders he considered degrading. Asked by an officer's servant girl to clean cutlery and boots, he refused. 'In a moment my metal was up and I said you can tell your Master, whoever he is, I did not enlist to turn Shoe black.' His stubbornness was reported to the officer who told him that 'the first duty of the soldier is Obedience'. The blunt reply – 'cleaning Boots, knives, Spoons and forks is not a Soldier's duty' – went unreproved and the young soldier shortly discovered that others had done these tasks without complaint.[31] Later, other soldiers also showed a marked distaste for domestic chores. During the Second World War Australian infantrymen were reluctant to become officers' servants, and during the 1950s the press made a fuss about national servicemen being ordered to do housework for officers' wives.

A boundary existed in the minds of some servicemen beyond which obedience became slavishness. At the turn of the century it was unofficial but common practice for officers in naval training depots to punish summarily minor offenders by ordering them to go down on their knees and stay there until ordered to stand. Such humiliation was inflicted on trainee stokers at Portsmouth by Lieutenant Bernard Collard, and it aroused much bitterness.[32] This exploded at the end of a training session on 4 November 1906 when Collard's familiar 'on the knee' was defied by many stokers. Petty officers took the names of the standing men, who were warned that their behaviour would jeopardise the award of good-conduct badges which brought with them additional pay. In the evening when the stokers were having a drink in the canteen there was a rumpus and marines had to be called in to restore order. Feeling about the kneeling order simmered during the next day and in the evening it was spread to civilians in public houses close to the barracks. After closing time on a night when mischief was traditional, stokers and civilian sympathisers rioted outside the barracks and the disorders were put down only after several hours and the intervention of mounted police and armed marines. Six stokers were arrested out of the hundreds who had joined in, and they were tried and given short prison sentences. The naval authorities excused the disorders on the grounds that the men had been stirred up by civilian agitators, none of whom was ever caught. An inquiry revealed more about Collard's treatment of the stokers ('Go down on your knee, you dirty dog, and learn your manners') and he lost six months' seniority.* His abundant use of this form of punishment was considered thoughtless and unnecessary by one of his colleagues and had directly caused two nights of rowdiness.

One of the stokers expressed his feelings to Edgar Wallace of the *Daily Mail* which, like the rest of the press, was deeply interested in the affair. 'There seems to be a set made against stokers by executive officers. We belong to another class, and it is because we

---

* Collard continued to embarrass the Navy. In 1915 he was appointed Captain and given command of a cruiser but ended the war in a staff post. Promoted to Rear-Admiral in 1926, he commanded the first battle squadron of the Mediterranean Fleet in 1927-8. He quarrelled with officers on board his flagship, *Royal Oak*, and swore at the bandmaster whose playing was not to his taste. The fuss led to courts martial of the officers, but the Admiralty did not endorse the findings and placed Collard on the retired list.

25

do belong to another class that we cannot get on with them. It is this way; seamen enter the Navy as boys and are used to being bullied. They never get out of the boyish stage of taking a bullying without resentment. Stokers enlist as men and an officer must treat them as men.' Strictness was not condemned in officers as long as it was balanced with fairness.

The stoker's sidelong reference to the class war suggests some acquaintanceship with socialist ideas. Most acts of defiance, however, drew little or no inspiration from ideology but were instead a personal reaction, and for this reason insubordination was usually an anarchic and spontaneous gesture. Examples are legion in both services. The insolence of Trumpeter John Shore of the 7th Hussars in September 1803 belonged to no particular time, place or service.[33] On being ordered to report to Lieutenant Campbell to explain his misconduct towards the bandmaster, Shore appeared 'walking very slow and leisurely with his hands in his pockets' and ignored calls to hurry. Asked for the reason behind his slow gait, Shore 'answered in an insolent manner that he was under Doctor's orders' which was enough to make Campbell threaten to knock him over. Shore doubted that he would dare to and when the Lieutenant grabbed his collar, he was felled by a blow to the jaw. A single man's rash assault on an officer was treated as seriously as mutiny and Shore was given 1,000 lashes.

Docility and biddability were not common forms of behaviour amongst the British working classes. In the services they had to be imposed on men who had had little acquaintanceship with them in civilian life. Here the main sources of discipline were employers, the law and the Church, all of which were struggling to impose habits of industry and morality on a population which seemed lamentably without them. From the mid-eighteenth to the nineteenth century, the expansion of manufacturing industry required an end to life which alternated intensive labour with idleness and entertainment. Factories and their machinery demanded that operatives worked regularly for fixed hours. Like soldiers and sailors, industrial workers found their working lives controlled by regulations drawn up to ensure good time-keeping, attentiveness, sobriety and discipline. Loyalty and the acceptance of subordination were required in factories and mines as they were on parade grounds and men-o'-war. Officers and industrialists shared a common aim, which was summed up by a Midlands ironmaster in 1851, when he applauded anything 'which was done to induce the working classes to be more steady, to promote temperance amongst them [and] to speed education amongst them' so that they would become industrious and reliable.

Religion also played a part, not only as a social discipline but as a vehicle for encouraging quietism. In 1798 Arthur Young insisted that 'The true Christian will never be a leveller.' Much the same view was taken by some service chaplains. In 1925 the Chaplain of the Fleet argued that the compulsory church parade was 'The one chance ... of talking to the men as a whole and explaining many things in everyday life they do not understand, e.g. newspaper articles; all of which is most important owing to the growth of a bad form of socialism.'[34] There was much need for such work since during the previous hundred years the Churches had made little progress in their missionary crusades against working-class indifference to religion. Save for the success of the Roman Catholics amongst the Irish immigrant community, there was, in 1900, little indication that the working classes were habitual churchgoers. There was little hostility to what the Churches preached, just an indifference towards them as institutions which were closely identified with the middle classes. This unconcern was reflected in the manners of soldiers. A recruit who joined in 1879 found that his bedside evening prayers provoked clownish ragging which soon subsided, and another, in 1891, discovered that older men used the pages of the officially issued Bibles and Prayer Books to wipe their razors clean.[35] The perils of the battlefield did, however, prompt a deeper interest in religion; soldiers in the Crimea proving susceptible to the persuasions of the evangelical Captain Hedley Vicars.

The discipline of the law was coercive and, with the spread of regular police forces to town and country between 1829 and 1856, meant greater supervision over the commonest offenders, drunkards and hooligans. Rowdy and often destructive public demonstrations did not disappear, and older traditions of working-class protest merged with the new trade unionism to produce a sequence of riots which extended up to the outbreak of the First World War and which sometimes had to be contained by troops. Vice could be eradicated by education, which taught discipline and the rewards of virtue. From 1870 onwards, governments passed measures to ensure mass literacy, but the results were slowly felt by the services. In 1899 sixty per cent of the Army's recruits were just literate, which did not reflect too well on nearly twenty years of compulsory elementary education. This education was putting the young in the way of other benefits, including discipline, for forms of semi-military exercises and drill were commonplace in the curriculum of many schools in the 1880s and 1890s. One teacher commented, 'The military ideal of automatic action is largely the ideal of much school discipline.'[35] Diluted military training, and an introduction to the merits of orderliness, were also available to working-class youth through the Boys' Brigade, Lads' Drill Association, and Boys' Empire League, where instruction was often in the hands of former NCOs. First-hand acquaintanceship with military discipline was provided by the militia which, between 1881 and 1898, attracted 656,000 men to its ranks from the unskilled and semi-skilled working class. During the same period a further million men were exposed to military training in the regular army and to the middle-class volunteers.

The cumulative result of these pressures is impossible to assess precisely. Those nineteenth-century men and women who were committed to extending the work ethic, sobriety, discipline and self-respect to those from whom the armed forces drew their recruits, found the task daunting and its achievement painfully slow. They had some assistance from the rising popularity of competitive sport, especially football, which offered a channel down which potentially disruptive energies could be directed. This was certainly recognised by the services, where sports were encouraged and inter-unit contests soon came to be widely enjoyed by participants and spectators. Football, hockey, long-distance running, water polo and cricket were enjoyed by Riflemen serving in India in 1913 and much was made of the cups and awards received by individuals and teams. Team spirit was a valuable concomitant to military discipline, since the individual had to submit to the orders of his captain and always look to the common rather than personal advantage.

Did all these influences make servicemen more tractable? The answer is probably no, thanks to the existence of counter-movements. From the mid-nineteenth century the working classes had come to learn how to organise themselves for the protection and promotion of their interests. Industrial unionism was forbidden in the Army and Navy, collective action of any kind being legally defined as mutinous, but soldiers' and sailors' benefit societies were permitted. In the 1900s there were unsuccessful efforts by sailors to sponsor MPs for dockyard constituencies, and in the 1930s the Labour Party's election manifestos promised that servicemen could join trade unions and that they could elect and instruct delegates to speak for them in negotiations over pay and conditions. These pledges were all but forgotten in 1945 when Labour came to power, although they have been resurrected recently. Service chiefs were distrustful of such proposals, which looked dangerously like measures which could limit their power to command. Anything which encouraged grumbling was to be discouraged, for it would weaken the bonds of discipline.

Discipline rested, in the end, in the hands of officers and NCOs who by a mixture of encouragement and coercion had to transform civilians into efficient fighting men. From the eighteenth to the twentieth century, officers were expected to be gentlemen; indeed until 1870 the Army made sure that they were, in terms of social background, by making them pay for their commissions. Afterwards limitations of pay and the need for an officer to maintain accustomed standards in the mess meant that most had to possess a private income. 'Gentlemen officers are a great advantage' for they alone could secure 'a ready and willing obedience', or so argued Sidney Herbert, who had been Secretary for War during the Crimean War.[37] The commissioned ranker was 'a somewhat inferior article' in the view of the Second Sea Lord, Admiral Battenberg, just before the First World War. In 1918 this opinion continued to dominate naval thinking when a scheme for the promotion of warrant officers was turned down by the Admiralty, even though there had been murmurings of discontent about wartime commissions being handed out to inexperienced and far from competent young men on the grounds that they were gentlemen.[38]

In both services, it was argued, the men recognised gentlemen and responded to their leadership which was based upon courage, a sense of fair play and open-handedness. What had been the 'moral economy' by which the gentry behaved towards their inferiors with benevolence and honesty was seen as the cement of service discipline long after it had all but vanished from civilian life. Mutual trust and respect also marked the relations between gentleman officers and native troops. One man who had more experience of this than most, General Sir James Willcocks, looked back on over forty years of commanding Indian troops and concluded that 'Indians of all classes are of any people I know the

29

easiest led when the leader understands their hearts, and the most difficult to manage when he does not.'[39] For the NCO the military ideal was expressed in a training manual of 1913 which urged 'such methods of command and treatment as will not only ensure respect for authority but also foster the feelings of self-respect and personal honour essential to military efficiency'. NCOs, drawn from the same background as the men they commanded, and gentlemen, whose upbringing and outlook qualified them to lead, were jointly responsible for the welfare and discipline of fighting men. When they failed in this duty, the outcome was often mutiny.

The officer, unlike the NCO, lived apart from his men, and this social separation was encouraged. In 1810 two ensigns of the 10th Regiment were reprimanded by a court martial for having danced with other ranks' wives in Malta, and in 1917 an Australian sub-altern was similarly chastened for sharing a bottle of whisky with a sergeant and some privates in France.[40] An American Intelligence assessment of the British Army drawn up in 1942 noted that 'a new generation of subalterns were, with the blessings of their seniors, upholding a renewed emphasis on privilege and social precedence'.[41] This was not, of course, completely absent from the United States army. By contrast officers and other ranks on board minesweepers which were clearing Malayan waters during 1946 worked together on familiar terms. This was, however, tightened up after the mutiny of the Indian Navy in that year.[42]

The system worked, and this was its most powerful justification in the face of criticism which was, by and large, voiced by civilians with political axes to grind. Beyond general grousing, there was never any widespread demand from soldiers and sailors for an end to leader-ship by gentlemen, although there were many for the removal of individual gentlemen whose behaviour was arbitrary or inclement. One of these, Sir Philip Wilkinson, the captain of the frigate *Hussar* in 1803, was reviled by his men for being not only cruel but the son of an Ipswich barber.[43] In 1914 Colonel Hugh de Montmorency came face to face with a type of officer whom he feared was too common in the army.[44] 'Scolding, blustering, fault-finding', such men thought that the only 'way to teach a man his job is to bully and frighten him'. His kind were also found in the Navy. One, Captain Leveson of the battlecruiser *Indefatigable*, defending the summary punishment by which offenders had to stand facing a bulkhead for fixed periods, stated in 1912 that 'Sailors were simply childish men, and must be treated as children.'[45]

Leveson's words were spoken to a committee of inquiry which had been created by Winston Churchill, then First Lord of the Admiralty, in response to public pressure. A few years earlier popular disquiet, expressed in Parliament and the newspapers, had led to the curtailment of flogging as a punishment for junior seamen, and a few years later there was similar unease about the widespread use of a form of crucifixion, in which men were tied spreadeagled to fences or cartwheels, known as Field Punishment Number 1, by the Army. It was abolished in 1923 largely as a result of public outcry. Whilst the Army and Navy defended their forms of punishment, they were both forced to make concessions in the face of public opinion, expressed through letters to ministers, newspaper editorials and criticism in Parliament. The public, through their representatives, were, in the final resort, the rulers of the Army and the Navy. Both services acknowledged this and both responded to the changing mood of society and, from the 1830s onwards, accepted the need for reform, which had become the creed of the politically powerful middle classes. There were some rearguard actions by ultra-conservatives who considered any kind of reform as political tampering with systems which worked and therefore should be left alone, but usually the Army and Navy accepted political control with good sense.

The close connection between the Navy and British world domination made its services particularly highly regarded by the public, as Tennyson appreciated:

> Her dauntless army scatter'd and so small,
> Her island myriads fed from alien lands –
> The fleet of England is her all-in-all.

The Army too, as the banner-bearer of civilisation in distant lands and the defender of the Empire, also rose in public adulation in the forty years before the First World War. As a side-product of the growth of public esteem for the forces, there was a growing affection towards the individual soldier and sailor, which had expressed itself in the humanitarian campaigns for the abolition of flogging. This disappeared from the Army in 1881 and was suspended from use in the Navy in the same year, although in practice it lingered on until 1906. By contrast, flogging was introduced as the penalty for some forms of robbery with violence in 1862, and retained until 1948.

Yet, whilst the public came to admire soldiers and sailors, and place a high value on the armed forces as the defenders of freedom

31

and the rights and prosperity of the British subjects, the men who performed these duties had to live and work under rules which excluded most of the liberties of their fellow countrymen. This was the price which Britain, like other democratic countries, had to pay for protection. The rights of representation, free speech and collective action which had been extended during the nineteenth and twentieth centuries meant little to soldiers and sailors, for whom they were severely curtailed. The profession of arms looked to the different values of duty, courage and honour.

WORM IN THE OAK:

Naval Mutinies, 1797-1806

Come, little drummer-boy, lay down your knapsack
here:
I am the soldier's friend – here are some books for you,
Nice, clever books by Tom Paine the philanthropist.
Here's half-a-crown for you – here are some handbills
too –
Go to the barracks and give all the soldiers some.
Tell them the sailors are all in a mutiny ...

The Anti-Jacobin (1797)

Come, all you bold Britons to the seas do belong
Of the seventeen Bright Stars I will sing you a song
On the 15 of April, at Spithead as we lay,
Lord Bridport he hove out a signal to weigh:
But we and all refused to obey.

Contemporary ballad

NO BETTER THAN SLAVES

To honour we call you, as free men, not slaves,
For who are so free as the sons of the waves?

'We are not free but now are slaves,' lamented some of the crew of
the frigate *Shannon* in 1796. A quartermaster on board the sloop
Perdrix in 1798 agreed with them. 'He was damning King and
Country, damning all Englishmen, for they were no better than

33

slaves and would soon go into Slavery.' A shipmate objected, 'I am a free-born Englishman!' and the two fell to blows.[1] In support of the free-born Englishman were the pro-government squibs and songs, the cartoons of Gillray which showed stout English yeomen, plump with beer and beef, their lives and livelihood guarded by the Law and Constitution. This was English liberty. Under King, Law and Parliament, men could employ their talents, grow rich, speak their minds, write what they wished and feel free from the tyranny of officials and arbitrary justice. On board a man-o'-war these were mere abstractions. The reality was closer to slavery, for the sailor obeyed his officers, did their will and when he did not, was punished at their discretion. If he answered back or deserted he might be flogged or hanged.

The contradiction between the lives of those who defended English liberty and the public face of that liberty was wryly noted by a sailor who joined the Navy in 1805.[2]

> Whatever may be said about this boasted land of liberty, whenever a youth resorts to a receiving ship, he, from that moment must take leave of the liberty to *speak*, or to act; he may *think*, but he must confine his thoughts to the *hold* of his mind, and never suffer them to escape the *hatchway* of utterance.

This young seaman, nicknamed 'Jack Nastyface' by his officers, soon appreciated that all he was allowed to say was 'Aye, aye, sir', touching the brim of his straw hat as he spoke. Another sailor, a pressed man, also learned the same lesson; his first few days aboard a man-o'-war convinced him that 'to be sober, Silent and Submissive, and above all to curb your tongue and temper was what I soon found to be the golden rule'. This was not new in the 1790s. Smollett's Roderick Random, press-ganged aboard a warship, found that his complaints about rough handling were answered with a squirt of chewed tobacco from the mouth of a midshipman who cursed him as 'a mutinous dog'. More followed in the same vein after a chance meeting with the same officer, who, when accused of inhumanity, responded, 'Damn you, you saucy son of a bitch, I'll teach you to talk so to an officer' and hit Random.

Fiction was close to reality. A less fortunate sailor than Random (who had friends amongst the officers) was given 50 lashes in 1797 for saying that he had been unduly picked on by a lieutenant.[3] Speech of this kind or any other which could be interpreted as grumbling, abuse of officers, or regrets about the service, was construed as insubordination or, at a captain's whim, as mutinous. The aptly named marine Thomas Broken refused a corporal's command to carry four muskets below deck on board HMS *Acasta* in 1801. 'I did carry them!' he replied. 'The sergeant made me carry down four muskets, the bugger! I have got my discharge in my pocket, I could show it to Captain Fellows if I thought proper, if that won't do, a Gentleman in Ireland will get me discharge or otherwise I have a hundred pounds in five Pound Notes in my pocket that will get another man, and woe to them who ever meets Broken on shore, I'll make them recollect the longest day they have to live.' Broken was sentenced to be hanged for mutinous language.[4]

It was understandable that some sailors compared their lot with that of the plantation slave and relished the irony that made their exertions the sheet-anchor of British 'Liberty'.

Quarter-deck declamations of the 'Articles of War' and the rituals of floggings and hanging at the yard-arm reminded sailors that on board ship they were not free. Their duty was to serve diligently, obey without question or hesitation and, by the careful performance of their tasks, make their man-o'-war an effective and efficient fighting machine. Each ship was vital in the maintenance of the Royal Navy's domination of the seas, which both safeguarded Britain from invasion and underwrote the expansion of her world trade. Victory in battle, whether in a ship-to-ship engagement or a fleet action, depended upon every sailor knowing his duties and undertaking them skilfully. This was achieved by training at sea and discipline. The furling and unfurling of sails and easy handling of guns gave British men-o'-war their advantages of speed, manoeuvrability and firepower. These were displayed in victory after victory during the eighteenth century and appeared to justify the Royal Navy's way of handling its men.

From the beginning of 1793, when Revolutionary France declared war on Britain, the Royal Navy faced its most formidable task. To meet the demands of upholding and advancing British seapower, it needed more men. William Pitt's ministry had answered the call for more sailors by a piecemeal recruiting policy which was hardly more than a sequence of emergency measures spatchcocked together in response to crises. In consequence ships of war were manned by townsfolk and countrymen drafted under the Quota Acts of 1795 and 1796 which ordered local authorities in the inland counties to produce a fixed number of seamen or face payment of an indemnity. These men from the shires rubbed shoulders with 'idle and disorderly' fellows, whom the magistrates were empowered to hound into the Navy and so turn the parish's misfortune to the kingdom's advantage. There were also more active miscreants sentenced by the Quarter Sessions to naval service as an alternative to gaol. Numbers from these unwelcome sources were mercifully small compared to the droves of disaffected young Irishmen whom their local justices had been authorised to send to the fleet in the hope that their exile might dampen down sedition. Such unwilling recruits were surrounded by others pressed from the quays and docksides of British and colonial ports, or taken from merchantmen on the high seas or as they entered harbour. This category included American, Scandinavian, Spanish, Italian, Negro and even French sailors. By 1800 just over 100,000 sailors had been drafted by these means.

It was the Navy's job to take these men, some reluctant, some stubborn and some supine, and transform them into obedient, responsive and skilled seamen who would beat the French. Whatever else officers may have thought of the influx of new men into the Navy, they soon became aware that they were having to handle sailors who possessed ideas of their own and were not only able to think for themselves, but were willing to risk mutiny to get what they wanted. In the spring of 1797, with the refusal to sail of the sixteen line-of-battle ships of the Channel Fleet and the mutiny of the various men-o'-war at the Nore anchorage at the mouth of the Thames, commanders and the Admiralty faced an impressive demonstration that sailors would not be treated as slaves.

Experienced officers were at a loss to explain what had happened. The First Lord of the Admiralty, Lord Spencer, attributed the mutiny to 'mischievous plotting persons' who were either recently arrived Quota Men or Irish nationalists.'5 Captain Collingwood agreed and specified those who had been educated at Sunday Schools and members of the Corresponding Societies as at the root of the agitation. It is hard to see how those who had learned to read the Bible and those dedicated to the imposition on Britain of the principles of the French Revolution could have collaborated, but Collingwood was perhaps happier with sailors who knew nothing of Tom Paine or the Bible. Another officer, who watched the Spithead mutiny from the shore, detected 'secret Jacobin springs' as the source of the poisoned waters of subversion and disobedience. Home Office agents, briefed to sniff out the dockside agitators, found none, nor did the officials who opened and read the letters which passed to and fro between the men at the Nore and their friends and families.

The sailors were both amused and horrified that they were thought to be instruments of revolutionary agitators. At the start of the mutiny, the crews of the Spithead ships had assured the House of Commons that they were 'as loyal to our sovereign, and zealous in the defence of our country as the army and militia'. 'We have not the least principle of the Jacobin spirit,' asserted the crew of the frigate *Jason*, who regretted that 'some people think proper to lay this to our charge'.[6] They were right, and those who wished to promote revolutionary ideas amongst the sailors would have agreed with them. Two men from the London Corresponding Society, on hearing of the mutiny, hurried to Portsmouth to fish in troubled waters. One, Robert Watson, was a French agent, but neither he nor his companion had any success in subverting the sailors. They had been taken by surprise by the event, as indeed had William Duckett, an Irishman in French employ and possibly their best agent. When news of the mutiny reached him at Hamburg, he made ready to sail, but his mission was called off when the news of the end of the mutinies reached him. Wolfe Tone, the exiled Irish nationalist, scented an advantage to his cause and later bewailed the slowness of his French allies to recognise and exploit it.[7]

The 'conspiracy theory' of the 1797 mutinies gained much publicity and credence over the following years when the government was anxious to suggest that Britain stood in peril from hidden plotters, paid and inspired by France. The opening years of the war had been a period of unparalleled political agitation and the spread of radical ideas from France coupled with the growth of purely internal discontent over conscription and high food prices had spread fear amongst the ruling classes. But ardent pro-revolutionary sentiments were confined to a narrow section of society and seldom spread to the labouring masses of the countryside and towns.

The most potent force for the dissemination of revolutionary ideas was Thomas Paine's *The Rights of Man*. It first appeared in 1792 and soon far outstripped other revolutionary books and pamphlets in its circulation and persuasiveness. Paine's assertion that 'Men are born, and always continue, free and equal in respect of their rights' and that they were bound to snatch these rights from the teeth of tyranny, had a powerful appeal. Like much else that he argued, this idea was discussed and broadcast by members of the Corresponding Societies which had sprung up during 1792 and 1793. For their members, the government of George III was a tyranny, and the boasted blessings of law and constitution a fraud. Other political dissidents expressed opinions which owed more to despair than ideology, like those of a seller of old clothes in Windsor who exclaimed, 'Damn and bugger the King and all that belong to him. I would as soon shoot the King as a mad dog.' Such words of angry frustration had their physical expression in riots, like that in which the King's carriage was stoned, noisy demonstrations about bread prices, and the sending of menacing letters to the rich and locally powerful. From 1795 a new grievance was added to the armoury of the discontented, war weariness. Save for the naval victories of The Glorious First of June in 1794, and off Cape St Vincent two years later, Britain's record of successes was dismal. The campaigns on land and sea in the Caribbean had been disheartening. Yellow fever carried away over half the troops sent, and by 1798 over 40,000 soldiers had died and about 10,000 sailors. In March 1797 the London Corresponding Society had sponsored a peace campaign and, a few months after, the Whig opposition demanded the abandonment of the captured French sugar islands.

It was inevitable that among the masses of men pressed or conscripted into the Navy were many who were conversant with political ideas. Evidence of their political knowledge and commitment is scattered, but together it suggests that before and during the 1797 mutinies there were men involved who were conscious of wider issues of freedom and tyranny. On a commonplace level everyday protests against shipboard conditions or overbearing officers were laced with the language of the radical squibs and demagogues. A grumbling seaman on board HMS *St Albans*, cruising on the North American station in April 1798, wished he was elsewhere.[8] '*St Albans* ought to be in the Channel Fleet, we ought to be with the Britons at home – but we are not – we are with the Tyrants of the Seas. Let those who are ignorant and have not eyes open come to me, and I will show it them in print.' Despite his claim, this sailor possessed no radical literature and when facing sentence for mutinous language, wisely avowed his loyalty to the King. In 1802 a lieutenant on board HMS *Dragon* in the Mediterranean was told by a drunken master's mate that: 'I was a Tyrant and had the law in my own hands.' Since he had threatened to shoot the master's mate, the reaction was understandable.[9] Elsewhere sailors who employed their right to petition the Admiralty used terms like 'free-born' and 'slaves' which, whilst they did not necessarily indicate an accord with novel, revolutionary ideas, did suggest that some at least of the new recruits believed themselves to be possessed of some rights and dignity. This was forcefully expressed, during the Spithead and Nore mutinies and, later, in the indignation against the careless and arbitrary use of corporal punishment. On *Pompée* its application was 'contrary to the spirit or intent of any laws of our country' whilst on *La Nymphe* men were treated 'more like convicts than free-born Britons'.[10] 'Cruel and Arbitrary Measures' were the captain's way aboard *Ramillies* together with 'Threats and Imprecations such as are by no means fit to repeat'.[11] The officers on *Bienpensant* hogged 'every prime Bit of Beef for Roasting the which we think not right' and to make matters worse 'the Beer is so weak as possible it can be', so that the sailors were in even more wretched conditions than prisoners of war.[12]

Sailors were not slaves, and their expectations as 'free-born' men embraced respect and honourable treatment from their officers. A few had had contact with Paineite ideas and made some effort to canvass them amongst their shipmates. William Guthrie, a Londoner with a reputation for 'respectful behaviour' on board the battleship *Pompée* and with four years' service behind him, was one of those involved in a plot to secure support from the ship's crew for a peace with France. He claimed that his conversion to the ideas of the London Corresponding Society had come from a member, Thomas Ashley.[13] Guthrie had spotted Ashley in deep conversation with a marine sergeant and later asked what they had been talking about. He was told 'Public Matters' and was given Ashley's opinions which included the observation that he 'had traced History and could not discover any one Good Quality belonging to him [George III]' '... He spoke on the Subject of Reform of Parliament and that upwards of sixty thousand People in London had Petitioned for Peace, which Petition had been rejected and that it could only be brought about by the sailors.' All this, Ashley admitted, he had learned from 'Letters from his friends in London informing him of that State of Public matters'.

Guthrie showed interest and was introduced to another London radical, James Galloway, 'the Captain of the Mast, the Man with the crooked nose', who offered him a paper to read, but Guthrie could not understand its meaning. He was, however, a convert, for, later, addressing his shipmates, he 'pointed his hand through the port towards France and said it is not our Enemys that live there, it is our Friends' and concluded with a few words about having left his wife at home with just a shilling, but their gist was inaudible to his audience, one of whom later stood evidence against him. A few weeks earlier *Pompée* had been involved in the Spithead mutiny, but there is no evidence to connect its intractability and militancy then with the presence on board of these radicals. One regretted the violence on board *London* and wished that the sailors had directed their energies towards securing a peace rather than higher wages. Not all radical sailors were so earnest. Thomas Jephson, an Ulsterman and former freemason, was a fiddler who strutted about the decks of HMS *Sandwich* during the Nore mutiny with a red cockade in his hat. He imagined himself the eyewitness of the dawn of revolution and proclaimed: 'A glorious thing it is, and it shouldn't end until the head is off King George and Billy Pitt.' Billy Pitt's effigy swung from the yardarms of *Nassau* and other ships of the Yarmouth squadron, and aboard one a Paineite coxswain declared, 'Damn and bugger the King! We want no king!'[14]

There were men in the Navy in 1797, and later, who were sympathetic to political radicalism and who supported its aim of overthrowing the King and Constitution and replacing them with a government on the French model. But, as in civil society, these revolutionaries and revolutionary fellow travellers were a minority. Whilst their political consciousness and literacy may well have helped the mutineers in organising themselves and drawing up petitions, these men were unable to put a political stamp on their fellow sailors' demands.

These demands, presented by the men of Spithead and their imitators at Nore, were solely concerned with conditions in the fleet. What outraged the seamen was their shipboard treatment by some captains and lieutenants and the seemingly callous indifference of the Admiralty. The chief symptom of the latter was the thinness of naval pay. It had not been raised since 1660, as both Thomas Paine and the sailors noted, and was delivered irregularly. In 1797 the ordinary seaman received 19 shillings monthly and the able seaman 24, which for most men represented a fall in income from what they could have earned on land or on a merchantman. An extreme case, recalled by 'Jack Nastyface', was of a man pressed from a transport ship who exchanged £5 10s a month for 32s.[15] At the same time food prices were rising which caused

40

distress to sailors with families. In 1798 petty officers, seeking a pay increase, complained to the Admiralty, 'That the price of every Species of Provisions &c for the support of their families is greatly advanced.'[16] The sailors' plight had been understood by one of their officers, Captain Thomas Pakenham, who wrote to Lord Spencer on 11 December 1796 and warned him of the problem. Sailors who served and endured financial loss 'with all the patience of subordination and all the zeal of patriotism' deserved a wage increase. Spencer was unconvinced. Higher wages meant a further drain on the public purse and 'public discussion of such a point ... would infallibly be productive of much mischief'.

Distress over low pay was the heart of the Spithead sailors' grievances, the cement which bound them together and kept them united in their cause. In their own words, addressed to Charles James Fox, the Whig opposition leader, 'It is indigence and extreme penury alone that is the cause of our complaint.' Yet other sources of discontent came quickly to the surface once the mutiny had begun. The sailors called for an end to the vicious system by which one-eighth of their rations was deducted before issue, a piece of typically eighteenth-century corruption which benefited pursers and victuallers and had never before been questioned. There were also calls for better-quality rations, particularly bread and greens, and the end of iniquitous penny-pinching which held down sailors' pensions and ensured that the sick and wounded got no pay whilst in sick bay. Such complaints were shared by all sailors. Individual ships yielded their own crop of grievances which were the direct consequence of brutal officers. Once the initial success of the mutiny was clear and the sailors were aware of their collective strength, various crews concocted their own petitions for the dismissal of unkind officers.

This was not an assault on naval discipline, although at the Nore there was a call for unspecified revisions in the Articles of War. What the sailors feared and hated was injustice and oppression. On board *Glory*, Captain Bruce's 'genteel kind behaviour' was not transmitted to his junior officers, 'who behaved tyrannically to the people with ordering them to be beat in a most cruel manner'. Blows were augmented by 'blacking, tarring, and putting the people's heads in bags'. Specific details of such maltreatment were set down by the crew of the frigate *La Nymphe*, nearly all of whom put signatures or crosses to the petition against their captain, John Cooke.[17]

We are kept more like convicts than free-born Britons. Flogging is carried on to extremes, one man received three dozen for what was termed silent contempt, which was nothing more than this. After being beat by a Boatswain's mate, the man smiled, this was an unpardonable crime. Another was flogged for not going up the rigging quick enough, and another for not sending him down as was supposed smart enough. In short the number that has been flogged for trifling offences would be too tedious to mention at present ... When we engaged with the enemy off Brest, March 9th 1797, they even beat us at our quarters tho' on the verge of eternity and said I'll beat you until I make you jump overboard or be God Damd. I will not send a boat after you ... Is this the way to encourage the service?

How harsh was Cooke's regime? Between 7 May 1796 and 12 May 1797, six crewmen of *La Nymphe* were flogged.[18] George Verrey, perhaps the man who smiled, received 36 lashes for 'contempt and neglect of duty' on 6 August 1796 at a time when *La Nymphe* was lying off Weymouth where George III was relishing the stimulation of sea-bathing and occasional salutes from the frigate's guns. On 27 June a sailor was given 48 lashes for neglect of duty and the remaining sentences were for insolence to a ship's corporal, drunken and mutinous behaviour and riotous disorder. Six floggings in six months was not exceptional and there is a disparity between the causes of the punishments as seen by *La Nymphe*'s crew and their description in the log. The log did not list startings, the commonest form of shipboard corporal punishment. It was vividly remembered by 'Jack Nastyface'.[19]

> The man is ordered to pull off his jacket, and sometimes his waistcoat, if he has one on at the time: the Boatswain's Mate then commences beating him, and continues to do so until he is ordered to stop, or unless his arm is tired, and then another Boatswain's Mate is called to go on with the ceremony. Some of those men's backs have often been so bad from the effects of the 'starting system', that they have not been able to bear their jackets on for several days; and as this punishment is inflicted without tying the man up, he will naturally endeavour to ward off or escape many of the blows as possible, and in so doing he frequently gets a serious cut in the face or hand.

This kind of bludgeoning appears to have been handed out to some of *La Nymphe* crew when their vessel engaged and took the frigate *La Résistance* and the corvette, *Constance*, off Brest on 9 March 1797.

42

La Nymphe's crew (which included many Cornish miners) was not notably obdurate. After Captain Cooke was sent ashore, his former company asked the Admiralty for a replacement and two lieutenants so 'that we may not be hindered from proceeding with . the fleet when ordered to sea'. Their eagerness for duty was satisfied when, on 13 May, the Secretary to the Admiralty, Evan Nepean, ordered Lord Bridport to do as he saw fit. Bridport sensibly, and perhaps with a good knowledge of Cooke's demeanour, replaced him with Percy Frazer. From 13 May 1797 to 30 June 1798 there were no floggings on *La Nymphe*.[20] Cooke redeemed himself, for he fell at Trafalgar in command of *Bellerophon*, a death which earned him the honour of burial in St Paul's.

His sailors on board *La Nymphe* had called themselves 'free-born Britons' and to all appearances were brave and dutiful sailors, who had proved their worth in action. Yet on 15 April they had ceased their duties, challenged their captain and admiral, and with thousands of others mutinied for what they considered the justice due to them as 'free-born' Englishmen, fighting for their country.

PROCEED IN CAUTION, PEACE AND GOOD BEHAVIOUR

The behaviour of the mutinous sailors at Spithead took their commanders and the Admiralty by surprise. No officer knew of the conspiracy which had developed for two months in complete secrecy.[21] Since those involved insisted on, and got, a royal pardon, there were no subsequent trials of the mutineers, and the mechanics of their planning were never revealed. More details came to light during the courts martial of the ringleaders of the Nore mutiny, although much of the evidence was presented to show how they had kept up the morale of the more hesitant rank and file. Since the events at Spithead and the Nore offered encouragement to other sailors to try their hand at mutiny, there was a series of trials of mutineers for the next five years in which much was uncovered about the mechanics of naval mutiny. From these not altogether perfect sources it is possible to isolate the ways in which mutiny was kindled and how those who planned it dealt with the problem of secrecy.

Combinations, and secret oath-taking, whether by servicemen or civilians, were illegal at the end of the eighteenth century. Both were recognised as the heart of mutiny and the legal prohibitions were reinforced after the Spithead and Nore upheavals. Collective action by working people was difficult anyway, since at this time factories and workshops were still small, and signs of illicit organisation by employees were easy to detect and frustrate. Few of the men who joined the Navy during the 1790s could have had any experience of this kind of activity, although not a few may have taken part in civilian riots. The 15,000 Irishmen in the fleet were an exception, for they would have brought with them knowledge of covert oath-taking and secret resistance brotherhoods which were gaining ground in Ireland. In Britain such revolutionary underground networks were insubstantial, both before and after the 1797 mutinies. It is, however, worth noting that one Corresponding Society member from Nottingham deliberately enlisted after he had heard the news of the mutinies in the hope that he could foment more unrest in the fleet.[22] In Ireland reports of the mutinies also encouraged trouble-makers to resort to the fleet, where they hoped to employ their experience in forming clandestine clubs. Sailors from such backgrounds and armed with a hatred of the government were natural participants in mutiny. In September 1797 the Belfast republican, Laurence Cronin, broke cover after the *Hermione* mutiny and advised and directed the mutineers. Save in the 1798-9 mutinies of United Irishmen this type of agitator seems to have remained a shadowy figure who rarely occupied the centre of the stage or assumed leadership. None of the six radicals who, a month after the end of the Spithead mutiny, tried to enlist their shipmates' backing for the peace petition appear to have played any significant part in the earlier unrest, although they may have been busy behind the scenes.

Mutiny required leadership, and to succeed would-be ringleaders had to get common approval for a cause and pledge men to it. Persuasion was hard, as the Articles of War insisted that knowledge of a mutiny and mutinous talk were punishable by death. Those who failed to resist, or even report what they knew of mutinous plans, found that courts martial were dismissive of any excuses. When on 23 November 1800 the mainly foreign crew of the bomb ketch *Albanaise* overpowered and imprisoned their captain and seized the vessel, the 'loyal' men found themselves outwitted and powerless. Thomas Parsons, a cook with twenty-one years of service, was roused from his hammock by 'John de Rook and Casalino', hustled on deck and confronted by Godfrey, a Dane and the mutineers' leader. He held a pistol in each hand and ordered Parsons to cook food for the mutineers as they sailed for the sanctuary of Malaga in Spain. 'There were very few Englishmen on board,' regretted Parsons, who had no choice but to do as he was told by the mutineers. Later he was exchanged and taken back to Gibraltar where he faced a court martial for assisting the mutineers. His excuses were ignored and he was sentenced to three months' imprisonment. Two fellow sailors were less lucky and were given 50 and 100 lashes each. The trials and verdicts were reminders that every sailor was expected to do all in his power to resist mutiny and that no excuse could exonerate those who failed in this duty.[23]

The men on board *Albanaise* had a ready-made cause for their mutiny. They were Spaniards, Portuguese and Italians who had been pressed into service, and they wanted no part in Britain's war and no doubt detested the hardships of life aboard a British man-o'-war. Such grievances were usually felt in the guts and their articulation took the form of sporadic grumbling, itself a crime if uttered within the hearing of an officer or petty officer. Leadership was needed to transform the discordance of many individual grumbles into a common cause. More than that, leadership was needed to suggest that through action the cause's object might be achieved. To make such suggestions was dangerous, for the man who played on the grievances of others ran the risk of detection by eavesdroppers or exposure by an informer. As in battle, where it helped stimulate courage, rum also stirred up the boldness of mutineers, helping them to throw off the restraint of fear. It was usual for many sailors to hoard their daily rum rations and augment them by purchase or cadging so that, off watch, they could settle down to prolonged drinking bouts. At such times grouses came lightly and often. John Wetherall recollected the temper and language of one such session on board the frigate *Hussar* in 1803.[24]

Says one, 'I cannot bear it much longer'. 'Nor either will I', says another. 'Well, but', says a third, 'we have to bear it all, and by what I understand of his [the Captain's] usage to the crew of the *Hermione* we shall grow worse and no better'. 'What is to be done?' says Jack Waddell, a wild daring young fellow. 'I don't know', says one. 'Nor I', says another.

45

Waddell, whose qualities had been appreciated by his captain, for he was in charge of the main topsails, suggested the swearing of an oath on the Bible by which each man who swore pledged himself to desert. This was futile, so later the malcontents turned to a legal way of securing relief from the enormities of their captain, and drew up a petition to his superior. Following the tradition which had been so clearly demonstrated at Spithead, they asked for Captain Wilkinson's dismissal.

Leadership in this enterprise came from a sailor who was experienced, considered responsible and capable by his officers, and in some position of authority over his shipmates. Yet, like them, he was vulnerable to the crabbed and vicious humour of his captain. Such men were dangerous, like the bosun's mates who led the mutineers on *Hermione*, or the bosun of the sloop *Ferret*, who helped to encourage her crew to mutiny in October 1806. All possessed grudges and all had some authority over their shipmates with whom they worked, and who looked to them for leadership. On *Hussar* the discontented considered an armed uprising (which was forestalled when their vessel ran on to shoals off the French coast), and on *Hermione* and *Ferret* the mutineers carried out attacks on their officers. Such behaviour was far from the minds of the Spithead mutineers, yet they chose for their leaders, or delegates as they were called, men who were experienced seamen and whose value had been acknowledged by their officers through promotion.

Valentine Joyce, a quartermaster's mate from Jersey from the *Royal George*, was regarded as the leading delegate, both by the Admiralty and the crews of the other ships. Whilst Edmund Burke was convinced he was a French agent, no connection with French or English revolutionaries was discovered either during or after the mutiny. He and his fellows were men in their mid-twenties to mid-thirties, many were petty officers and there were five ageing midshipmen who had given up hope of passing their lieutenantcy examinations. Three were Irish, one American and the rest English, Welsh and Scottish. In all, the spokesmen of the line-of-battle ships were sober, intelligent and dignified in their dealings with their officers, and firm in handling their followers. Joyce showed courage when he intervened to save the life of a lieutenant after a violent incident on the *London*, and was respectful without obsequiousness in his contacts with admirals. John Fleming, a sailor from *London*, elected by his shipmates to stand in for a wounded delegate, gave some notice of their minds in choosing him and also his own when he cautioned them against precipitate action in putting their admiral on trial.[25]

> Now, my brethren, your general cry is 'Blood for Blood'. Do you mean that as a compliment indeed; or do you, let me ask you, think it justice? I hope not; if you do, pray, from whence do you derive your authority to sit as a court over the life of even the meanest subject? The only answer you can give me is, that you are authorised by your respective ship's companies. But is that authority sufficient to quiet your conscience for taking the life even of a criminal, much more that of a deserving worthy gentleman, who is an ornament to his profession in every respect; I can safely say you will say 'No'.

Not all the delegates or men actively involved in the mutiny at Spithead were of this kind. William Milner, a delegate from the frigate *Jason* who had been involved in the tussle on board the *London*, deserted once the mutiny was over, whether out of a lack of faith in the royal pardon or out of disaffection with naval life is not known. John Sullivan, who was busy in the mutiny on board *Defence*, was subsequently revealed as a deserter from another ship. Both were men with a grudge against the Navy and were of a less reliable type than the delegates from the sixteen capital ships. Such sailors were more in evidence during the Nore mutiny and may have done much to give it its violent complexion. One, John Blake of the *Inflexible*, had had the red flag hoisted and when the mutiny began to collapse, he fled with seventeen shipmates to France. All offered their services to the French navy, either out of conviction or desperation.[26]

The volatile and anarchic spirit of the Nore mutiny, to which men of Blake's kind contributed, also owed much to their leader, Richard Parker, self-styled president of what a news-sheet called 'The Floating Republic'. Parker was a thirty-year-old draftee on the *Sandwich*, which he had joined earlier in 1797 after a career of tergiversation and squabbles with authority. Fourteen years before he had joined the Navy as a midshipman, but his life in the Navy and on merchantmen was stormy. It ended at Leith where he tried his hand at schoolmastering without success and found himself in debt. He had qualities which made the self-elected delegates from the warships at the Nore draw him from the fringe of the mutiny to its centre. Mercurial and vain, Parker upheld his power in a meretricious masquerade in which he was rowed from ship to ship in an admiral's state. He had much to say, boring many crews with his harangues, which in the end did nothing to convince them their cause was anything but hopeless. He learned from his follies: shortly before his execution he wrote:

> Remember never to make yourself the busybody of the lower classes, for they are cowardly, selfish and ungrateful; the least trifle will intimidate them, and him whom they have exalted one moment as their Demagogue, the next they will not scruple to exalt upon the gallows.

Parker and his cronies were able to draw strength from what was happening at Spithead. They started their mutiny in support of the Spithead men and sent representatives to Portsmouth, where they met Lord Howe on 14 May. These men returned with copies of the original Spithead petitions and details of what had been conceded by the Admiralty.[27] What followed was a mutiny in which organisation and planning were haphazard and the mutineers' gestures were a series of increasingly desperate reactions to an obstinate government. From the beginning the nucleus of ships involved was thrown back on coercion as the means to persuade others to join the cause. In part this was because the Nore was no more than an anchorage where ships came for revictualling or refitting, and so the ships which became involved in the mutiny lacked the cohesion of a fleet, which was possessed by the squadrons at Spithead. The 74-gun *Inflexible* had therefore to be used as a cudgel with which to menace smaller vessels like the sloop *Pylades*, which joined the mutiny only 'through dread of being fired into'.[28] Indeed, *Inflexible* had set the mood of the mutiny from the start when, on 13 May, she had fired on the frigate *San Fiorenzo*, damaged her bowsprit and secured her brief allegiance to the cause. The decision to blockade the Thames, taken once the government's firmness was clear and the mutinous vessels found themselves under siege from the land, was another sign of this willingness to use force which marked out the Nore mutiny from that at Spithead.

Coercion played a vital part in many naval mutinies. No more than forty men from the crew of about 180 on the *Hermione* were able to seize the vessel and murder several officers without interference from their shipmates. A loyal marine, Thomas Holford, recollected that, 'I heard many people, the next day, say it was a great pity there was no Resistance made against the Mutineers.'[29] One who shared this regret was a maintopman:[30]

> At the time of the Mutiny I was on the after part of the quarter deck between the two aftermost carronades when I heard cries of Murder in the cabin from Captain Pigot and several people coming upon the quarterdeck, being shocked at the bloody scene that soon ensued, I endeavoured to keep out of the way and lay down between the two guns. I would, with all my heart, have joined in any attempt to recover possession of the ship, but seeing such number awed by so few, a poor weak individual could not possibly do anything.

The court martial accepted this tale and acquitted the man. Pleas of duress, based upon moral weakness did not, however, diminish culpability and a *Hermione* mutineer, John Hayes, was hanged in spite of his excuse:[31]

> At the time when the detestable and horrid mutiny took place on board his Majesty's ship *Hermione* I was a boy in my fourteenth year with all the disadvantages of education and moral example. Necessity drove me to sea in my ninth year. Driven by the torrent of mutiny I took the oath administered to me on the occasion. The examples of death which were before my eyes drove me for shelter amongst the mutineers dreading a similar fate with those who fell, if I sided with, or showed the smallest inclination to mercy.

Hayes may well have been scared, but once he had seen which way the wind was blowing, he moved amongst the mutineers and urged them to kill his master, the vessel's surgeon. The initial success of a mutiny was a powerful force to convince waverers or else encourage them to add their private grievance to the general.

The successful *Hermione* mutineers, like others, used the supernatural to gain co-operation and cohesion. All the crew (save for the loyal men) were made to swear an oath by which each man promised not to betray the others. Two days after the first defiance by the Channel Fleet at Spithead, each man swore to stand by the common objective. The Nore delegates and their circle went from ship to ship between 13 and 16 May, exhorted the crews to solidarity and when took over a cabin to which seamen were called, one by one, and made to swear support for the cause. The method suggests unease about the overall enthusiasms of the sailors.

Yet, before any mutineers could show their hands, they had first to find supporters. The would-be leaders had to take the plunge, move amongst their shipmates, buttonhole them, gain their confidence and induce them to pledge support for action. Canvassing help for a mutiny had to be a stealthy business, undertaken in the quiet parts of the ship with eye and ear alert for an eavesdropper. Many were willing to play the part of the spy. The bosun of the sloop *Proserpine* stole about the vessel and told the captain of what he had overheard, much to the annoyance of the crew who, during the Nore mutiny, demanded his dismissal.[32] Aboard the frigate *Diadem* in September 1799, a seaman of eight months' standing, who had been watching a shipmate writing, later snooped in his music book where a letter had been hidden, read it by candlelight and found it contained references to the captain and his officers. His nosiness helped to convict the writer of making false charges.[33]

This man was a plain busybody. There were others whose duty it was to keep eyes and ears open for dissension. Petty officers traditionally carried out this task, like the captain of the forecastle of the *St Albans* who, on hearing a seaman utter seditious words, immediately reported him to the captain.[34] Plotters on the *Princess Royal* in 1798 knew that, once they saw a man whom they had just approached 'in deep discussion with the Master-at-Arms', their scheme was on the verge of discovery.[35] One reason for the successful underground movements which preceded the Spithead mutiny must have been the sympathy of petty officers. Like the sailors they were suffering from low pay at a time of rising prices, for in March 1798, the bosuns, gunners and carpenters of the Channel Fleet petitioned the Admiralty for higher wages.[36]

The informer always ran risks of retaliation from the friends of those whom his information brought to trial. William Oliver, captain of the forecastle of the *Caesar*, who, on behalf of the 'respectable' men of the ship, informed his captain of the Irish sailors' mutinous plot in 1798, suffered at the hands of their mates. According to his evidence:[37]

> Daniel Davis the Boatswain's mate came Forward into my Berth and said, 'Oliver did you ever hang a Man?' I was so struck with such a Question that I could not answer him. The Prisoner followed close after, said, 'Yes, Mr Oliver, you and buggers like you, hung them poor fellows recently.'

Oliver's persecutor, John Mahoney, an Irishman and former tailor, later asked him whether he had reported the plans of the Irish to murder the Protestants. Oliver said he had, and Mahoney shouted: 'Were you not a damned deceitful Rascall for so doing!' and warned that Oliver would pay for it, before scurrying off, 'murmuring to himself'. Neither Mahoney nor Oliver's other tormentor offered any excuse for their words and were each given 50 lashes which could have done little to reduce their rancour. Still, a sense of duty and a knowledge of what the 'Articles of War' offered for those who kept knowledge of mutiny to themselves were sufficient to ensure that many mutineers were exposed by their shipmates. When one asked Daniel Murphy of HMS *Volage* for his aid in a plot to take over the ship, Murphy answered that it was 'an affair which would have bad consequences' and he advised his questioner to think no further of it. This coolness angered the mutineer, who bullied Murphy into an oath of secrecy. Murphy immediately repeated the incident to an officer.[38]

Once a knot of men had found their cause, they had to brave discovery and seek out supporters. Three men on the *Princess Royal* in 1798 wrote down their plan and sent it as a round robin from berth to berth in the hope that others would join them and rescue some shipmates held in irons. To give encouragement, they assured readers and listeners that other ships in the Mediterranean Fleet would join them.[39] This was good sense, since any mutinous man-o'-war which declared itself might well risk attack by loyal consorts. The *Pompée* ringleaders in June 1797 told the men they canvassed that other ships were party to the conspiracy. Their method was to approach seamen and marines directly and explain the purpose of the mutiny.[40] Reactions varied greatly, as did approach. Martin Welsh spurned the business: 'I said I would not as it might hurt the nation.' Against this patriotism, the agitator found he could make no headway and so he went his way cursing, 'Damn and Bugger you and the nation too, you old Bugger!' Another mutineer threatened those who would not sign the peace petition with a hanging, but a sergeant of marines was more gently urged with the question, 'Did I not wish for a peace and if I had no person dear to me on shore?'

For many sailors such approaches put them in a moral quandary – whether to inform on a shipmate or to remain neutral. Some tried to dissuade the mutineer, like William Gilbert of the gun vessel *Haughty*.[41] He had been approached by William Timmings ('a Troublesome Man when in liquor') during May 1798 with a scheme to seize the ship and take it to the nearby French coast. Timmings was an isolated figure with a brooding grievance, for he had been recently flogged for insolence to the ship's doctor. Gilbert pointed out that he imperilled himself by talking to others about his planned mutiny, that even if he got twenty converts they could not cover all the hatchways and that if they got to a French port, they might be ill-received. Several sailors were approached but Timmings found only one helpmate. Both were revealed and hanged.

When he was brooding over his many misfortunes, Timmings became desperate and moaned that he was 'wearied of his life'. A few mutinies were truly the offspring of hopelessness, but most were conceived more rationally as petitions for the redress of grievances. The Navy tolerated the right of sailors to join together and offer petitions, either to their commanders or else the Admiralty. Sometimes these were acted upon, like the petition from the crew of *Ceres* in 1795, when allegations against the vessel's officers were investigated by three captains. These inquiries did not please the *Ceres*'s captain and first lieutenant who were keen to get their revenge on the crew, once the commission had gone ashore.[42]

The borderline between drawing up a petition and getting it signed or marked by sailors, and mutiny, was a narrow one. In their passage between decks, the organisers of a petition often stirred up violent passions which could quickly pass out of control. In June 1798, the crew of the line-of-battle ship, *Adamant*, asked Admiral Parker to investigate their grievances. These embraced thin beer, officers' monopolising the best cuts of meat, and the lack of 'every Indulgence wich Every other ship get after coming from Sea'. They added, plaintively that 'our wifes and children [were] Turned out Three Days before the Ship was payed wich was verry Piercing for they had no money to Subsist on.'

In consequence the *Adamant*'s crew wanted some new officers, or else drafting to another ship. On 30 June there were disturbances below deck, which were reported by the Master-at-Arms, and Captain Hotham found himself faced with several sailors who, 'in a very mutinous manner', called to be moved to other ships. The fuss subsided when Hotham warned them their behaviour was mutinous and several were arrested. 142 of their shipmates stood by them and asked for their reprieve:[43]

We never had the Least thought about any such thing as mutiny. It was owin to our be too much Intoxicated or Els we should not have gone aft and your Honours knows the ways of Seamen when they are in Liquor that they are always [a] Very unruly set of men.

The Admiralty knew this too well. Its board members also knew that the making of petitions was often a step towards mutiny, with or without rum. Knots of men getting together and talking about their misfortunes and considering ways in which those might be reversed, were the seeds of mutiny. The Spithead mutiny had started in February 1797 with below-decks agitation about pay when the Channel Fleet was in port. The *Queen Charlotte*'s men may well have set the ball rolling and on 27 February were exchanging letters with the *London*'s crew on how to approach the authorities over pay. 'Proceed in caution, peace and good behaviour', counselled the *London*'s crew, who knew that deviation from such a path would mean suspicion of mutiny. The result was a petition from *Queen Charlotte* to the Fleet's commander, the seventy-year-old Lord Howe, who was at Bath, taking the waters as a cure for gout. His discomfort was increased by more unsigned letters from other ships which were 'decently expressed', but, to his mind, the work of one 'malicious individual'. Inquiries made in Portsmouth yielded no evidence of conspiracy and so, on 22 March, Howe dropped the letters at the Admiralty. The board's reaction was that it was never accustomed to handle anonymous petitions.

What the Admiralty Board did not realise was that the unsigned papers were the result of a formidable and concealed movement which had grown between decks in every ship of the Channel Fleet. The framing of these petitions had been the work of an organisation which had, by some hidden means, secured the loyalty of every sailor in that fleet, although none of this was apparent from the letters themselves.

VIGOROUS AND EFFECTUAL MEASURES

When the Spithead sailors realised that their requests to Howe had been ignored, they decided on a new course of action. How far their plans had advanced by 15 April 1797 is not known, but by this date Lord Bridport, who had superseded the ailing Howe as commander, was aware that something was amiss with his crews.

He suspected that there were 'combinations' amongst the sailors and so did the Admiralty, which forced the issue by sending orders for the fleet to weigh anchor. In a display of awesome solidarity, the crews refused. For the next four weeks the fleet passed from Bridport's control to that of the Delegates whilst the sailors waited for their grievances to be redressed. Throughout this period, the Delegates gave clear notice that their quarrel was not with the government but with the naval hierarchy, and pledged themselves to put to sea once intelligence was received that the French fleet had left Brest for its expected foray against Ireland. Vessels such as brigs, sloops and frigates required for routine convoy and patrol duties were ordered to fulfil their normal duties. Proper order was maintained on ships, although the Delegates took to themselves the honours due to flag officers.

Once the mutiny had begun, its course was dictated by the reactions of Lord Spencer, Bridport and his junior admirals, Sir John Colpoys and Sir Alan Gardner, and the captains of the mutinous ships who had been allowed to stay aboard. The more peppery officers were quickly sent ashore by the Delegates who rightly anticipated that their choler might easily provoke incidents. Lord Spencer, First Lord of the Admiralty, who arrived in Portsmouth on 18 April, was a patrician public servant whose mediocrity and assiduity passed for virtue in the eyes of his contemporaries. He was stirred to no sense of urgency by what he found at Portsmouth and later played his part in the delays which so alarmed the sailors, but he was to some extent the victim of the cumbersome machinery of state which he served. Bridport, a seventy-year-old member of the Hood naval dynasty, was at the end of a career which had been respectable if not spectacular. He possessed calm and wisdom, and restrained his fire-eating subordinates, Colpoys and Gardner. Still, the responsibility proved all but too much for him, for, after a fortnight, he informed Evan Nepean, the Secretary to the Admiralty, 'I am so unwell that I can scarcely hold my pen to write.'

Colpoys and Gardner suffered no infirmities save for enlarged spleens. At the start of the mutiny, Colpoys, flying his flag in *London*, had wanted to order his marines to fire on the Delegates as they were rowed to his ship. Bridport forbade him, but on 7 May he was unfettered and his attempt to stop the Delegates boarding *London* ended in bloodshed. This incident worsened the temper of the mutineers and led directly to the expulsion of officers from all

ships. It also secured his own dismissal, for a week later the
Admiralty ordered Bridport to remove him from his command. His
sea-going record was dismal, as the mutineers acknowledged in a
ballad:

> The murdering Colpoys, Vice-Admiral of the Blue,
> Gave orders to fire on the 'London' ship's crew;
> While the enemy of Britain was ploughing the sea,
> He, like a base coward, let them get away
> When the French and their transports sailed for Bantry Bay.

Gardner also fell out with the mutineers, calling the Delegates 'a
damned mutinous blackguard set' who were too scared to fight the
French. His affirmation that he would hang every fifth man aroused
deep fears and forced Spencer to ride to Windsor to get a full royal
pardon.

Like the unimaginative bureaucrat that he was, Spencer was
both niggardly and cautious in his dealings with the Delegates,
fearing all the time the costs of any concession. He gave way on 20
April, after hearing Bridport and the fleet's officers pooh-pooh his
suggestion of a *coup de main* against the mutinous ships. The
monthly wages of the ordinary seamen rose to 23s 6d. and those of
the able seamen to 29s 6d., and measures were taken in hand to
rectify faults in the distribution and quality of rations. This
resignation to circumstances had not been easy for Spencer, and it
rankled with many officers. It did not, however, end the mutiny, for
the sailors continued to press for a royal pardon which was seen as
the only guarantee against official retaliation at a later date, and
there was a flurry of demands for the dismissal of individual officers
whose wayward application of punishments antagonised their
crews. Matters were made worse by the administration's slowness
in getting the original concessions enrolled on the Parliamentary
statute book. By 7 May the sailors' suspicions were aroused as they
began to interpret procrastination as betrayal. Colpoys's clumsy
efforts to regain control of *London* and the bloodshed which followed
created new tensions, which were in part relieved by the expulsion
of all officers from their ships.

By now the Admiralty had recovered from its initial shock at the
outbreak of the mutiny, and was seeking ways to get the men back
to their duties and to forestall any further disruptions in other
ships. On 28 April the Board's mood was indicated in a letter
which hoped that, now the sailors had been allowed 'very liberal

indulgences', they would return to discipline.[44] If the sailors could not be coaxed, they had to be coerced, and on 1 May orders were sent to all officers which enjoined them to take special care of arms and ammunition held by the marines and 'on the first appearance of mutiny to use the most vigorous means to suppress it' and punish the ringleaders. The contagion had to be contained, and a day later Nepean warned Lord St Vincent that three mutinous ships, *Bellerophon, Audacious* and *Theseus*, would be shortly bound to join his Mediterranean Fleet. 'You may be prepared to take most vigorous and effectual measures for the counter acting any attempt that may be made by ill-designing Persons to excite the Spirit of Mutiny among the crews of the Ships of HM squadron under your Command.'[45] Commanders of ships lying in the anchorages at Cawsand Bay, Torbay and Hamoaze were commanded to have no truck with 'irregular conduct', and the Torbay flotilla was ordered to make sail for the Lizard so as to keep them away from ships already infected with mutiny.[46] The quarantine was unsuccessful, for the Cawsand crews knew what was happening at Spithead and on 11 May their commander was advised not to tempt trouble by giving orders.[47] The planned isolation of the Torbay squadron also failed, as on 13 May their commander was told to take them to Spithead, where it was hoped that their crews would be placated by the general conciliation planned by Lord Howe.[48]

The secondary developments which had followed the first outbreak of mutiny at Spithead placed the Admiralty in an intolerable position. Calls for the dismissal of unpopular officers were a direct challenge to the structure of command and were a far cry from grievances over pay and victuals, both of which the Admiralty admitted had been indifferent.[49] The Admiralty was faced with another problem, that of the French fleet at Brest, whose preparations to sail were almost completed. On 9 May intelligence reached London through an American skipper, whose vessel had sailed from Brest eight days before, that sixteen ships of the line and a dozen frigates were ready to put to sea. Thirty thousand French troops were in the port and six transports had just arrived. On the following day news arrived of the other French invasion force which had been gathering in the mouth of the Texel. Here forty ships of war and thirty-three transports were lying at anchor and apparently ready to put to sea.[50] The destination of these two formidable fleets was not known for certain, but the common guess was Ireland where troops were to be put ashore to assist local rebels. With the Channel Fleet in a state of mutiny and other squadrons becoming involved, the French seemed guaranteed to have a clear passage. 'Total destruction is near,' one of the Admiralty Board warned Pitt.

The solution was further concessions to the sailors. The task was helped by the Commons and Lords passing the Act for the Navy in a day – the extra cash needed for the wages and victuals being estimated at £563,000 a year.[51] This did much to pacify the sailors and helped Lord and Lady Howe, who were sent to Portsmouth on 10 May, to tour the fleet. The sailors had much affection for their old commander and this, coupled with the good news he brought from London, reassured them that at last they had got what they wanted. Howe and Bridport were ordered to use their discretion over the dismissal of officers and, bowing to pressure, they agreed that over fifty were to be kept on shore. Howe, the Act of Parliament, and the reluctant concession over the officers did the trick, and on 17 May the fleet put to sea in good heart.

NO FURTHER CONCESSIONS

What had been gained by the sailors at Spithead was more than better pay and food. The sailors had shown their strength, caught their officers and the Admiralty hopping and, by example, shown what could be achieved by determined, collective action. The floodgates of indiscipline had been opened, as the Admiralty had been quick to recognise. Fears that the spirit of collective insubordination would spread were soon justified, for there were more serious mutinies on board ships of the Channel Squadron, anchored at the Nore, and the North Sea Fleet, lying off Yarmouth. As ships from home waters were dispersed to foreign stations, their crews carried with them tales of what had happened at Spithead and the Nore, and so excited sailors in the Mediterranean, West Indies, Cape and Indian Ocean squadrons. For the next four years, sailors in all these fleets tried their hand at mutiny to gain concessions from their officers.

The response of the Admiralty and individual commanders was unbending; there would be no more stepping down in the face of threats or defiance. On 20 May 1797, the port admiral at Plymouth

57

was told that, whilst it was not worth pressing for the return of officers who had been expelled from their ships if this hindered the sailors' return to their duties, he was to offer 'no further concessions'. Sailors who continued to show obduracy were to be warned that their pardons were in jeopardy.[52] An even firmer line was being taken against the mutineers at the Nore whose flotilla had been placed under a state of siege by the government.

The ships involved in the Nore mutiny were of less strategic importance than the Channel Fleet and the wild behaviour of the mutineers left the Admiralty little choice but to show intractability. The demands made by Parker and the Nore Delegates were a gross trespass on the Admiralty's power to govern the Navy and individual captains to command their ships, and went far beyond anything sought at Spithead. The Nore men wanted statutory and generous leave, the right of crews to vote as to whether unpopular officers should be permitted back on their ships, an indemnity for deserters who had re-enlisted, and a modification of the Articles of War. Spencer, who faced the Delegates and many of their adherents on 25 May, rejected these demands and insisted that the mutineers return to discipline. The message could have surprised few who heard it, for, three days before, the first of many detachments of militia had appeared on the north Kent coast, tokens of the government's will to break the mutiny. On 27 May, the Admiralty ordered Admiral Duncan to stand by with his squadron, which was to be ready to attack the mutinous ships, and the following day the wavering loyalties of the crews of the frigates *San Fiorenzo* and *Clyde* were put to the test when their captains were commanded to take the vessels to Dover. Undeterred by the bullying of the larger ships' crews, the *San Fiorenzo*'s seamen rallied to their captain and on 30 May broke from the fleet. She was fired upon 'with Musquetry and great Guns loaded with Rounds of Grape shot' which cut away the main topgallant and mizzen shrouds. Four topmen were wounded before the frigate escaped from the anchorage.[53]

The Nore mutineers were now at war in earnest, although Parker pleaded that he and his followers were not fighting the government, the government was fighting them. It was an unconvincing appeal and many of the mutineers, unnerved by the Admiralty's firmness and unwilling to act as agents of the country's undoing, were having second thoughts about a mutiny which looked very like rebellion. This was what the Admiralty had intended, for it knew well that the mutineers were riven by dissensions which could be plainly seen when brawls broke out on several ships over whether or not to raise the Red Flag. It was a flag of defiance, and the ships which flew it were determined to wear down their opponents with a blockade of the Port of London.

Fearing that they were losing ground, in spite of the blockade, the Delegates had decided on 23 May to send representatives to the North Sea Fleet at Yarmouth. The enterprise failed, for their cutter was taken at sea, since Admiral Duncan had been forewarned of their coming. Not that their seizure had much effect, as his own squadron had been agitated for some time and by 29-30 May all but two ships were in a state of mutiny. Duncan, by the force of his own personality and the warmth of feeling he generated in his crews, had tried to stem the unrest. He sympathised with the sailors over pay and had asked the Admiralty to reduce the number of lashes which a captain could award. As his fleet disintegrated and he faced the shame of having his crews desert in the face of the enemy, he insisted that his men had no grievances.[54]

The refusal to sail to the Dutch coast of nine of Duncan's line-of-battle ships and their defection to the Nore on 29-30 May was a bonus to the mutineers there, and a blow to the Admiralty's policy of intransigence. Parker now had under his control a formidable force, including ships which the Admiralty had hoped to use against the mutiny. But the commitment of the Yarmouth mutineers was fragile. For some, the unrest had been an excuse for getting drunk, rough-handling civilians and breaking windows in Yarmouth, and for others a carnival in which they hung effigies of the Prime Minister from yardarms and got even with some of their officers. This was certainly so on the 64-gun *Nassau*, where the crew had unsuccessfully petitioned for the removal of the 'tyrant' Captain Herbert Sawyer and his first lieutenant two years before.[55] Once at the Nore, *Nassau* and her consorts helped to enforce the blockade and hoped that it would undermine the government's resolve. But there were no signs of any flinching and the mutinous ships stood at anchor, cut off from the land, waiting for concessions which never came. All the time Parker and his sympathisers attempted to maintain morale, but their harangues left the sailors puzzled and anxious.

On 10 June the mutineers' cohesion began to break up. The first vessels to desert were the *Repulse* and the *Leopard*, both of which came under fire from the more militant, with Parker himself frenziedly commanding one gun. On these ships and on many others, sailors were debating amongst themselves what was best to be done. All the Admiralty offered was a pardon, whilst the more extreme mutineers were openly discussing defection to the French, which was tantamount to an admission that the 'good cause' was lost and its supporters had no choice but to run away from whatever retribution the Admiralty was preparing for them. Cut off from land, where patrols of soldiers seized and arrested any sailors who came ashore, and forced to play the part of traitors at war with their country, the sailors were bewildered. This was not how matters had proceeded at Spithead, and very few of the mutineers had ever had any wish to come to blows with a country which was now united against them. Rather than stumble along a road whose end they could not discern, the seamen drew back towards their duty. Their old world, with all its imperfections, was preferable to the airy promises of Parker and his cronies. Officers, who sensed the change of mood, played on the sailors' doubts and exhorted them to return to obedience and with it the possibility of pardon.

By 13 June, the sailors' will had been broken and the Admiralty's inflexibility had been justified. Parker was arrested, tried and hanged at the yardarm, and over 500 of his closest adherents were detained. Of these, fifty-nine were tried and found guilty of mutiny and thirty-six were executed.[56] The Nore mutiny had achieved nothing for its participants, but its defeat had restored the confidence of the Admiralty. It had shown that it would go no further in making concessions and that a policy of firmness could work. In the future, naval mutineers who tried to bludgeon either their officers or the Admiralty would find both unyielding and could expect condign punishment; there would be no more compromise after Spithead.

MISCHIEVOUS PLOTTING PERSONS

The resolution of the Admiralty was conveyed to all captains on every station. They were commanded to be watchful for signs of restlessness and to respond swiftly to any manifestation of lower-deck unrest the moment it showed itself. Within weeks of this order being despatched, men-o'-war which had been involved in the Spithead and Nore mutinies were sailing to new squadrons and taking with them sailors who were either still disaffected or possessed of a knowledge of what could be achieved by collective action. At the same time more Irishmen were joining the Navy, bringing with them the discontents of their homeland and a determination to transfer the methods of clandestine organisation to its warships. The virus of mutiny was moving across the seas.

The first sign of the impact of the two major mutinies on distant squadrons was felt in the Mediterranean Fleet. On 27 June 1797, the frigate *Latona*, whose crew had taken part in the Nore mutiny, anchored in St Michael's Roads off the Azores and soon the sailors were telling their mates from other vessels the news from England. The *Latona*'s crew wrote to the crew of the frigate *Romulus* and let them know what had been conceded by the Admiralty in the way of higher wages and better victuals. 'Moreover,' they added, 'we are to have better Usage than we have had of late ... nor a bad officer is allowed to stay in any ship.' Furthermore, they asserted, sailors only had to put their complaints in writing, using precise terms, 'and you May Depend on getting redress even from the Captain to the Least officer in the ship'. Nothing of this kind had been promised, but the dismissal of unpopular officers by Bridport and Howe had clearly excited the sailors' hopes. This news certainly agitated the *Romulus*'s crew, who, two days after hearing it, became restive, mutinied and turned two for'ard guns aft. They called for the expulsion of two officers, but were calmed by their captain who promised that there would be no repercussions.[57]

Such a conciliatory approach incensed Lord St Vincent, the commander of the Mediterranean Fleet, who once he had heard of the disturbances on board the *Romulus* drafted the ringleaders to a tighter ship and replaced them with men 'of inferior stature' from two line-of-battle ships. This was, he assured the Admiralty, 'a measure I judge highly necessary to put an end to these daring attempts to carry his Majesty's Ships whenever it pleases a few Ruffians who keep the rest of the crew in fear'.[58] Discipline concerned St Vincent and he had already taken measures designed to see that it was strictly enforced on his ships. For some time he had actively encouraged marines to regard themselves as men apart from sailors, to mess separately and to be ready to quell disturbances at their officers' orders. Forewarned by the Admiralty that the restlessness of sailors in home waters might spread to his crews, St Vincent was vigilant and ready to crush any sign of mutiny with condign punishment.

He served notice of his mood at the end of June 1797 when he approved the death sentence passed on two sailors from the *St George* who had been found guilty of buggery. He had no choice, he assured the Admiralty, since 'the crime of which they were convicted was of so horrid and detestable a nature, and the times requiring summary punishment'.[59] The two sailors' messmates thought otherwise, for whilst it was common for sailors to feel nothing but loathing for such unnatural behaviour, the evidence set before the court martial suggested that the pair were too drunk to have performed the act.[60] On 4 July the crew of the *St George* mutinied and attempted to rescue the condemned men, but were checked by the courage of their captain, who was assisted by a company of the 25th Regiment, serving aboard in lieu of marines. The mutineers were tried and six were hanged, a few days after the men they had tried to save.

This display of determination was only partially successful, for unrest continued to erupt on board ships of St Vincent's fleet. It was made worse by the presence on board of many Irish sailors, and in May 1798 St Vincent decided on a trial of strength combined with a spectacle of the awesomeness of the discipline which he demanded. The immediate cause was the arrival of the *Marlborough*, which the year before had been involved in the Spithead mutiny and had secured the expulsion of its captain. During the *Marlborough*'s cruise from England, there had been a small-scale mutiny, prompted by some of the Irishmen amongst the crew. Warned of this, St Vincent ordered the newcomer to anchor between the rest of the line-of-battle ships which had been drawn up in two lines. The mutineers were then put on trial, found guilty and sentenced to death. St Vincent insisted that one of the men sentenced was to be hanged the next morning and was to be hauled aloft by his own shipmates. The *Marlborough*'s captain expressed fears that his men would refuse to obey such a command. St Vincent was furious. 'What, do you mean to tell me, Captain Ellison, that you cannot command his Majesty's ship the *Marlborough*? For, if that is the case, sir, I will immediately send on board an officer who can.'

The following morning, orders were issued for the other ships in the Fleet to send launches, armed with carronades ready for action and manned by trustworthy gunners, to surround the *Marlborough*. Isolated between the lines of men-o'-war and surrounded by launches, less than a hundred yards from her hull, the *Marlborough* was ready for a trial of strength. There was no resistance from her crew who obeyed orders to lower the gunports and hauled the condemned man up the yardarm. 'Discipline is preserved, sir,' observed St Vincent, well pleased with his success. He was, perhaps, too optimistic, for Irishmen on board the *Princess Royal* had been waiting for a sign from the *Marlborough* as a signal to rush their officers and kill them.[61] They imagined that the crews of the *Prince* and the *Hector* would rise up as well. A few weeks later their plan – to seize the *Princess Royal*, kill their officers and St Vincent as well, and carry the ship to a Spanish port – was revealed. The three men at the heart of the conspiracy were tried, found guilty and hanged.

The hesitancy of these mutineers had been their downfall and vindicated St Vincent's firm line over the *Marlborough*. Yet they had no doubt exaggerated the strength of their movement, a common failing with mutineers after the Spithead and Nore, for, beyond a resentment against the service, they lacked a cause which could unite them with other crews. Above all, there was the fear created by St Vincent's well-known inflexibility; he would uphold the law and not be trifled with. Another stern officer, Sir Edward Pellew, recognised this and, after Lord Bridport had refused him permission to court martial some men from his ship, the *Impéteux*, for drawing up a petition, he applied to St Vincent. He knew his man and was allowed his court martial in which the petitioners were found guilty and executed.

Like the Admiralty, St Vincent recognised that the Navy was facing a crisis during the months after the Nore and Spithead. The concessions made at the end of the Spithead mutiny had called into question the right of officers to command as they wished. Although the Admiralty had been quick to claim that no further toleration would be given to demands for the dismissal of unpopular officers, sailors clung to the belief that they now possessed the right to secure the removal of such men. It took some time to disabuse them of this fancy. Sailors from the *Suffolk*, then attached to the East Indies squadron, had learned from the *Bombay Courier* of 9 October 1797 of the allowances granted at Spithead. On 13 January 1798, 'considering ourselves to be upon an equilibrium with those at home', the *Suffolk*'s crew sought their captain's confirmation of the new conditions of service and wages. They pressed him further and demanded that he dismissed the Master and two lieutenants, mention of whom provoked cries of 'Put them on shore'. The sailors were temporarily calmed by their captain but two days later they again pressed their right to get rid of the three men by a demonstration. 'In a mode of Defiance', they clambered up the rigging and in imitation of the Spithead and Nore mutineers began cheering. The captain and his officers moved for'ard to mark out the ringleaders and arrest them. One man fought back with a handspike, but the rest gave up without a struggle. The man who resisted was executed and four others were flogged but, as elsewhere, the mutinous spirit was not completely eradicated by such examples, for there were further disturbances a few months later after a seaman had refused to paint a mast.[62] Similar unrest ran through the ships of the Cape Squadron during September 1797 when its sailors heard of what had happened at the Nore and Spithead. Again the main source of disorder were calls for the removal of heavy-handed officers, one of whom, the captain of the *Tremendous*, was taken and tried by his own crew. The commanding Admiral, Thomas Pringle, settled the matter by giving the officer concerned a formal trial which, after hearing the case against him, recommended his dismissal. Sterner measures were needed later and in January 1799 two of *Tremendous*'s crew were hanged for insolence to a midshipman.[63]

On one hand, the Admiralty and individual officers were anxious to advertise that the 'rights' secured at Spithead did not extend to seeking the expulsion of officers or questioning their methods of command, and on the other, many sailors believed that they could challenge their officers' authority with impunity. During the first eight months of 1799 the crew of the frigate *Diadem* chafed against the shortage of food and the poorness of its quality, as well as the vindictiveness of their officers. In their own eyes they were good sailors, who had won approbation from many commanders, including Lord Nelson. Their officers saw them in a different light as 'a set of Lazy good for nothing Rascalls', a view which had been shared by St Vincent during *Diadem*'s Mediterranean service, when he had found them a 'dirty blackguard crew' fortunately kept on a tight leash by their captain. As a result, the *Diadem*'s crew complained, 'We are not allowed to speak and when stripped at the gangway it was plain to see our backs are as much cut as is a Negro's in the West Indies with the whip.'[64] The petition which sought redress was treated as mutiny. Likewise the demand made in August 1799 for the dismissal of Captain Rowley and Lieutenant French of the *Ramillies* and their replacement by Lieutenant Frost was interpreted as mutiny, in spite of the accused men's claim that they had been angered by their captain's ban on bumboats coming to his ship whilst it was in harbour. What mattered here was that *Ramillies* had been involved in the Spithead mutiny, where the crew had unsuccessfully demanded their captain's removal on the grounds of his ferocity.[65] A petition for duty on another ship from the crew of the *Pluto*, who had just heard that they were to be sent to Newfoundland, was similarly construed as mutiny. Two of those who helped frame the petition were subsequently hanged. Another protest against foreign service, this time in the West Indies, led to the mutiny by the crew of the *Téméraire* in January 1802, which was accompanied by violence and threats to kill the captain and his officers.[66]

ENOUGH TO MAKE A MAN MAD

During the final stages of the Nore mutiny, a handful of the more desperate mutineers had claimed that they would take their ships to France and surrender to the French. This type of mutiny had hitherto been rare. In 1795 the crew of the 4-gun *Shark* had taken over their boat, steered it to The Hague and handed it over to the Dutch and, a year later, petitioners from the frigate *Shannon* contemplated similar action in the face of cruel and oppressive officers.[57] The mutineers on *Princess Royal* in 1798 had planned to take their ship to Spain, and a series of similar acts of piracy were planned by Irish nationalist mutineers in the same year.* These men had a political axe to grind, for most hoped that the men-o'-war they had taken would eventually join the French service and play a part in the struggle for Irish freedom.

The Irish shipboard plots of 1798, and the increase in similar, non-political attempts to take over warships between 1797 and 1800, disturbed the Admiralty. Great efforts were made to track down, capture and punish the men responsible in order to deter others, and with the *Hermione* mutineers the uncommon procedure of placing the bodies of executed men in gibbets overlooking naval anchorages was adopted. Vessels such as frigates, sloops and bomb

* See pages 185-96

65

ketches with small crews and on solitary patrols were particularly vulnerable. It was remarkably easy for a small body of sailors to plan and execute a *coup* as long as they had surprise on their side. In March 1800 mutineers were able to overpower the officers of the watch on board the 12-gun *Danae* whilst she was patrolling off Brest. Twenty men out of the crew of 139 guarded the hatches, leaving the captain, Lord William Proby, with forty loyal armed men below decks, powerless to intervene. The mutineers steered *Danae* into Cameret Bay, where they were able to summon a detachment of French infantrymen. With his ship boarded and under the guns of the French forts, Proby found himself without 'the most distant prospect of doing my country a service' and accordingly surrendered. He was well treated by the French, but the mutineers found to their dismay that the France of the Consulate looked less kindly on them. They were locked up in the prison of Dinan and later drafted aboard men-o'-war. One had the mischance of being taken prisoner and was later identified in an English prison.[68]

It is impossible to identify the motive for this mutiny. Proby's log suggests that he was a humane officer and the contention that the ringleader of the mutiny was a Nore mutineer, who had served as Parker's secretary, is conjecture.[69] Unquestionably the commonest explanation for this type of mutiny was the presence on board a vessel of a handful of bitter men who wanted revenge on their officers and had the nerve to carry out an attack on them. The plot to take the sloop *Volage* in 1799 possessed all these ingredients, and began with three conspirators exchanging grievances with a man being held in irons. The prisoner wished that they would be taken by an enemy man-o'-war and one of the conspirators, Timothy Donovan, concurred, adding that he would like to take their vessel into Havana. The two others approved and hoped that they would have the chance to kill two of their officers. Later, when accused of mutiny, Donovan claimed that he was drunk, but this did not prevent his being found guilty and given 500 lashes. A victim of such punishment on board the gun-vessel *Haughty* in 1798 nursed a sore back and confided to his messmates that he would be glad to murder two or three officers and be hanged for it. His misfortunes were 'enough to make a man mad' and later he toyed with the idea of seizing the ship and sailing it to a French port, where he hoped he and his fellow plotters would be rewarded with prize money. He needed just twenty men but found none who would share in the venture. One whom he approached was doubtful of the reception which would be offered by the French and warned him that 'he would not get half the value of the vessel' and that afterwards the mutineers would be 'looked on as scoundrels'.[70]

The core of plotters on board *Volage* and *Haughty* received no support and little encouragement from their shipmates, who were either overawed by the risks involved or else were satisfied with their officers and conditions. On board the frigate *Hermione* no such goodwill towards officers and service seems to have existed. Hugh Pigot, who had taken command of the vessel in February 1797 soon after he was twenty-eight, had been marked out by Lord St Vincent as 'a very promising officer and spirited fellow', but has subsequently secured a reputation as one of the most sadistic officers in the Navy. This odium is solely the result of the mutiny on board the *Hermione* in September 1797, in which he was murdered, and the repetition of subsequent gossip about the events which led up to it. Pigot was certainly a skilful seaman who demanded a high standard of professionalism from his crew which he was prepared to enforce with the lash. In manner he was irascible and volatile, the victim of wayward moods and ever liable to erupt into a fury. When this burnt itself out, Pigot regretted his passion and seems to have been genuinely sorry for the victims of his temper. Yet, as a commander, his mercurial spasms could not be checked and his crew therefore lay at the mercy of sudden rages.

The mutiny on board the *Hermione* on the night of 21-22 September 1797 had been preceded by two sombre incidents, both the result of Pigot's capriciousness. Since 1 September, *Hermione*, accompanied by the brig *Diligence*, had been patrolling the Mona Channel between Puerto Rico and the eastern tip of Saint-Dominique (Santo Domingo) but had taken no prizes, a misfortune which may have added to Pigot's irritability. Six days into the patrol, Pigot had fallen out with David O'Casey, an Irish midshipman and an experienced officer, and as a result of the squabble had demanded that O'Casey kneel before him and apologise. O'Casey did not, and was given 6 lashes, a punishment which Pigot later wished undone. The second incident followed what Pigot considered a piece of poor seamanship in which the topmen fumbled their reefing of the topsails during the pursuit of an American merchantman. The mizzen-men were noticeably hamfisted and the enraged Pigot warned them, 'I'll flog the last man down.' The topmen knew their captain and three missed their footing in the scramble and fell to the deck. Two, Peter Bascombe,

67

a Negro from Jamaica, and a sixteen-year-old lad, Francis Stainton, died immediately. 'Throw the lubbers overboard!' ordered Pigot and the corpses were hurled over the side. According to Casey, then confined to his quarters, 'this melancholy circumstance ... which greatly increased the previous dislike of the captain ... no doubt hastened, if not entirely decided the mutiny.'

The next day, 21 September, twelve main-topmen were flogged for the previous day's mishandling of the sails. Some, but not all, of those chastised joined the attack on Pigot's cabin that same night. For several days there had been mutinous mutterings amongst the crew, some of which had been overheard, but not reported, by Midshipman Wiltshire. He climbed into the shrouds during the evening and remained a neutral observer who, after the mutiny, secured for himself anonymity, perhaps out of fear that a naval inquiry would reveal his abdication of duty. The actual opportunity for mutiny came in the late evening when the *Diligence* steered on a northward tack which took her out of sight of *Hermione*. This chance was exploited by twenty-six or so of the *Hermione*'s starboard watch, who, having stirred themselves up with rum, finally rushed aft and stormed Pigot's cabin, armed with cutlasses. What followed was recounted by Marine John Holford, who was Pigot's cook:

> James Phillips, the sailmaker, who has since become a soldier [in the Spanish army] told me he stabbed the Captain in the guts, that John Farrel a seaman told me that the Captain was ill-used and he went into the cabin and saw him leaning on the couch and he said to the Captain, 'You bugger are you not dead yet?' and on the Captain's answering, 'No you villain, I'm not', Farrel struck him over the head and knocked him down.

The dying Pigot was then thrown overboard. One of his assailants, an Italian foretopman called to him, 'You've showed no mercy yourself and therefore deserve none.' Old scores were settled elsewhere and the first lieutenant was cut down by a group which included his servant, who bawled, 'Let me have a chop at him, he shall not make me jump about the gunroom any more.' A fourteen-year-old midshipman was also murdered at the instigation of a sailor whom he had had flogged.

In less than thirty minutes, a tenth of the crew, all from one watch, had murdered the captain and several officers and taken control of the ship. After revenge, their first thought was drink and

Pigot's wine was consumed and the first attacks made on the barrels which contained 1,000 gallons of rum. Leadership came from the Master's mate, who had steered the ship away from the *Diligence* at the first sign of disturbance, the two bosun's mates, who a couple of days before had been the instruments of Pigot's tyranny and, latterly, Laurence Cronin, the surgeon's mate. Cronin had played no part in the first uprising, but once it was over he called the crew to him and read them an address which he had prepared. He announced himself a Belfast Republican and applauded what had taken place, having already made a record of the behaviour of the Captain and his officers. He proceeded to give the crew a lesson in the General Will and told them that they must kill all the remaining officers who were imprisoned below to complete the deed of tyrranicide. Nine were hauled on deck and thrown overboard. The following morning kangaroo courts 'tried' Midshipman Casey, who refused to throw in his lot with the mutineers, and the vessel's Master, Edward Southcott. Both had enough friends to outvote those who called for their murder and they were set free.

The 'assembly' of mutineers, willing and unwilling, then debated another matter, their future. This was, by general agreement, thought to be most assured at La Guira, on the coast of Venezuela, where it was hoped that the Spanish authorities would give them reward and sanctuary. Then Cronin, drawing on his Ulster Jacobin experience, administered an oath to each mutineer in which they swore loyalty to each other and pledged not to betray their mates. Several, either conscience-stricken or frightened by the gallows, later abjured this oath. In the meantime the *Hermione* sailed to La Guira and for six days the mutineers held a carnival in which officers' goods and clothes were doled out, what cash there was aboard was shared, dances were held on the quarterdeck in mock of authority, and rum was drunk. The days of revelry over, the mutineers took the *Hermione* under the guns of La Guira and threw themselves on the mercy of the Spaniards there, taking care not to be too explicit about the fate of their officers. They were given asylum, but soon their presence proved an embarrassment. Many soon found to their dismay that they had merely exchanged the rigours of Pigot's command for menial labour in the Spanish army and, without the means of livelihood, they drifted into berths on French or American merchantmen.

Details of what had happened to the *Hermione* gradually reached

Admiral Sir Hyde Parker, then commanding the West Indies station, and by the end of the year were known to the Admiralty in London. Fellow seamen were horrified and their reaction may be judged by that of the crew of the *Diligence*, who were amongst the first to hear the news. In La Guira the *Hermione*'s crew had boasted that the men from *Diligence* were party to the conspiracy, a *canard* which angered the Diligences.[71]

> Never could any body of Men be more shocked at hearing of such unexampled barbarism, nor ever was indignation marked stronger than when they were told of the intention of breeding Mutiny in, or seizing the Diligence by force, to a Man I was assured, that had we been in company when this fatal catastrophe took place that they would have retaken the Hermione, or perished alongside her.

The Admiralty was alarmed by the news of the *Hermione* mutiny since it arrived within a few months of the end of Spithead and Nore outbreaks and seemed to presage further and more violent upheavals. In the end no more than forty men were involved, but they had taken control of the frigate with a crew of just under 200, leaving their shipmates either lukewarm adherents or horrified spectators. Given that there were still rumblings of discontent elsewhere, the Admiralty was determined to strain every muscle and nerve of the Navy to discover, arrest and punish the *Hermione* mutineers. Over the next years over forty were uncovered from the anonymity of merchantmen in the West Indies and even, in two cases, aboard British men-o'-war, and over half of them were executed.

When brought to trial, the *Hermione* mutineers told a story of what was little more than a mindless *jacquerie* upon which Cronin imposed a democratic charade. Once they had killed their enemies, the mutineers' only aim was to escape. Pigot was undoubtedly a severe captain; in command of *Success* between September 1794 and September 1795 he had sentenced eighty-five men to be flogged. This was excessive but not unusual, and several *Success* men, including some mutineers, had followed him from that vessel to the *Hermione*. What may have tipped the balance was his capricious and choleric behaviour in the fortnight before the mutiny. This was most cruelly felt by the most insecure men on the ship, the topmen. Normally an élite of the crew, the topmen reefed the sails balanced high over the deck, and on *Hermione* their everyday perils were

70

augmented by Pigot's impatience. Not surprisingly, topmen played a crucial part in the mutiny.

The maltreatment of topmen caused a copycat mutiny in October 1806 on board the brig *Ferret*. Her commander, the Honourable George Cadogan, was a pitiless officer whose remorseless use of the lash made Pigot appear gentle. During April and May 1807 he ordered three floggings, two of 24 strokes for sleeping on watch and negligence, and one of 36 strokes for drunkenness. On board his next command, HMS *Crocodile*, he awarded forty-four floggings during a round cruise from Spithead to the Cape, which lasted from 15 December 1807 to 9 May 1808. Just over 600 lashes were given, and several men were whipped two or three times.[72] He had been given his earlier command, *Ferret*, in March 1806 and within a short while 'a majority' of its crew of 118 had turned against him.[73] He had shown displeasure with the way in which the topmen were furling and unfurling sails and just before the mutiny he had threatened the foretopmen with a flogging 'if they did not reef the foretopsail as quick as the main'. His hectoring stung one of the foretopmen to answer, 'If any of the men was tied up, they would cut him down and turn to like good fellows.' A colleague agreed and added that Cadogan deserved to be shot like a dog.

Both men became ringleaders in the mutiny, aided by a disaffected bosun, whom Cadogan had wanted to demote. The bosun was, at first, prepared only to compile a petition for Cadogan's removal which he intended to submit to Rear-Admiral Dacres, the commander at Jamaica. Martin had no time for such a course, perhaps in the knowledge that the well-connected Cadogan could easily sidestep any censure, which would mean more trouble for the crew of *Ferret*. Instead he proposed to seize the ship and take it to La Guira, the *Hermione*'s former sanctuary. Earlier, in 1806, the 6-gun *Dominica* had been seized by her crew and taken to Guadeloupe, and, shortly before *Ferret* had sailed, a *Hermione* mutineer had been taken to Jamaica for trial. Having agreed to follow the examples of the *Hermione* and *Dominica*, the *Ferret* mutineers developed their plans. Revenge on Cadogan was uppermost in their minds ('If I had the cruel raskal on the Spanish shore, I would send him to Hell to beg his bread and shoot him like a mad dog'), but the final plan was faulty, for it relied on a marine, Thomas Grey, who was to use his musket to shoot Cadogan. Grey had no stomach for mutiny but his misgivings were overborne by

71

Martin's assurance that the mutineers 'would blow my brains out, and the Captain would also blow my brains out if I did not take care of him'. In the event, the mutineers would seize the boarding weapons stored on the deck – cutlasses, pikes and tomahawks – and secure the hatches.

When the moment came, on the night of 2 October, the mutineers' nerve failed. They were all 'chicken-hearted fellows' according to the bosun, who had used the disturbances as a cover to settle a private vendetta and murder the Master's mate. What took place was vividly recalled by the First Lieutenant, who had been roused from his cot by three loud cheers, a pounding of feet on the deck above and shouts of 'Guard the hatches!' A few moments later Cadogan appeared at the gunroom door, naked, with a pistol in one hand and a cutlass in the other. He cried out, 'Officers are you armed?' and then rushed up the after-hatchway, which was already blocked by a crowd of sailors. White hurried after him and described what happened next.

> Then Captain Cadogan with his pistol pointing to the breast of Edward Jones, who was the only man I saw armed, with a Cutlass in the face of his Captain, who was asking him at the same time the cause of their mutinous and dastardly conduct. The answer was 'ill-usage'. Captain Cadogan immediately disarmed the man, saying that he had but one life to lose and he would have one of them.

Faced with this boldness, the mutineers' courage withered and they flinched. Pikes and cutlasses were dropped and the men shuffled away. Marines and officers who were now alerted and armed, moved amongst them and arrested those whom Cadogan marked out as 'most active in the business'. They were put in irons. The reluctant Marine Grey, holding the primed musket with which he had been told to shoot his captain, was asked by Cadogan what had caused the trouble. 'Ill-usage by flogging and starving' was the reply. Cadogan assured the marine that he would not shoot him 'for I am more of a gentleman', and six days later Grey spoke in evidence against his sometime comrades. Twelve were found guilty and duly hanged. Less than twelve months later, Cadogan was replaced by Captain Lannock as captain of the *Ferret*; he too found the crew obdurate. Seven men were flogged between August and December 1807.[74]

The *Ferret* mutineers died at Port Royal in October 1806, hanged

a short time after the last *Hermione* mutineer whose example they
had set out to follow. (Cadogan, by a series of family deaths,
became the 5th Earl: he died in 1864.) Theirs was the last attempt
by a crew to seize their ship and take it to the enemy. It was a
desperate form of mutiny, a last resort whose frequency after 1797
may indicate that some sailors at least were aware that the use of
conventional naval channels was no guarantee that an officer would
be replaced or even that their grievances would be investigated.
Purblind anger, drink and greed may also have played their part in
the genesis of such action. Yet the fruits of such mutiny were often
sour. Neither conservative and hierarchical Spain nor the France of
the Directory and Consulate offered a warm welcome to mutineers
and traitors, and their proven unreliability made them all but
unemployable. Most, like the men from the *Danae* and *Hermione*,
drifted back to sea and the risks of discovery by Navy patrols.

Some of the *Hermione* mutineers appear to have thought their
crime and its price worthwhile. They had, after all, the primitive
satisfaction of revenge. Others felt remorse. One, Richard Redman,
facing sentence of death, was moved to tears by his recollection of
Pigot's openhandedness towards him in the past. His whimpering
so sickened one of his judges, the stiff-necked Sir Edward Pellew,
that he wanted him hanged from the yardarm immediately on the
grounds that it would be good for other sailors to witness the death
throes of a cringing mutineer.[75] Given the date, March 1799, this
was not undue harshness. For two years the old order of naval
discipline had seemed, to men like Pellew, to be under a systematic
assault. The Royal Navy had not lost its will to fight, very much the
contrary. Crews which had shown recalcitrance at Yarmouth and
the Nore in June 1797 were able to fight bravely and trounce the
Dutch at Camperdown a few months later, and other victims of
disaffection fought just as well at Aboukir Bay in 1798. There was
no correlation between shipboard unrest, even mutiny, and a lack
of enthusiasm for battle. Later the more paranoid government
supporters thought they detected a connection between the
Spithead mutiny and French plans for an invasion of Ireland. This
bogey of a plot by which the naval mutiny had been planned to
coincide with the French fleet's departure from Brest was a will-
o'-the-wisp. There were sympathisers with Revolutionary France
amongst the drafted sailors, and many more who believed in
political reform in Britain, but none were able to win converts
enough to influence the mutinies in any way. Save amongst a few

73

extremists at the Nore there were no mutineers who seriously considered refusing battle. The actual fighting efficiency of the Navy was not impaired by the mutinies of 1797 or later, although contemporaries, alarmed by what they were witnessing, may justifiably have imagined otherwise.

Naval discipline was, however, under attack. At Spithead and after, many sailors expressed their aversion to officers whose enforcement of the Articles of War was considered spiteful and unjust. Under pressure, the Admiralty had faltered and to secure a settlement it had given way on this point. Soon after and in the face of further demands of this kind from the Nore mutineers, the Admiralty recovered its resolve and denied the existence let alone exercise of this 'right'. In the end the Admiralty won. The traditional methods of command remained unquestioned and unquestionable and the challenges were fended off. The Admiralty's intransigence on this matter had been transmitted to its commanders, who, after the summer of 1797, were universally zealous to detect and frustrate disruption on board their ships. The consequence was a spate of isolated mutinies during the next three years, all of which were countered with firmness and the rigorous application of the draconian Articles of War. Not only mutiny was checked. Allied offences such as insubordination and seditious language were severely punished, and the public punishments inflicted on offenders may have done much to convince waverers of the risks involved in offering any kind of affront to naval authority.

The Admiralty and its captains were, in part, helped by the fact that during 1798 many of the openly mutinous were Irishmen in pursuit of treasonous political goals which divided them from their English and Scottish shipmates. Moreover, mutineers who sought to limit their officers' right to command were never able to secure the cohesion which had been obtained before the Spithead mutiny. By the time of the Peace of Amiens in 1802, the concerted efforts of the Admiralty and naval officers were bearing fruit and a semblance of calm had been obtained. The re-opening of the war in 1804 did not bring with it a recrudescence of restlessness and mutiny. There were still inhumane officers, as the example of *Ferret* indicates, but there were also others, like Collingwood, who conducted themselves with honour and kindness and accordingly won much affection from their crews. 'A seaman will as soon risk his life for his kind and good captain, as he would to defend his country's honour,' observed Jack Nastyface. Yet such men were

74

still uncommon, for he also noted that the traditional collection and purchase of a plate by grateful seamen who wished to thank generous officers was confined to two ships out of his squadron of nine.[76] Still, a sturdy and residual patriotism felt by many of his shipmates ensured that they did their duty. The rest of their lives was endured with stoicism; 'I became inured to the roughness and hardships of a sailor's life. I had made up my mind to be obedient, however irksome my feelings.'[77]

The sailors had made some gains. The Spithead mutiny had raised wages and improved conditions of service. It had also served for a warning. Shortly afterwards, soldiers' wages were raised in anticipation that the Army might well be tempted to copy the Navy, and in 1806 sailors' pay was again put up. Ordinary seamen received a further sixpence a week, able-seamen a shilling, and petty officers between five shillings and nine and sixpence a week. Still their pay lagged behind that offered to civilians and would do so for over a hundred years.

Late eighteenth-century Britain had committed itself to wage a war in which manpower was a crucial, indeed decisive, weapon, and the government therefore had to make unparalleled demands on its subjects. They were fighting, so they were told, because they were free-born Britons, and their enemy was first the ideological then the military tyranny of France. In 1797 and later, the sailors took propaganda at its face value and insisted that they should be treated as free-born Englishmen. They would do their duty, but did not accept poverty, humiliation and the contempt of their officers as part of that duty. Their protests had been partly successful, for the government had, mindful of their strength and the vital part they were undertaking in the war, acceded to some of their demands. The mutineers had, unknowingly, established a pattern, which would re-emerge over a hundred years later during the First World War, when the government would again ask for its subjects to make sacrifices to wage total war.

A JUST CAUSE:

Army Mutinies, 1917-19

The fighting man has a grim sense of justice, which it is
dangerous to affront.

Winston Churchill

IF WE BREAK, ALL BREAK

The year 1917 marked a turning point in the course of the First
World War. For Britain and her Allies it was a year of crises. In
March the revolution in Russia heralded the disintegration of an
empire whose peoples and armies soon ceased resistance to the
Germans. The following November the Bolsheviks snatched power
from the debilitated Provisional Government and a month later
signed an armistice. Over half the divisions of the French army
mutinied between April and June; some of the mutineers
denounced inept generals and demanded an end to suicidal
offensives, whilst others clamoured for a revolution to overthrow the
corrupt government in Paris. Order was gradually reimposed by
the patience and good sense of Marshal Pétain, but at the price of
no further major French offensives. In April the United States had
joined the Allies, but the bulk of her army was not ready for combat
in France until the late spring of 1918. Britain alone now had the
full burden of holding the line and providing the cutting edge for
the Allied war machine. 'If we fail, all fail. If we break, all break,'
concluded Churchill, the Minister for Munitions, in July.[1]

77

He and his fellow ministers could, however, draw some consolation from the misfortunes of the Allies' principal opponent, Germany, which was also facing a crisis of nerve. Between June 1917 and January 1918, there had been a disturbing series of protests and mutinies by sailors of the High Seas Fleet at Kiel. There were indications of war-weariness and a wish for peace among front-line troops in the east and west. At home, civilian morale was dissolving under the pressure of high prices and food shortages, both the consequence of the Allied naval blockade. Increased privations led, in turn, to strikes and political unrest fomented by trade unions and revolutionary socialists who sensed the onset of a crisis for capitalism.

As the antagonists faced the winter of 1917-18, their rulers were being forced to ask the uncomfortable but unavoidable question, whose will to fight would crumble next? Three years of striving for decisive victory on the battlefield had proved fruitless. Often detached from the realities of fighting, the opposing High Commands had failed to discover a strategy which could break the stalemate established at the end of 1914. All that had changed were the casualty lists, which had expanded to grotesque and demoralising proportions. The events in Russia suggested that a period did exist to the demands which governments could make of their populations. When this was reached, the old order stood in peril with its shortcomings and contradictions exposed by failure in a war which had exhausted the patience of the ruled. France had narrowly avoided a revolution and, at the end of 1917, the German High Command was convinced that another year without victory would lead to civil disturbances, perhaps even revolution.

Britain was not immune from this malaise, which was sometimes described as a mixture of war-weariness and defeatism. For some time members of Lloyd George's coalition ministry had been studying secret reports which assessed the morale of civilians and fighting men and investigated the activities of those groups and individuals on the left who questioned the purpose of the war and agitated for its termination. In November 1917, Sir Basil Thompson, the Assistant-Commissioner of the Metropolitan Police, summarised his agents' findings. He anticipated the growth of pacifist activity during the coming winter, but optimistically predicted that 'in this respect we shall have had twelve months advantage of the enemy'.[2] In other words, Britain's will to wage war would outlast Germany's.

Since the beginning of the war in August 1914, the British government had asked for and obtained the co-operation of its subjects. The will to wage war had been healthiest during the first twelve months, when it had justified official faith in the voluntary principle as the best way to create a mass army which would engage and beat the Germans on the Western Front. Between August and December 1914, 1.1 million men had voluntarily enlisted, but the flow began to dry up during the next year. The 1.2 million men who came forward during the twelve months of 1915 were not enough and the government had, unwillingly, to turn to compulsion. Lord Milner was so distressed by the shortfall that he seriously suggested the re-introduction of press-gangs who would collar 'loafers' at race meetings and drag them off to barracks. Conscription was the only answer and the Military Service Act was passed in the spring of 1916, making all men between eighteen and forty-one liable to call-up after June. The catastrophic losses during the Somme offensive between July and November 1916 and its equally ill-starred successor, called the battle of Passchendaele, between June and November 1917, meant that by the beginning of 1918 the army in France was 130,000 men short.[3] With a massive German offensive expected in the spring, a further conscription act had to be hurried through Parliament and the upper age limit for men liable for service was pushed to fifty. The measures worked. By the date of the Armistice, 11 November 1918, Britain had 5.6 million men under arms, of whom 4.9 million were in the Army. This created new problems, for once the servicemen knew that Germany and her allies had surrendered, they wanted to be demobilised immediately and either get back to their old jobs or find new ones.

In terms of fighting spirit, the determination and dedication of the volunteer army, the men of the 97 battalions of 'Kitchener's' or the 'New' Army, were unquestioned. This was the army of the 'Pals Battalions', the volunteers who joined and served together in a moving spirit of patriotism, comradeship and adventure. Drawn from the lower middle and working classes of the great commercial and industrial centres of South Wales, the Midlands, the North and Clydeside, the men of the 'New Army' displayed 'spirit and devotion' according to Field-Marshal Lord Haig, the Commander-in-Chief of British and Dominion forces in France. The same was also true of the great mass of men who followed them, drawn into the Army by the two conscription acts. Yet since the net was widely

79

and indiscriminately cast, the drafted men included many bad soldiers. 'Men who were temperamentally unfitted to be soldiers', in the judgement of Major-General Childs of the Adjutant-General's staff, were sent into the trenches alongside others better suited to soldiering.[4] Haig too was apprehensive about misfits in his army. On 3 October 1917, he confided to the Cabinet that the new intake of soldiers included, 'a leaven of men whose desire to serve their country is negligible' ... 'They come from a class which likes to air real or fancied grievances' and were therefore a potential force for the undermining of discipline and, with it, the will to fight.[5]

Both kinds of bad soldier, the psychologically unsound and the inveterate grouser with political and social grudges, were coming into the Army at a difficult time. The determination to fight on was still strong, but its edge had been dulled by the experience of the past three years of war. The changing mood was sensed by a Regular artillery officer, Colonel Hugh de Montmorency.[6]

In the early days of the War our men were like crusaders; chivalrous, confident in the justice of our cause, and ready and willing for sacrifice. But in 1917 the years of savagery and cruelty of war had undoubtedly blunted the enthusiasm of our soldiers: everyone was longing for the end.

Another officer, R.H. Mottram, was also aware of a new attitude, which, he thought, stemmed from the temper of the freshly arrived conscripts. They, 'showed rather less spring and good-humour, perhaps, but on the other hand they never regarded the War as a picnic. Their one thought was to get it done.'[7] The novelist's judgement was supported by the findings of the Army's censorship department which regularly sampled soldiers' letters to measure morale. The Chief Censor's report to the Cabinet on 8 February 1918 assessed morale as higher amongst men serving on quiet sections of the front, but added that, overall, 'the British Army is firmly convinced, not only of its ability to defeat the enemy and its superiority man to man, but also of the dangers of a premature peace'.[8] 'War weariness' and 'an almost universal longing for peace' were detectable among what the censors judged the great mass of 'cheery ordinary letters'. These symptoms did not indicate that the patient was seriously infected. The British Army fought bravely and well, both in resisting the Ludendorff offensive in the spring of 1918 and in the counter-attacks of the summer and autumn which finally broke the German army and forced its commanders to ask for an armistice.

Nevertheless, the combination of war-weariness and the presence in the Army of a small minority of men who, for various reasons, were eager to spread discord and play upon their comrades' discontent, caused a number of incidents during 1916, 1917 and in the winter of 1918-19. Chief amongst these was the five days of disorder at the base camp at Etaples at the beginning of September 1917, which was the largest disturbance amongst British servicemen during the whole war. There were further expressions of unrest and often violent demonstrations amongst troops in Britain, northern France and the Middle East during the first weeks of 1919. Some of these were protests against the muddle and procrastination of the demobilisation procedures, and others reflected a feeling among many behind-the-lines technicians that they were being overworked and inadequately paid. The attitudes and some of the methods of industrial trade unionism had taken root in the Royal Navy in the years before the outbreak of war. As a consequence the Navy was troubled by agitation over rates of pay during 1917 and again in 1918-19. Together, this restlessness did not add up to very much and in no theatre of war did it impair the fighting efficiency of British forces. Still, the coincidence of a number of isolated mutinies with civilian unrest during this period, and the example of the formidable mutinies in the Russian and French forces, gave the British military and naval authorities cause for anxiety.

NOISY MEETINGS

'Moral fibre' was essential for every soldier under his command – or so Haig insisted.[9] Men who possessed little or none of this quality 'would give way at the moment of stress', were it not for the makeweight of 'the daily fear of punishment'. This judgement, delivered at the end of 1916, was understandable since Haig's strategy of wearing down the numbers and willpower of the German army by a series of grinding offensives demanded steadfastness and endurance from his soldiers. To make certain that men in the trenches did not falter in the attack or flinch in defence, Haig was stubborn in his support for the wide use of condign punishment. His views were shared by many of his subordinate commanders who had first-hand experience of the results of panic on the battlefield. In May 1918, an infantry colonel asked permission from Headquarters for the men in his battalion to witness the execution of a soldier due to be shot for desertion from the front. It would be salutary, he thought, 'in order to restore discipline and show the men of my battalion that the death sentence is sometimes carried out'.[10] Why they should have thought otherwise is difficult to understand. Since September 1914, the names, crimes and death sentences of men convicted of cowardice and desertion from the battlefield had been habitually read out to soldiers during battalion parades. If this litany of retribution was not enough, certain units had, from time to time, been ordered to watch the firing squads at work.

Soldiers could not expect 'to be treated like civilians and on active service punishment must be short and sharp,' argued General Milne, who commanded the Salonika Expeditionary Force.[11] Major-General Childs added a further principle. 'Any penalty inflicted upon troops must be one that will not cause a shortage of men', in other words, frequent recourse to Field Punishment Number 1.[12] Strapping men to cart wheels or limbers for eight hours a day was also needed to compensate for the loss of the old regimental spirit, which, in Child's opinion, had been destroyed along with the 'Old Army' in the battles of 1914 and 1915.

Like other senior officers who expressed misgivings about the courage and discipline of civilians-turned-soldiers during the First World War, Childs's views had been coloured by what had happened during the Boer War. In May 1918 the Army Council lamented that 'in the South African war an idea became prevalent that officers and men were justified in surrendering to save unnecessary waste of life', but added, 'that on more than one occasion a Victoria Cross was awarded to an officer who chose the clear path of duty and came off victorious'.[13] The path of martial duty which seemed clear enough from Whitehall was less obvious from the perspective of the front line. Here the futile last-man stand seemed less attractive.[14]

To tell you the truth, I did'nt want to die but I thought we were going to. I did'nt think we were going to see the sunset but I remember thinking that, whatever they did to us, we had at least earned our bob that day. Mind you we had no fancy ideas about fighting to the last man.

This statement, from a private in the Leicesters, was made about the hard fighting during April 1918. A month later the Army Council insisted on more fights to the last man, and called on the public to show no sympathy to unwounded POWs who 'should be looked upon as having failed to carry out their duty as soldiers'.[15]

In the light of the fortitude and doggedness of the men in the trenches, such a judgement was both harsh and absurd. Yet it reflected a common mentality which insisted that the stamina and bravery of the soldier rested in part upon the use of coercive punishments. For many who joined the Army, the borderline between the justifiable and necessary use of punishments and bullying was hard to appreciate. In May 1915 a battalion of Welsh volunteers went on strike in protest against rough-handling by their drill-instructors, who had been drawn from the Guards and the Metropolitan Police. The Army's first reaction to this mutiny was to summon up another battalion, but this intimidation failed, no doubt because the Welsh were quite used to troops after the 1912-14 coalfield strikes. In the end the Army sensibly backed down and sent the over-zealous instructors away. Later the same battalion went on strike again in protest against too much recourse to Field Punishment Number 1.[16]

This type of mutiny seems to have been exceptional, although the use of Field Punishment aroused considerable unease outside the Army and was the subject of newspaper and Parliamentary agitation during 1916. Opposition to its use came from the ex-soldier journalist, Robert Blatchford, who campaigned in the socialist *Herald*, Labour MPs and trade unions. Individuals also protested to the War Office, like an anonymous correspondent from Wickford in Essex who alleged that a soldier at a nearby camp, who had returned late from leave, underwent the punishment holding a pail of water in each hand for eight hours a day. Another soldier, returning from leave, informed a fellow rail passenger on Grantham station that 'About six bullies have been murdered at Belton Park', a nearby training camp.[17] Extravagant rumour like this did much to fuel the campaign against Field Punishment, which was strenuously defended by the Army authorities. Their arguments, based upon practical military necessity and the need to win the war, prevailed.

The widespread use of Field Punishment Number 1 had been sanctioned by the Suspension of Sentences Act of 1915 which had had as its aim the need to keep soldiers in the field. General Milne had noted, drawing on his Boer War experience, that front-line soldiers were not deterred by the fear of prison sentences. 'Many men, even good characters, when they get war weary, are ready to commit themselves with a view of getting into prison to get away from the field.'[18] Such men existed and a group was seen by Major-General Childs, early in the war.[19]

> I was walking through the streets of St. Omer just after we got there when I met about a hundred and twenty soldiers being marched under escort through the streets. They were singing and whistling and in very good humour. I ascertained that they were all on their way to the base to undergo punishment in the military prisons there.

If these men believed that their woes were behind them, they were soon disabused. The regime of the military prisons was so rigorous that inmates were left in no doubt that front-line soldiering was preferable.

The resort to harsh coercive measures provoked two mutinies, both in the late autumn of 1916, at Blargies prison, not far from infantry headquarters at Rouen. The first hint of unrest in this grim place had been a demonstration by a group of newly arrived Australian convicts which had led to some softening of the conditions. This step-down by the prison administration encouraged a further demonstration by sixty-seven prisoners who refused to obey their sergeant-major's orders and called out to speak with the deputy governor. He refused to treat with them and, in the face of catcalls and booing, ordered the guards to handcuff the demonstrators. This was an easy task since the mutineers were already manacled – a common practice at Blargies and other military prisons – and they were herded into a compound. During this operation there were scuffles and an NCO was attacked, but later the mutineers, aware of the hopelessness of their position, submitted. Seven ringleaders were subsequently tried for mutiny. In mitigation of their behaviour, the accused listed the humiliations and inconveniences they had suffered. There were fourteen lavatories for 300 prisoners, their use was limited to a quarter of an hour each day, there was no soap, dietary restrictions were too common a form of punishment, convicts were manhandled by their guards, underwear and bedding were louse-ridden, men on additional punishments were tied to poles for long periods, and men undergoing Field Punishments were blindfolded. The Director of Military Prisons, called in evidence, admitted that none of these circumstances was unusual and added that blindfolding dis-couraged men from making insolent grimaces – which suggests that Field Punishment did not always induce a sense of shame in the victim.

All the seven ringleaders were found guilty and six were sentenced to death.[20] Only one, an artilleryman, was shot, whilst the rest had their sentences commuted to between two and fifteen years' penal servitude. Shortly after there was another riot at Blargies, for which a New Zealand infantry private was sentenced to death and executed, and four other mutineers were given two years' hard labour. The severity of the sentences was exceptional. No British soldier had been executed for mutiny since 1898, when eight Sudanese infantrymen had been shot at Kampala for their part in a mutiny which had resulted in heavy loss of life.* During the Boer War, what was described as a 'mild case' of mutiny by a dozen men from an Irish regiment earned sentences of between 56 days' and twelve months' imprisonment. Another, which involved local volunteer cavalrymen, resulted in sentences of between seven and twelve years, but these were not confirmed.[21] Thirteen mutineers from the Army Service Corps each received three years from a court martial at Marseilles in December 1915. The two death sentences for the mutinies at Blargies suggest that Haig, who confirmed all capital sentences, was determined to give no toleration to any kind of resistance to military discipline from men already under sentence for crimes committed in the field. This would have been made clear to men serving in the field when the details of the sentences were announced at battalion parades.

The case of the New Zealander who was executed raised a further problem, for two of his fellow ringleaders were Australians. The difficulty was remembered, not entirely accurately, by Major-General Childs.[22]

A serious mutiny took place in a military prison in the field, which culminated in the arrest of the ringleaders. Unfortunately one of them was an Australian and, as I have said elsewhere,

* See page 250

under the Australian Army Act the death penalty cannot be carried out. Some five men were sentenced to death, but it would have been impossible to shoot an English soldier who had taken no greater part in the mutiny than the Australian, so the sentences were commuted to penal servitude.

This was not completely true. The sentences were not all commuted and under the Australia Army Act mutineers were liable to the death penalty, although it had to be confirmed by a civilian, the Governor-General, who was susceptible to local political pressures. Childs's confusion over detail may be excused on the grounds of his frequently expressed exasperation with the Australian forces. Haig also considered their easy-going attitude a permanent threat to the discipline of British forces. From July 1916 he pestered the Australian government for the right to bring men of the Australian Expeditionary Force under the British Army Act. His own efforts and those of the War Office and Army Council were unsuccessful.[23]

There were five Australian divisions in France by 1918 and, with New Zealand and Canadian contingents, they comprised one sixth of the British Army's strength. All the Australians were volunteers, mostly aged between eighteen and twenty-four, and, in four cases out of ten, drawn from the labouring and working classes. Every Australian serviceman was subject to the Australia Army Act which exempted him from the death sentence save in cases of mutiny, desertion to the enemy, and treason. This independence from British military law was a source of national pride. According to the official Australian war history, officers and men who listened to the parade recitals of the death sentences carried out on British deserters shared 'a sullen sympathy and a fierce pride that their own people was strong enough to refuse this instrument to their rulers'.[24] A different kind of anger was felt by Major-General Childs who wanted to shoot Australian deserters, who were 'a menace and a terror' to the French civilians whom they molested and plundered.[25] Whilst the desertion rate amongst Australians troops in 1918 was 0.9 per cent compared to 0.2 per cent from the British Army, the details of evidence offered in courts martial for desertion suggest that few deserters took up robbery. Most chose to lie low or try to escape across the Channel to England where they could find anonymity more easily than in France.

Evidence for the cussedness and unruliness of Australians is plentiful and does much to explain the exasperation and fears of British generals. The Australian attitude to soldiering was summed up in the understatement of Lord Chandos, who fought alongside them in 1918. 'They are not the best of troops to handle when there is no one to fight, but let them get a sight or scent of battle, and they are superb.'[26] This was borne out by the conduct of Australian forces in Egypt, a country which one of them called 'a land of sin, sand, shit and syphilis'.[27] The latter was too abundant, so during April and July 1915 mobs of Australian and New Zealand servicemen ransacked the Wassa district of Cairo as a protest against infection from the many prostitutes in the brothels which were concentrated there. Whorehouses were sacked, pimps thrown into the streets and furniture, including pianos, after them.[28] 'The conduct of Australian and New Zealand troops in the Canal Zone during October [1918] has been far from satisfactory,' went the Provost-Marshal's report on discipline along lines of com-munication in Egypt and Palestine. Men returning from France went ashore and assaulted Egyptians, local police and French officers. Other Australians, passing through Jerusalem, also caused havoc. During December gangs of Australians in Port Said became involved in brawls with Italian troops in which revolvers were fired, and in March 1919 Australian convalescents, returning from France, found the strength to come ashore at Port Said and other ports and damage property.[29]

The same turbulent behaviour was evident in France. Towards the end of 1916 Australian soldiers, evacuated from the Dardanelles, were put in camps close to Canadian battalions on the grounds that colonials of one kind were likely to get on with those of another. Headquarters were woefully mistaken.[30]

> Somebody with a big mouth on the Australian side said they'd come up to finish the job the Canadians couldn't finish. So the next fellow turned around and said, 'Why didn't you finish where you were before you came?' ... And that started a riot. Unfortunately, in those days, the sergeants always carried what they called sidearms, they carried their bayonets in their belts ... There were some men killed.

Destructiveness and brawling were not of themselves mutinous. They were, however, manifestations of an attitude towards military order which worried those responsible for its enforcement. For their part, Dominion troops, particularly Australians and Canadians, regarded themselves as volunteers who had crossed the seas to fight in a quarrel which was not their own. Having come to fight of their own free will, the Dominion soldiers saw no reason to submit themselves unquestionably to British military rules and regulations. A Canadian nurse, serving in a British Military Hospital in France, was overawed and perplexed by the strictness. When she was reprimanded by an officious sister, she answered back, 'I haven't come 3,000 miles to work voluntarily to be spoken to like that by anybody.'[31] Her indignation was shared by many other Dominion volunteers.

At the root of the friction between Dominion volunteers and representatives of the British military system was a contrast in social attitudes and assumptions. Many emigrants from nineteenth- and early twentieth-century Britain had settled in the Dominions in the hope that they would find opportunities open to them for advancement. The social hurdles which they had left behind them in Britain had not been exported to Australia, Canada or New Zealand, where ability and ambition alone were the credentials for success, and respect was earned by effort. In consequence, the gulf between master and man was not as wide as in Britain. Australian, New Zealand and Canadian servicemen, the sons and grandsons of pioneers, came to the war without the belief that respect and obedience were owed to officers automatically on account of their birth, upbringing and education. Since social background did not provide the foundations for authority in the dominions, it was commoner for Australian and Canadian officers to have served in the ranks before being commissioned and there was a closer camaraderie between officers and men. For the Australian officers, in particular, it was not easy for them to distance themselves from their men since it had been customary for each of them to serve six months or more in the ranks before being considered for a commission. They were often at a loss to understand why the British soldiers accepted his lot, which included lower pay (1 shilling a day compared to 5 shillings), without complaint, and sometimes urged him to stand up for himself. Haig believed that his men could do without such advice and the restlessness and jealousy which it could easily stir up. Aware of the uncomfortable consequences of over-close association between British and Australian troops, he ordered measures to be taken to separate them, where possible, in base camps and hospitals, at the beginning of 1918.[32]

Yet there seemed slight grounds to fear for the morale of the British
Expeditionary Force in France. A report, based on the censorship
department's survey of 4,500 letters at the beginning of September
1917, revealed just twenty-eight complaints about war weariness.
'The love of fighting has eradicated the peacetime habit of
grumbling,' concluded the Chief Censor.[33] The soldiers' will and
sturdy doggedness ensured a stable army which would fulfil its
Commander-in-Chief's objective, the erosion of his opponent's
numbers and will to fight. Just before the censorship department's
reassuring memorandum was sent to the Cabinet, there had been a
spontaneous riot by several thousand soldiers at the Etaples base
camp on the French coast, ten miles south of Boulogne.

Etaples base camp served the 6th Army and was a cheerless
accumulation of encampments, set up to house a transient
population of soldiers passing to and from the front line. It was also
a concentration of hospitals, marshalling yards, stores, workshops,
training areas and punishment camps. During August 1917, 30,000
other ranks and 2,700 officers arrived in the camp as reinforcements
from Britain, and over 50,000 were despatched to their units in
northern France.[34] Whilst they waited at Etaples, many underwent
additional training at the hands of instructors – nicknamed
'Canaries' on account of their yellow armbands – who were
universally detested for their hectoring and bullying. They and
their training ground were remembered by Edmund Blunden who
later wrote, 'I associate, [Etaples] as millions do, with "The Bull
Ring", that thirsty, savage, interminable training ground.' Another
soldier who passed through remembered Etaples as a place where
discipline was aggressively enforced and there was always someone
undergoing Field Punishment.[35] There was no respite from war at
Etaples. Five days before the first disturbances at the camp, it
suffered an air raid in which two bombs fell on one of the training
camps and seven on one of the hospitals. Three American troops
were killed and twenty-five patients were wounded; the
anti-aircraft batteries made no attempt to fire back.[36]

A day later, on 5 September, a large draft of men arrived from
Britain, mainly from Irish, Welsh, Scottish and North Country
regiments. There were also forty men from the New Zealand Field
Artillery who appear to have soon fallen foul of the Military Police,
responsible for camp discipline. On Sunday, 9 September, a
corporal from one of the Infantry Base Depots warned that the New
Zealanders had planned a raid on the Military Police lines. The

matter was not taken seriously for, as the base diary commented, 'threats by colonials were fairly common'. At three in the afternoon, the Military Police arrested Gunner A.J. Healy, a New Zealand artilleryman, who claimed that he had been taken into custody without any cause and had been subsequently knocked about. His tale aroused his comrades, who gathered outside a police hut by a railway bridge which led into the town. Sunday afternoon was a period when men had time on their hands, for once church parade had ended there were no further duties. The hubbub outside the police hut attracted a crowd, including soldiers who had just left a nearby cinema. At half-past five, a New Zealander from the crowd called for Healy's release, was taken inside and shown that he had been discharged. This did not satisfy the crowd, which by now numbered between three and four thousand. There were attempts to rush the hut during which a Military Policeman, Private Reeve, drew his revolver and fired two wild shots. One hit a corporal from the Gordon Highlanders who was passing by and fatally wounded him, and the other wounded a French woman in a nearby street. One eyewitness claimed that Reeve had become involved in a brawl with an Australian and, in his own defence, he stated that he snatched the gun from the Australian – which is unlikely, since no private soldier would have carried a revolver. Reeve's court martial did accept his plea of self-defence and generously sentenced him to twelve months' imprisonment for manslaughter.

The shooting incensed the crowd, whose wrath was concentrated on the Military Police. They withdrew from their hut, and when the officer responsible for them, Captain Strachan, the Assistant Provost-Marshal, rode up he was stoned. Another officer, the Adjutant, Captain Guinness, also came to see what was happening and realised that the police had lost all control. He reported to Colonel Nason, the officer in charge of reinforcements, who immediately ordered a piquet to be collected from the New Zealand depot. One officer and twenty-five men with rifles and bayonets but no ammunition were sent to the bridge. Nason went too and, 'seeing the serious state of affairs', called up two further piquets of over a hundred men from three other base depots. He also went to the officers' club and ordered all inside to return to their depots, each of which was to send three officers who were to try and persuade the men to return. They did so and were well received by some of the soldiers, since 'Feeling in the crowd was only against the Police and Officers were treated respectfully.'[37]

Some soldiers were moved by the officers' appeals. A Scottish soldier remembered one officer who 'appealed very strongly' to the men to get back to their base depots 'and like true Scots we did'. Others did not and moved off into Etaples where about a thousand gathered outside the Sévigné Café, where two Military Policemen were hiding. The crowd was prevented from entering by a cordon of officers, and by nine the town was clear. Inside the camp the disturbances petered out an hour later. The base commander, Brigadier-General A.G. Thomson, emphasised that no animus was shown towards officers, but members of his staff had been stoned and one later recalled that Thomson's own office was broken into and he was manhandled.[38]

An uglier incident occurred on one of the bridges when a piquet of British and Canadian soldiers under a captain confronted a band of seventy or eighty men who were marching from the camp towards the town, some carrying red flags and wrenched-up notice-boards. The men of the piquet were unwilling to impede the mutineers and so the captain quickly reorganised it into regimental groups with the men under their own NCOs. He then exhorted them to do their duty, words which provoked one of the mutineers to come back and call upon the piquet guard to join the mutiny. 'Don't listen to the bloody officer. What you want to do with that bugger is to tie a rope round his neck with a stone attached to it and throw him into the river.' The speaker was a regular soldier, a thirty-year-old corporal from a northern regiment; he was subsequently arrested, returning from Etaples. He was charged with mutiny, found guilty, sentenced to death and executed three weeks later.[39]

The severity of his sentence was a reflection of the alarm felt by the officers responsible for Etaples after the riots of Sunday. Yet, the next day, routine duties continued as usual with forces coming and going. Brigadier-General Thomson had summoned his superior, the General Officer Commanding Lines of Communication, Lieutenant-General Asser, from Abbeville, who arrived with Major Dugdale of the Military Police to investigate the disorders. 'The Police being unable to cope with the situation', a major from one the depots was placed in charge of Etaples, and a committee of inquiry was set up to discover what had happened and why. Meanwhile, at four in the afternoon, a mob broke through the piquet lines on the bridges and crossed into Etaples, where they 'held noisy meetings'. Several motor cars were tampered with and a 'mob' of between two and three hundred moved towards the Detention Camp. They were intercepted by Brigadier-General Thomson with Captain Strachan, Major Dugdale and another staff officer who together persuaded them to return to the camp. Thomson also spoke to about a thousand men who had gathered by a bridge and induced them to go away. Others in Etaples were busy hunting for Military Policemen. At eight in the evening a hundred or so tried to enter the Field Punishment compound where Redcaps were thought to be, and an hour later another group gathered opposite the railway station in search of the same quarry. These men were also persuaded to return to the camp. Thomson recorded in the base diary that 'The demeanour of all crowds towards officers was perfectly good.'

This may well have been so, but the problem remained that the piquets, drawn from the Infantry Base Depots, were clearly unwilling or unable to stop their comrades from crossing into Etaples. Thomson required assistance from outside and on Tuesday 10 September he set about securing it. He persuaded Brigadier- General Horwood, the Chief Provost-Marshal, to report that outside troops were necessary for the restoration of order. General Headquarters agreed and promised 800 men from the Honourable Artillery Company. Thomson thought that cavalry would be useful and, by telephone and through one of his staff officers, who drove over to the 9th Cavalry HQ at Frencq, he attempted to secure the services of two squadrons of the 15th Hussars. This request was refused by General Headquarters.

While Thomson was trying to get together a force to put down the daily disturbances, the normal life of the camp proceeded. At four in the afternoon, when duties ended, men again broke out of camp and set off towards Paris Plage and the seaside. 'None of the piquets made any determined effort to prevent these men', but Major Cruikshank, the Railway Transport Officer, was able to stop them and get them to return. In Etaples there were more disturbances in which one man was injured lying down in front of a motor car. Five men were arrested, and by ten the crowds had returned to camp.

The next day, Wednesday 13 September, saw the return of Lieutenant-General Asser who agreed to bringing the Honourable Artillery Company detachment from Montreuil. Captain Strachan, the Assistant Provost-Marshal, was replaced by Captain Long-ridge, and a force of ten mounted, and twenty-five foot, Military

Police were brought over from Boulogne. At half-past three, Thomson was informed that two squadrons of the 19th Hussars with a machine-gun section were standing by. At half-past six, sixteen officers and 364 men of the Honourable Artillery Company arrived at Etaples. They were too late to hinder the progress of a thousand men from the camp who set off for Paris Plage in despite of an order which confined all men to their depots save for training.

The disturbances ended on Thursday 14 September. Thomson now had considerable forces at his disposal. The Honourable Artillery Company men had taken over from the reluctant piquets and were placed under the control of Major Dugdale, whilst Captain Longridge took charge of 120 Military Policemen who had been drafted in from Calais, Abbeville and Le Havre. The 19th Hussars were standing by, as were the 22nd Manchesters and the 1st Royal Welch Fusiliers, a total of over 2,000 men. The men in the Infantry Base Depots were ordered to hand in all their ammunition, which they did. A hundred broke camp in the afternoon, and a further 200 in the evening. The latter had a tussle with the HAC men, who were armed with entrenching tool handles, and two ringleaders suffered minor injuries. A roll-call was subsequently taken and it was found that twenty-three men had deserted. The next day between fifty and sixty men tried to enter Etaples, but were all arrested.

What had the disturbances been about? One participant wrote a letter on 30 September to the revolutionary socialist journal *Workers Dreadnought*, which, for some inexplicable reason, escaped the censor. The author first complained about thin rations ('We are getting fed like whippets') and then proceeded to recite his version of what had occurred at Etaples.[40]

About four weeks ago about 10,000 men had a big racket at Etaples and cleared the place from one end to the other, and when the General asked what was wrong, they said they wanted the war stopped.

This was no doubt encouraging news for the journal's anti-war readership, but is nowhere else substantiated. One band of mutineers had carried red flags and there had been a meeting, on the second day of the unrest, at which, one eyewitness recalled, a committee was elected. What, if any, representations it may have made to the authorities is not known, for neither participants nor the base diary make reference to any dealings with the mutineers' spokesmen. Sixty years later extravagant claims were put forward on behalf of an RAMC deserter, Percy Toplis, who, it has been alleged, was chosen as chairman of the mutineers' committee.[41] A number of deserters lurked about base camps and made a living scavenging from the supply dumps and scrounging off soldiers, but there is no evidence to connect Toplis or anyone else with the leadership of the mutiny. It is also extremely unlikely that the soldiers would have chosen a deserter, petty criminal and *fantasiste* to represent them with the Army authorities.* Yet it was inevitable that the disturbances at Etaples, which at the time were shrouded in official secrecy, would later generate much rumour and sensationalist speculation.

Official records refer to 'ringleaders', and the executed mutineer seems have been one of these, but he appears to have been no more than the vociferous leader of one small party. His objective, and that of all the other groups which passed from the camp into Etaples on the five afternoons and evenings, was to get into the town. While there the mutineers did little damage, save to official cars, although their presence worried the local French authorities, and the Mayor and *chef des gendarmes* called on Brigadier-General Thomson on the Wednesday. On several occasions mutineers set off for the pleasant seaside resort of Paris Plage but were headed off. There is nothing in these actions which suggests anything more than a wish to enjoy the pleasures of the French seaside, which was probably why, on 15 September, Etaples was officially thrown open to all the troops at the base camp. This seems to have satisfied everyone, for two days later the additional forces which had been called in were removed. In so far that one of the mutineers' consistent aims was to pass their off-duty hours in Etaples, they had been successful.

Whilst in Etaples, several groups of mutineers made efforts to track down fugitive Military Policemen. A Military Policeman had started the disturbances, for Private Reeve's wild shots

* Toplis remained on the run from the law until 1920, when, under suspicion for murder, he was shot dead resisting arrest in the churchyard at Penrith. Claims for his dominant role in the Etaples mutiny put forward by Allison and Fairley in *The Monocled Mutineer* cannot be substantiated since the book lacks any useful footnotes. The tale has been lately retold for BBC Television by an author who claimed, 'I've written about the truth, not necessarily the facts' (*New Statesman* 5.9.86). The result was lurid and distorted.

undoubtedly provoked the disorders on Sunday evening. Almost immediately, the camp's police force of 150 men lost control and they were withdrawn from their duties. On 13 and 14 September all were ordered out of the area and transferred to other postings, their place being taken by drafts from other camps nearby. These men were under the command of a new Assistant Provost-Marshal. The relief force of the HAC were under the impression that all the trouble stemmed from 'the unpopular edicts and actions of a certain Provost-Marshal'.[42] The removal of Captain Strachan, and the entire camp police, suggests that Thomson and his superiors were well aware that much of the mutineers' rage was directed towards them. Officers fared better, in spite of a handful of incidents, and throughout the disturbances the mutineers responded obediently to exhortations to return to camp. The fate of the one man who openly called on men to attack their officer may well have discouraged others. There were no indications that the overbearing drill instructors from 'The Bull Ring' were singled out. More importantly, the daily work of the camp proceeded as usual, men arrived and drafts passed out to their front-line units without incident.

The troubles were therefore confined to off-duty hours which the men were determined to spend in Etaples. The piquets, whose duty it was to stop them, clearly thought that their comrades were doing no harm and made no effort to hinder them. These men were drawn from the same Infantry Base Depots as the mutineers and, sharing the same quarters, must have felt disinclined to take actions for which they might well suffer in the future. There were some efforts to approach the detention compounds, but there is no definite evidence to suggest that this represented an attempt to rescue the men held there. Rather, it was probably part of the hunt for Redcaps, although at the end of the disturbances Thomson took the precaution of placing a guard of the Royal Welch over these camps.

Final responsibility for all that had happened at Etaples fell on the shoulders of Brigadier-General Thomson, the base commandant. He was an experienced officer of engineers, who had served in Egypt, the Sudan and South Africa. His chief problem had been a lack of forces which could be relied on to stop the men from leaving the camp and entering Etaples, although he also had to take the blame for the regulations which they were breaking. The findings of the local Committee of Inquiry and of Captain Joy of the Intelligence Corps, who arrived at Etaples with two assistants on 13 September 'for special duty', have never been revealed, but Thomson was shortly superseded by Brigadier-General Rawcliffe.

The despatch from General Headquarters of an intelligence officer suggests that a decision had been taken to trace, where possible, the role of 'agitators' in the disturbances. During the summer, intelligence officers had investigated the circulation of the anti-war journals, *Labour Leader* and *Herald*, amongst troops serving with the Cavalry Division and Army Service Corps, but they found no indications that the readership was in sympathy with pacifism.[43] Rather, the men concerned were interested in ideas about the shape of post-war society, and their officers were recommended to take more care of their welfare and provide more extensive recreational facilities. Men with strong socialist and revolutionary views were certainly serving in the forces – in July 1917 soldiers at Shoreham camp left behind them a placard calling on their comrades to imitate the Russians, and, in September, a soldier on leave asked the audience at a Birmingham political meeting, 'Why don't you people start the revolution? You are too peaceful, look at Russia. You do not care what life you sacrifice, all manhood is gone!'[46] These were isolated incidents, but their background was an effort by the Independent Labour Party, and allied socialist and anti-war groups, to create Councils of Workmen's and Soldiers' Delegates, in imitation of the soviets which were springing up in Russia. The movement, which started in June 1917, had fizzled out ignominiously by the autumn.[95] Its few meetings were broken up by patriots and soldiers on leave.

One meeting which did not end in chaos was held at Tonbridge on 26 June and attended by men who claimed to be representatives of various Home Counties battalions which were stationed in the area. The delegates called themselves the 'Home Counties and Training Reserve Branch of the Workers and Soldiers Council' and issued a manifesto. It called for higher allowances for soldiers' families to meet the growing cost of food, no civilian work for soldiers and the employment of civilian doctors to examine men and pronounce them fit for service. There were also calls for the relaxation of the Defence of the Realm Act and censorship, and better education for children. There was a trade union tone to this document with an insistence that soldiers should not be used as strike-breakers ('The using of soldiers as Blacklegs revolts the instinct of every decent man'), and the enjoyment of citizens' rights

96

by soldiers ('We plead as beggars for what our comrades can demand as citizens'). A word was also found for young officers, who suffered such heavy casualties and who, it was argued, deserved better treatment of the Army.[46]

The group which drew up these resolutions disappeared from sight soon after, probably as a consequence of its members being drafted to the front. Whilst it is interesting as an indication of the views of some trade unionists and Labour supporters on the Army, there is no reason to believe that such ideas were in evidence at Etaples, where, given the units which were present, the bulk of the mutineers must have been Scottish, Northern and Irish soldiers, with some New Zealanders. Nor is there any likelihood that Haig's memorandum about agitators and men with grievances, written within a month of the disturbances at Etaples, was coloured by what had happened at the base camp. His main concern in compiling the report was the anticipation of restlessness in the wake of demobilisation.[47]

What had occurred at Etaples was a spontaneous outburst against high-handed and allegedly brutal agents of military authority. What followed was an extended carnival in which bored, off-duty soldiers behaved in the way they wanted. There were efforts to catch and chastise the Redcaps, but they were easily deflected. Since the picquets ordered to stop the demonstrations were made up of men who sympathised with the mutineers, the trouble went on for several days. In the end they were stopped by less than 400 men armed with spade-shafts, although the presence nearby of reinforcements may well have convinced would-be mutineers that the game was no longer worth the candle.

The events at Etaples in September 1917 have been the subject of much fanciful invention, but there is no evidence to suggest that the rumpus was a protest against the war or the men responsible for waging it. Neither was it an isolated incident. On 21 July 1918, when soldiers and civilians were celebrating Belgian National Day, there was a similar outburst, when, according to the Base Camp War Diary, 'certain Scotch Reinforcements became troublesome at and after the Sports Day and in the evening about 200 broke into Calais, making a demonstration against the Military Police'. Everything was calm by 11.00 p.m and, the following morning, the Base Commandant went and spoke to the Scotsmen at their camp and found no signs of disorder. In the afternoon, there were rumours that a foray was planned that evening, and two groups of

Scots got into the town and ransacked the Redcaps' billet in the Rue Amsterdam. The next day, 23 July, piquets were placed at all entrances from the town and the Field Punishment prisoners (who might well have included miscreants from the previous two days of disorder) were moved to camps outside the town. There appears to have been no further disorder, although half a battalion of the East Lancashires were ordered to patrol the town. After an address to Lieutenant-General Asser, the Scotsmen went on their way to the front line.[48] On 6 September there were further minor incidents with reinforcements.

Military Policemen, like their civilian counterparts in industrial cities, did not command much affection and were often targets for attacks by hooligans. Hooligan was a word which first gained common currency in the two decades before the First World War when there was a series of spasms of newspaper indignation against the prevalence of public rowdiness. This, in turn, prompted much editorial and public heart-searching and alarms about moral decline and, in some areas, about the degeneracy of the 'Imperial Breed'. The outbreak of war did not mean an end to noisy and violent behaviour in the streets of large towns and cities, nor did the imposition of military discipline mean that those addicted to such a pastime abandoned their old habits. At Etaples and, on a smaller scale, at Calais, soldiers kicked over the traces, made a lot of noise, did a little damage, and baited the Military Police. When it was over, they calmed down and got on with their military training and, in some cases, passed on to the front line. Such behaviour was perturbing to the military authorities for whom it was unexpected, but then they would have had little experience of what often occurred nightly on the streets of Glasgow, Liverpool or the East End of London.

FIRST IN, FIRST OUT

The rumpus at Etaples may well have concentrated Haig's mind on what would happen when the war was over and the time came to disband the vast volunteer and conscript army. On 3 October 1917 he warned the Cabinet that, 'as soon as demobilisation commences a feeling of jealousy will arise, men will keenly watch the dates of departure of others and will institute comparisons as to their respective claims, there will be generally an unsettled state, and as the natural consequence of a prolonged and arduous war, nerves will be in an irritable and unstable condition.'[49] This would be to the advantage of agitators, and to counter the trouble they might foment, it was necessary 'to retain formed units whose tone is healthy and whose spirit is wholesome, for so long a time as is practical'. Whether or not the final sentiment was a reflection of the dismal performance of the men called to undertake piquet duty at Etaples is not known, but clearly Haig expected demobilisation to be marked by disturbances which would require steady troops to quell them. He was correct in his judgement.

The signing of the Armistice on 11 November 1918 was greeted with exhilaration by all servicemen. In some cases celebration turned into a violent carnival. At Malta revellers damaged barracks and at Kantara, the Middle East Army's major base, there were violent junketings.[50] Canteens were plundered and, in a gesture of defiance, the sergeants' mess was attacked and its piano hurled into the Suez Canal. There were 8,000 men in the Infantry Base Depot and only a small percentage were involved, mainly, it would appear, from the Rifle Brigade.[51] In common with thousands of other servicemen, the merry-makers believed that the Armistice meant an end to the war. They were mistaken; Germany had merely signed a truce, and final peace would only follow the agreement of German delegates to the terms offered them at the Paris Conference, which was scheduled to open early in 1919. The war officially ended on 28 June, when the Germans signed the Versailles Treaty. In the meantime, the campaigns against Bolshevik Russia continued, and troops were required to garrison the Rhineland, Constantinople and former Turkish territories in the Middle East. Men were also required for the suppression of an Egyptian nationalist uprising in March 1919; to repel an Afghan invasion on the North-West Frontier in May, and in Ireland.

The inevitable upheavals of the demobilisation of nearly five million men coincided with a period of political and industrial unrest. From the viewpoint of the government, strikes and demonstrations by soldiers looked dangerously like revolution, and there was much officially inspired scaremongering about Bolshevism in Britain. This was given some substance by the speeches and behaviour of many on the extreme left, who hoped to exploit the troubles. The riots by soldiers gave rise to fears that

99

troops might not be reliable and could even make common cause with political agitators. This anxiety was intensified after the police strike at the end of August 1918, following which Lloyd George had made concessions on pay and had given permission for the continued existence of the National Union of Police and Prison Officers. Within a year a new Police Act was passed which outlawed the union, and policemen who remained members faced summary dismissal. The Metropolitan Commissioner, General Macready, feared trouble from the militant policemen and, when the new Act's terms were explained to them, he had detachments of Guards in readiness for trouble.[52]

Care was taken that soldiers were kept up to the mark in matters of discipline. General orders for the Fourth Army, issued in December 1918, deprecated the widespread slackness which had followed the Armistice, which was manifested by slouching, untidily dressed junior officers and casualness in saluting.[53] Steps were also to be taken to stamp out disaffection. 'Agitators and discontented men are not to be allowed to address assemblies of soldiers' and every officer, NCO and Military Policeman was to report such meetings immediately to his Headquarters which would take the appropriate action against the ringleaders. Four months later there were still fears that soldiers in the army of occupation in Germany might be approached by Bolshevik agitators.[54]

Soldiers were also reminded that they might have to handle civil disturbances in Britain. The path of duty in this direction was made clear by General Sir Henry Horne in a speech made to the 14th Battalion the Worcester Regiment and four battalions of the Royal Naval Division, to whom he had just presented new colours, on 14 February 1919.[57]

Europe is in a state of great unrest, and this unrest has spread in a minor degree to our own country ... Let me tell you, as an old soldier, one who has spent his life amongst the troops, and loves the British Soldier with all his heart, that I wish to warn you that when you go home you will meet perhaps with influences which will not be either for your good or the good of the country. At the present moment Germany, recognising that she has been beaten in war, is doing her utmost to gain victory in peace. Germany agents are at work endeavouring to stir up and foment unrest at home. Don't allow yourself to be led astray in this direction. You have learned loyalty and discipline out here: when you go home, help properly constituted authorities to maintain law and order at home. If you can help in this direction you will have done your duty not only on the field of battle, but also in the pursuit of peace.

Those who were sowing the seeds of unrest were not German agents. They were socialists who hoped to mobilise the working classes and soldiers against the government, as had happened in Russia. 'Well-known Revolutionary agitators' had met covertly in Glasgow during January 1919 and, according to the Special Branch report, planned to turn the strike there for a forty-hour week into the forerunner of a revolution. Having overturned law and order in Glasgow, the plotters would turn their attentions to other militant areas, South Wales and Belfast.[56] Siegfried Sassoon and Robert Graves toyed briefly with the idea of a 'general anti-Governmental uprising by ex-servicemen'. Presumably they had in mind the various discharged soldiers' organisations which had mushroomed since 1916 and which, for the most part, concerned themselves with matters which closely touched their members' welfare, such as better pensions for the disabled. The Soldiers', Sailors' and Airmen's Union (SSAU), which had emerged at the end of 1918, went much further. It was allied to extremist groups and at one of its meetings at the beginning of 1919 there was wild talk of stockpiles of arms ready for mutinous soldiers. In support, the *Herald* published, on 11 January 1919, an article called 'The Great Mutiny', which applauded the recent mutinies by men demanding swift demobilisation.[57] Later the SSAU promoted a campaign for men to demobilise themselves without consulting the authorities. It argued that the volunteers of 1915 had pledged to fight until six months after the end of the war and, since the Armistice had been signed on 11 November, these men were free to go on 11 May 1919. It was hoped that, if successful, this mass unofficial demobilisation might provoke a confrontation with the forces of the government. Like other such groups the SSAU was monitored by the intelligence services which were also concerned about the way in which political groups on the left were seeking to convert ex-soldiers.[58]

It was natural that soldiers returning from the war and others still in uniform should attend political meetings. Many heard the Labour MP Colonel Wedgwood address a meeting at Liverpool at the end of April 1919, where he warned that conscription was an official plot 'to discipline the youth of the country, so that they

101

would not answer back the foreman'.[59] This may not have been what they wanted to hear, for local concern was about the availability of jobs. Discharged soldiers were 'disturbed because the girls who threw white feathers about in 1914 are holding on to their jobs with the connivance of the Government and employers'.[60] Yet many soldiers did share common ground with the left over the issue of sending troops to Russia, although their opposition was not so much based on sympathy with the 'Workers' Republic', as with a lack of desire to continue soldiering now that Germany was beaten.

Opposition to drafts to Russia surfaced several times during the sequence of mutinies during January 1919. Often called 'strikes' by those who took part, these demonstrations were, by and large, protests against the injustice and inefficiency of the demobilisation scheme, often coupled with complaints about inadequate rations and excessive duties. They began at Folkestone on 3 January and spread like a wave across the various depots and camps of South-Eastern England in the next three days. There were outlying demonstrations in the West Country and Midlands and, at the end of the month, a serious mutiny at Calais. Suffering much the same misfortunes, forces in the Middle East also staged a series of demonstrations.

At the heart of the troubles was the first demobilisation scheme. It was complicated and, in the minds of many servicemen, iniquitous. First priority was given to men who had jobs awaiting them in Britain, irrespective of their length of service. Then followed a long list of forty-two different groups of men, each category being determined by the nature of a soldier's future employment. Advantages attached to what were known as 'pivotal' men, who in peacetime occupied crucial jobs in their industry. Their privileges were a consequence of the government's determination to get industry working after the war. Soldiers did not see matters in that way. They believed that simple equity demanded that those who had joined first should be demobilised first. Haig concurred and warned that the operation of the government's initial plan would damage morale.[61] His advice was given to the new Secretary for War and Air, Winston Churchill, who took up office on 9 January 1919, arriving at the War Ministry in the midst of a grave crisis occasioned by the rioting soldiers demanding demobilisation.

Immediately, Churchill insisted on length of service as the only criterion for demobilisation, the 'First in, first out' principle which

Haig had wanted and which was enthusiastically championed in the popular press. Before it could be promulgated, this scheme had to be discussed and, in the end, approved by Lloyd George who was already in France for the peace conference. Apart from ministerial timorousness in the form of Sir Austen Chamberlain, there was a fear that too swift demobilisation would weaken the forces, which had to remain strong as a means of giving political weight to Britain at the peace conference. Still, on 17 January, the specially created committee came down in favour of Churchill's plan which, in turn, was endorsed by Lloyd George. At the same time, Army pay was to be increased and the 80,000 newly conscripted young men, who were still in training, were to be kept in the Army for service abroad. The principles agreed on needed some time to be shaped into official orders, and so the details of the new plan for demobilisation and the higher wages were not made public until 29 January. As during the Spithead mutiny, the slow-moving wheels of government had ground on against a background of growing disorder and mutiny amongst servicemen.

By 1 January 1919 there were three and a half million men waiting to be demobilised, the majority in northern France. Practical problems added to the men's growing feeling of irritation, for the French railways were unable to cope with the movement of 10,000 men daily. Frustration first exploded on 3 January at Folkestone when detachments who had just detrained prior to embarkation for France refused to parade. The pattern of unrest here was soon copied elsewhere. An orderly crowd of 3,000 marched through the town to the Town Hall where they asked to speak to the mayor. As they marched, the soldiers chanted, 'Are we going to France? – No! Are we going home? – Yes.' The mayor's assurance that if they went back to their camps they would be satisfied was met with a chorus of 'Tell Me the Old, Old Story'. Matters then passed to the town commandant who pledged that all individual complaints would be listened to. The 'pivotal' men with jobs could be immediately discharged, and men with complaints would be allowed seven days' leave to follow up their cases. This did not satisfy the men and on the next day there were further disturbances. Following trade union habits, bodies of men picketed the railway station and the harbour, and urged men returning from leave to join them. At the harbour some challenged the armed guard which withdrew. There was little rowdiness, although a 'For Officers Only' sign outside a station waiting room was torn off and there was some shouting of slogans such as 'The war is over! We won't fight Russia! We mean to go home!'

A second meeting was held at the Town Hall, attended by about 10,000 men, and a 'Soldiers' Union' was formed with a committee which included a few former trade unionists. This committee negotiated with the local military authorities, who were joined by civil servants from the Ministry of Labour sent from London to assist with the formalities of demobilisation. A few miles away, at Dover, there were similar incidents in which the demonstrators were joined by Canadians and Australians. Again there was an appeal to the mayor and later discussions with local army commanders. As at Folkestone, soldiers were allowed to contact employers and, if they received assurances of jobs, were free to leave. The temper of all involved had been good-natured but determined.

Evening and morning newspapers carried accounts of these events and those which followed, at least until 8 January. There had already been a campaign in the press about the unfairnesses of demobilisation and when lorry-loads of Army Service Corps men descended on Whitehall, they repeated commonplace popular press criticism of army staff officers. 'They used the most offensive epiphets towards us, calling us "brass-hats", "red-tab officials" and so forth, and insinuated that we did not work,' recalled Major-General Childs, who thought they had picked up all this from newspapers. Churchill noticed lorries which were adorned with the slogan, 'Get on or Get out Geddes', a remark directed against the Minister of Labour in a *Daily Express* cartoon. *The Times* refused, on 8 January, to publish any more letters on demobilisation, for it was clear to the leader writer that such material was 'fanning an agitation which is already mischievous and may become dangerous'. The government agreed and, from 5 January, insisted that no further reports of servicemen's demonstrations were to be published.

The ban was too late. Copycat mutinies broke out all over the Home Counties between 5 and 8 January. At Shortlands Army Service Corps depot, 1,500 men held an impromptu meeting, elected a committee of twenty-eight and marched to Bromley Town Hall where they called for an end to demobilisation delays and being kept in the Army to undertake civilian jobs. They also agreed to send a sub-committee on a tour of other ASC depots around London to whip up support. The Maidstone mutiny of infantrymen was marked by a march down the town's High Street, a request to the mayor for his aid and an open-air meeting. Regimental officers who spoke with the men agreed to their demands, and there was an end to unnecessary fatigues, guard duty and drill.

Purely service grievances dominated the mutiny of 700 RAF technical staff at Biggin Hill on 7 January. They occupied the camp and only after appeals by an officer did they abandon a plan to drive in lorries to Whitehall. Their complaints concerned sparse and ill-cooked rations, poor washing facilities, undertaking private work for officers, and demobilisation delays. Two days later a party of officials visited the camp, instigated improvements and offered most of the men ten days' leave.

Bases and depots close to London were infected by the mutinous mood between 6 and 7 January, and many of them took their protests directly to Whitehall. ASC men from Osterley Park commandeered lorries and drove to the demobilisation head-quarters in Richmond Terrace where a deputation of six was seen by staff. Other ASC men from Grove Park and Uxbridge broke out from camps and demonstrated. Four hundred marched along Uxbridge High Street singing 'Britons never shall be slaves' and what had become the battle hymn of those displeased with demobilisation, 'Tell Me the Old, Old Story'. They also told journalists that their rations were scanty – one loaf to five men; and monotonous – sausages five days a week. Soldiers from Kempton Park drove to the War Office in lorries on which were chalked, 'No red tape', 'We want fair play', 'We're fed up', 'No more sausage and rabbits' and 'Kempton is on strike'. Church parades antagonised the Ordnance Corps men from White City, who called for their ending as well as swifter demobilisation.

The most formidable demonstration in the London region was on 7 January when 4,000 ASC men chose a committee which demanded faster demobilisation, reveille at 6.30 and not 5.30, the end of all training, no men over forty-one to be sent abroad, no compulsory church parades, no drafts for Russia and no victimisation. The next day the men from Park Royal took their grievances to Whitehall where they hoped to see Lloyd George. At Paddington Station they were stopped by General Feilding, the Commander-in-Chief of the London District, who said that they would be demobilised as soon as possible. He cautioned them that 'they were soldiers and would have to obey orders', which might include serving in Russia. They ignored his warning about the use

105

of police and marched to Downing Street, and were finally calmed by Field-Marshal Robertson.

There were a handful of further disturbances on camps in the provinces. Aldershot, Winchester, Shoreham, the Isle of Wight and the RAF camp at Beaulieu were all convulsed by the usual pattern of refusals to obey orders, demonstrations and representations to officers. At Falmouth on 7 January 600 men from the 25th Battalion Royal Rifles would not parade and demanded a reduction of drill and no further night exercises. At Luton the pattern of relative orderliness was broken when civilians joined in the disturbances and the local Town Hall caught fire and was burned down. Elsewhere there was not much destructive rowdyism, although a handful of ASC men in London proposed to form a 'soviet' and fraternise with local workers.[62] By contrast, the marchers at Shoreham displayed Union Jacks.

These brief mutinies by men described by Churchill as 'newly released from the iron discipline of war' and 'the inexorable compulsions of what they believed to be a righteous cause', caused much official disquiet. Revolutionary extremists were making attempts to attract former soldiers, and, in the case of the SSAU, men still in khaki, in the hope that their discontents might be harnessed towards political aims. The danger was recognised by Churchill with a typical theatrical flourish.[63]

If these armies formed a united resolve, if they were seduced from the standards of duty and patriotism, there was no power which could even have attempted to withstand them.

That there were no serious disturbances involving the men from these armies Churchill credited to 'the renowned sagacity and political education of the British Democracy'. Yet the men who paraded through the streets of English towns and careered through Whitehall on hijacked lorries were not concerned with replacing the government. They wanted to get out of the Army, and if they had to stay there, some saw no reason why their final weeks or months should be marked out by the wartime regime of compulsory church parades, drill, guard duty and the like. Their grievances stemmed from conditions of service life, and, for their part, senior and junior officers were willing to listen and do what they could to put matters right. They also had the sound sense to ignore the unorthodox

106

methods of the soldiers and overlook often gross insubordination. The waves of discontent which broke across southern and western England for three or four days quickly petered out, although the example of this rough and ready way of securing justice was taken up by others a few weeks later.

A second spasm of mutinies at the end of January was taken more seriously by the Army authorities and with good reason. The so-called strike at the Calais base, and its attendant mutiny by men returning from leave, was a danger to forces in northern France and Germany. What Haig acknowledged as 'the very serious Mutiny' at Calais imperilled his armies in France and Germany, for it left them without rail transport, petrol, and supplies of food. It came at a difficult time for the government, for it coincided with the general strike in Glasgow and riots in Belfast, both of which needed the deployment of large forces – 8,000 soldiers, including tank units, were stationed in Glasgow by 1 February. The unrest at Calais and subsequent riots by soldiers in London during the second week of February raised the question of the reliability of the Army.

The origins of the troubles at Calais lay in the attitudes of many of the men employed behind the lines. Former trade unionists, who played a significant part in the strikes, had already shown on earlier occasions that they had not abandoned deeply held convictions about collective bargaining when they joined the armed forces. At the beginning of the war, Field-Marshal Slim, then a junior officer, discovered that a platoon of former miners had gone on strike when they found what they considered irregularities in their pay.[64] He entered the hut where they had confined themselves and talked the matter over with them until it was concluded to their satisfaction. The incident was kept from the battalion commander who would have regarded it as a case of mutiny and acted accordingly. 'To me, as a soldier,' wrote Major-General Childs, 'any strike among disciplined men means mutiny', and many other officers would have agreed with him.[65] Soldiers had orthodox ways of seeking redress, but these were not always understood, nor, at times, did they appear very effective. Ex-trade unionists could, therefore, fall back on the methods which they were wont to use in peacetime and which, in the years before the war, had often proved highly fruitful. Recourse to such syndicalist approaches was commonest amongst the masses of skilled and unskilled specialists

107

who worked behind the lines and whose jobs had obvious civilian equivalents.

The supply, equipping, feeding and transport of the front-line Army and the servicing of its weaponry and transport had caused a massive increase in the personnel of the Army's technical corps. It was often the case that peacetime skills were deliberately exploited by the Army so that former bus-drivers found themselves at the wheels of supply lorries. Such soldiers worked in the Ordnance and Transport workshops and storehouses, ran trains, kept up rolling stock and even manned dockside cranes at French ports. They repaired artillery, tanks and motor vehicles, and serviced base camps and hospitals. They took no part in the fighting, but were vital for the efficiency and success of those who did. They were also paid more, 8s 2d. weekly as opposed to 7s, which was the infantryman's wage. In return they were expected to work far longer hours than civilians doing similar tasks.

The soldiers' reaction to this discrepancy was sensed by some of their officers. At the end of November 1918, Colonel Paul, the Chief Inspector of Ordnance Machinery, noted an intensification of grousing by his men.[66] 'The workmen are getting restless and more than ever inclined to contrast their lot with that of men employed in munitions in England.' There, industrial workers were paid more for a 48-hour week, whilst on the lines of communication, Ordnance Corps men worked nine hours daily for six days. Officers were aware that their men were making comparisons and were sympathetic to demands for a reduction in hours and an increase in wages. But their hands were tied. The men's work was necessary for the maintenance of the forces still in northern France and the army of occupation in Germany. This had to be kept in a state of high efficiency in case the German government refused to sign a peace treaty and the war re-opened. Any proposals for changes in the pay of, and hours worked by, technical and support staff would have to be laid before General Headquarters, where they would inevitably require examination before they were approved. These delays were not understood by the men, who became increasingly impatient during December and January.

This impatience was worked on by a handful of men who were socialist and trade union militants. 'We had a real hard-core of trade unionists and socialists,' remembered one man from the Valdelièvre camp near Calais, who also claimed that the circulation of *Weekly Herald* in the camp rose to 500 copies a week during the last six months of 1918.[67] Valdelièvre was an Ordnance depot, and Churchill later remarked that Ordnance and Mechanical Transport soldiers 'were the least-disciplined part of the army ... and were most closely associated with political Trade Unionism'. Major-General Sir Charles Mathew, the Director of Ordnance Services, felt certain that the strikes had been stage-managed from afar and detected the hidden hand of 'Bolshevism' behind the men's behaviour. When, on 30 January, the strike collapsed, one of the men noted that its downfall coincided with the end of the general strike in Glasgow 'to which our eyes were anxiously turned'.[68] Yet, whilst the strikers contained men whose minds were fixed on what they considered a wider social and political struggle, the demands of the delegates were limited to improvements in service conditions.

The prelude to the Calais strike was a period of unrest in various camps in northern France. On 18 December 1918 Ordnance men at Le Havre went on strike and called for shorter hours, more leave out of camp, holidays for Christmas and New Year, and an additional ration of bread. Colonel Langhorne, the local Chief Ordnance Officer, was later confronted with calls for a 48-hour week. He appreciated the men's position, especially those who were facing long waits before demobilisation. They deserved more money, he argued, so that they would not be 'at any disadvantage as regards pay etc., as compared with fellow workers who are fortunate enough to be sent home early'.[69] At Calais there were similar signs of restlessness amongst Tank Corps technicians who went on strike on 21 December when asked to work on Saturday afternoons. They were placed under arrest.

Measures were immediately taken to investigate the complaints raised by the strikers. Major-General Mathew toured depots at Dieppe, Le Havre and Rouen between 29 and 31 December, and on 8 January 1919 a conference at General Headquarters examined the problems of pay and hours. It soon emerged that concessions to one group of men would provoke an outcry from others who would have claimed discrimination. Contact with the strikers had already taught the staff officers concerned something about the trade union mentality and its obsession with demarcation of jobs and differentials. Nevertheless, compromises were made, and Royal Engineers doing vital railway jobs at Calais had their hours reduced.

This in turn encouraged others to press their claims. The Calais

Ordnance men sent a delegation to the Chief Ordnance Office on 21 January with demands for an acceleration of demobilisation, better rations and improved conditions. Soon after this meeting, one of the spokesmen, John Pantling, was arrested for a minor offence. His colleagues immediately cried 'victimisation' and clamoured for his release. The authorities caved in and Pantling emerged from the guard room, unpunished; but on 26 January he was re-arrested for making what was interpreted as a 'seditious' speech.

Pantling had now become a martyr, a cause on which the men in the Calais Ordnance camps could focus attention. On 27 January, what approximated to a general strike was called in the Calais region. During the afternoon about 4,000 men from two Ordnance depots, joined by women from the Queen Mary's Army Auxiliary Corps, marched to Headquarters' offices in Calais and called for Pantling's release. By this time the strike was embracing men from other units, including Royal Engineers serving on the railways, and the whole apparatus of supply and transport collapsed. Co-ordination and, where necessary, intimidation, followed the pattern of trade unionists' activities in peacetime. The Ordnance men were the moving spirits, and provided the organisation. 'Parties of picked men were sent out to visit the different camps in the area' and persuade them to contribute pickets. One of these 'picked men', who seemed to have had some experience of this sort of thing, came across a handful of NCOs still at their clerical duties. They were ordered out: 'Don't you know there's a strike on?' When they showed signs of not being interested, they were ordered again. 'I've no time to waste arguing with you, come on now, out of it.'[70] Like soldiers, strikers were not expected to think for themselves.

The strike was well under way when pickets from the Ordnance depots turned their attention to the 5,000 infantrymen stranded in Number 6 Leave Camp at Calais. These men had returned from leave in Britain and were expecting to be entrained for their units in France and Germany. On 28 January they took their cue from the strikers, formed a committee and expelled officers from the camp. Their principle objective was to secure additional leave and with it the opportunity to get jobs and so jump the demobilisation queue.

News of these events had been passed by Major-General Mathew to General Headquarters. Haig was troubled by the cessation of all activity at a focal point in his army's transport system and by the 'serious' mutiny of a large body of front-line troops who were clearly trying to bully the Army into demobilising them. 'Their attitude was threatening, insubordinate and mutinous', and so Haig summoned General Sir Julian Byng, commander of the Third Army, and ordered him to take over at Calais and bring the unrest to an end. Troops of the 104th and 105th Brigades were placed at Byng's disposal; these were then moved by motor lorry to Calais, which some of them reached by the night of the 28th.

Byng's primary objective was to overthrow the mutiny at the Leave Camp, which was immediately surrounded by pickets from the 4th Battalion, North Staffordshire Regiment. Attempts by the mutineers to subvert the newly arrived men were unsuccessful. By the morning of 30 January, Byng had the camp besieged by troops from the 104th and 105th Brigades, supported by 60 machine-guns. The 104th, led by its commander, Brigadier-General Sandilands, entered the camp with fixed bayonets. Sandilands called to the groups of men he came across: 'Fall in those who wish to return to their units.' The men gave up quickly, ignoring efforts by the ringleaders, one of whom, a sergeant from the Scottish Rifles, shouted to them to 'stand fast and united'. Slowly, the soldiers from the 104th moved through the camp, leaving the 'delegates' isolated. Within two and a half hours, the mutiny had been broken. The four ringleaders had been arrested, and when two hundred of their hard-core supporters approached Byng with demands for their release, he gave notice that he would have no truck with deputations. 'I have heard of Field-Marshals in the Army, of Generals, Colonels, Captains, Sergeants and Privates, but I have never heard of a deputation. Surrender unconditionally in half an hour or bear the consequences.'

The promise of no reprisals against those who had given themselves up and gone to their trains, together with Byng's firmness, was enough to persuade the mutineers to surrender. The four delegates, three of them NCOs, were arrested and court-martialled for mutiny. Haig was relieved, and later praised the 'staunch behaviour of such troops as were able to concentrate' and put an end to the disturbances. He was, at the same time, fearful that there would be further mutinies and therefore wanted the death penalty for the ringleaders, otherwise 'the discipline of the whole Army will suffer, both immediately and for many years to come'. Churchill replied to this request by a telegram on 31 January. He dismissed the idea of shooting the ringleaders, an act which he thought would distress the public. 'Unless there was

111

serious violence attended by bloodshed or actual loss of life', the
death penalty should not be invoked, he argued. Haig was irked
and complained in his diary, 'no *telegram* from [the] Secretary of
State can affect my right to do what I think is necessary for the
Army'.[71] The four men were, however, imprisoned.

Byng's attitude towards the other mutineers, the Ordnance and
support troops at Calais, was more conciliatory. Their delegates
were invited to negotiations in the afternoon of 30 January. A
divergence of interest was quickly revealed, for the extremists from
the Ordnance Corps demanded a 36-hour working week, official
recognition of the soldiers' council and permission for its delegates
to attend a political rally at the Albert Hall. The RASC men were
satisfied with a 45-hour working week. Byng, Mathew and
Brigadier-General Wroughton, who had previously sanctioned
Pantling's release, refused these demands. They insisted that all the
'strikers' should be back at work by 6.30 the next morning and that
all grievances should be treated in the accustomed Army way. The
delegates agreed.

Several factors contributed to the sudden end of the Calais strike.
The example of the determined action against the men in the Leave
Camp may have unnerved many strikers, who were also well aware
that the authorities had adequate troops at hand to meet further
troubles. These men gave no indication of any sympathy with the
strikers. The release of Pantling had removed one, unifying
grievance. One of the more militant men recollected that a local
cinema had been opened and was showing a popular programme of
British films that evening, and this proved more attractive to many
strikers than attendance at negotiations. A few months later, after a
mutiny by men of the Machine Gun Corps at Evinghoven, a mobile
cinema was immediately brought over to the unit's camp.[72] The
Army may well have realised the strange power of the movies to
deflect unrest. Certainly it was argued in the 1930s that the picture
houses were of value in inducing quietism and escapism among the
unemployed. Whether or not the evening's films took the strikers'
minds off their grievances is not known, but the bottom was
knocked out of their will to resist by the announcement of the new
demobilisation scheme and higher wages which had been made on
29 January. By the morning of 31 January the men and women at
Calais were back at work.

With the men back at work, Churchill believed it was possible to
open negotiations about hours of work and pay. He suggested that

the Army authorities might make use of the talents of Sir George Askwith, who had been the Board of Trade arbitrator during the strikes of 1912-13. Yet whilst Churchill contemplated making this concession to civilian practice, he was firm on the matter of soldiers' strikes. 'They must return to their duty and no bargaining or negotiation can take place between them and the Army authorities.' Only 'when order and discipline have been thoroughly restored and the ringleaders punished with fitting severity', could matters about hours and pay be discussed. Between 24 January and 4 February, forty-two men from various units, including the Army Service Corps, were court-martialled at Rouen for mutiny. Nine got three years and the rest between fifty-six and ninety days' detention.

Even so, the sequence of disturbances during January left many soldiers with the belief that they could get their way by a resort to disorder. On 7 February, about 3,000 men, returning from leave, found themselves stranded at London stations, thanks to the incompetence of the military transport authorities. They made their way to Horse Guards Parade where there was a noisy demonstration. A rifle was hurled into Major-General Ashmore's office but its owner, 'a diminutive private', later came for it with the excuse that it had 'slipped out of his hand'. Ashmore returned it, but later had to rescue a hijacked Headquarters motor car which was being taken for a joy-ride. Ashmore recognised it was a harmless prank, for the driver 'was quite a good sort and didn't really mean any harm'. This may have been so, but the Army authorities were now nervous about large and noisy gatherings of servicemen, and the following day strong measures were taken. Many of the soldiers, still without transport and in many cases with no money, were armed and their gathering looked ominous. Ashmore watched them from his window, and the approach of troops from the Household Division and the Guards who had been called in to restore order.[73]

At a signal, a squadron of Household Cavalry trotted up from the Mall and formed a line on the edge of the mob. A battalion of the Scots Guards marched up from the other side and completed the rounding up. The rioters were hemmed in against the line of buildings. The authorities, with tact and judgement, had left a 'Golden Bridge', a free passage close to the wall, and through this a great many of the less mutinous people could, and did, fade away. The more determined were sorted out and pacified.

113

They were then marched off to barracks under escort.

The deployment of troops had been undertaken at Churchill's orders. He had first asked Field-Marshal Robertson and General Feilding whether the Guardsmen would obey orders and was told, 'The officers believe so.' Luckily, the incident passed off without anyone being hurt and the 'mutineers' were given breakfast and trains were found for them.[74] Both Ashmore and Churchill agreed that they had had a genuine grievance.

There were echoes of Army discontent from other areas. In Egypt the disbandment of the British Army was slow and the many hitches led to a series of disorders during April and May at the Kantara base depot. The problem here was exacerbated by the need to keep troops for garrison duty in Palestine and in Egypt, where additional forces were required for the suppression of a nationalist insurrection during March. Australians were to the forefront of the restlessness and many, finding themselves delayed in Egypt, turned their anger on the local population. Another Imperial difficulty, the insurgency in the Punjab in the spring of 1919 and the subsequent half-hearted Afghan invasion of the North-West Frontier Province, hindered the demobilisation of troops in India and Mesopotamia. As a result there was a rash of insubordination which verged on mutiny by various units serving behind the lines in India, and a marked reluctance to serve in the Afghan campaign by some battalions which had been expecting demobilisation.

DEFENDING THE HONOUR
OF HIS COUNTRY

The worst disorders which arose out of delays in the demobilisation programme were the last. They occurred at the Canadian Army camp at Kinmel Park, near Rhyl, on 4-5 March 1919, and ended in many casualties including five dead, four of them mutineers.[75] News of the incident was extensively reported, and in the press there were a number of lurid and unsubstantiated claims. To this day, the Canadian government is reluctant to offer its own version of the sombre incident.

Kinmel Park was a concentration of camps, twenty in all, conveniently close to Liverpool, the port through which Canadian forces passed. During the first months of 1919 the troops here had become increasingly despondent. Living conditions were squalid, the camps were infected by Spanish Influenza and there was much disgruntlement about the inadequacy of the pensions which the Canadian government was prepared to offer wounded men. Further and more bitter distress was felt during February when the Canadian government's demobilisation scheme appeared to have broken down completely, the official excuse being a lack of ships. This was not believed by the Canadians who were incensed by the fact that shipping seemed to be available for United States troops, some of whom had done little fighting, but not for them, many of whom had been involved in the great battles of 1918. An officer recalled the circumstances and the soldiers' temper.[76]

> They were there without any pay, and without any money, and stuck in this camp at Rhyl, and no idea as to when they were going to get home. They got *mad*, and they started to make a fuss. When the authorities didn't pay any attention to them, they wrecked the damn camp from one end to the other. They just burnt the damn thing right down.

At some time during the evening of 4 March the upheavals began. By half-past ten there had been a number of meetings at which a Russian immigrant, Sapper William Tsarevitch of the Railway Company, was elected the leader of the mutineers. According to *The Times*, the cry 'Come on the Bolsheviks!' had been the signal for an attempted take-over of the camps in the Kinmel complex. There was some resistance, which was overcome by force, but the mutineers failed to occupy Camps 19 and 20, which housed officers and administration buildings. There was also a certain amount of looting, especially of drink which was taken from canteens, and the 'Tin Town' Stores, a collection of shanties near Bodelwyddan, was destroyed, although here the mutineers were joined by a number of civilians. The rumpus and the sight of the fires at the camp caused alarm in nearby Rhyl whose inhabitants remembered what one of them called a 'feeling of terror'.

The following morning the mutineers appear to have been inactive, in contrast to their officers who were determined to put down the rising. One of them, Lieutenant Gauthier, removed his badges and wandered amongst the men in an effort to identify who

115

were the ringleaders. In anticipation of an attack on Camp 20, trenches had been dug to form a perimeter defence, and at 1.30 forty of the officers and loyal men were issued with rifles at the orders of Captain Maclean. Just after two, Lieutenant Gauthier warned some mutineers against approaching the camp, but his address was met with derision.

At about 2.30, an advance-guard of mutineers under a Red Flag came towards the entrance to the camp. Behind them was a second party, also bearing Red Flags, and behind them a larger body. Some of these men were seen to have been carrying stones and rifles and, earlier, an eyewitness to the first unrest, had seen men with cut-throat razors attached to sticks. The guards immediately made a sally towards the first party of mutineers and were able to seize and arrest twenty, who were taken back to the Camp 20 guardroom. This, in turn, prompted the mutineers to rescue their comrades and so an assault was launched on the guardroom and records office. A company sergeant-major witnessed the foray:

> Two men were leading, with a red flag on two poles. The crowd went into the Guard Room and I could hear their leaders say, 'Let's have them out'. Stones were thrown through the windows of the Guard Room and two or three of their leaders seized fire buckets from their hooks and smashed windows with them. Then they moved off towards No.18 Camp canteen. Shortly afterwards I saw a crowd collect near the roadway and make a rush between the huts of No.18 camp. They were armed with sticks and stones and one or two rifles. I noticed that one of the rifles had a bayonet fixed. Immediately afterwards, I heard shots coming from the direction of No.20 Camp.

The second attack on Camp 20 was a more determined affair. The mutineers had briefly paused when they saw the guards, who then took the opportunity to rush them. Eyewitnesses were confused as to exactly what followed, but there was certainly some hand-to-hand fighting, a withdrawal by the guards and an exchange of fire. Gunner Hickman was shot dead in Camp 18 and several men in one of its huts were wounded. Private Gillan, one of the guards, was hit in the crossfire as he was moving towards a group of mutineers who were in an ASC stables. Gunner Haney was shot in the head, Corporal Young killed by a bayonet wound in the head and Tsarevitch, allegedly the leader, died from a bayonet wound in the lower stomach. The last two men must have been wounded during

116

the sharp hand-to-hand fighting between the guards and the mutineers. The fierceness of the resistance led to the mutineers hoisting a white flag. Four had been killed, twenty-one wounded, and seventy-five were arrested. Fifty men were charged with mutiny, of whom twenty-seven were convicted and sentenced to between 90 days and ten years.

One immediate consequence of the disorders was a Coroner's inquest on the dead in which the Canadian authorities offered limited assistance and several eyewitnesses gave evidence. Pressed to explain why the riot had taken place, one officer replied that the causes were 'part Russian, part drink'. The obvious explanation was frustration over the delays and inequities of the demobilisation system, and this was indirectly admitted by the Canadian army when they suddenly speeded up the process of shipping men home. So swift were their measures that several of the witnesses needed by the Coroner were already on the seas when his court convened on 20 March.

One question troubled the Coroner's jury, and that was who started the shooting. The mutineers possessed no arms or ammunition, at least in theory, but it was likely that, in common with so many soldiers returning from the war, a few men had kept rifles and bullets. Whether or not the guards on Camp 20 had been ordered to open fire, they could have had little choice when confronted by the mutineers who were armed and who outnumbered them. One of the guards killed in the crossfire has inscribed on his grave: 'To the proud memory of Private David Gillan, who was killed at Kinmel Park defending the honour of his country'. The honour of the Canadian army was emphasised in the statement in *The Times* of 8 March, which also pointed out that the camp was now quiet and that the looting had been the work of no more than sixty men.

Just how many of the 20,000 men in the camps took part in the mutiny is not known. Of these, how many joined in the attacks on Camp 20 is also unknown, although their demeanour appears to have been such as to have provoked a formidable defence. This was strong enough to convince those who survived the attacks to surrender. It is not known whether their original objectives extended beyond mere protest at demobilisation delays and camp conditions. The participation of a Russian, the Red Flags and the alleged use of 'Come on the Bolsheviks' may well have indicated the sympathies of a few mutineers. The mutiny was described in *The*

Call, the official organ of English-speaking Communists in Russia, on 2 April, in which it was set alongside accounts of the insurrection in Egypt. It was claimed that thirteen officers had been killed and over 40,000 men took part.

Looking back on the disruption and strains which marked the demobilisation of the British Army, Churchill concluded that 'The fighting man has a grim sense of justice, which it is dangerous to affront.' The handful of mutinies in the British Army had been started by men who had felt themselves affronted by an injustice. which took different forms; at Blargies it was a vindictive prison system, at Etaples the clumsy exercise of authority by the Military Police and, in the months after the armistice, the ineptness and unfairness of the demobilisation procedures. There were also complaints about pay and hours, together with the traditional grievances over food and duties, many of which seemed superfluous after Germany's surrender. All injustices stemmed from negligence and human error by officers who, for the greater part, handled disturbances with forbearance and good sense.

Soldiers' unrest during these two years has been a field which has been well beaten in the hope of starting the hares of class-warfare. Radical agitators did exist and were obviously keen to make what they could of discontentment, but soldiers' grievances never assumed a political complexion. Nor did mutineers question the basis of officers' authority or their right to command. Expressions of open unrest were confined to areas behind the fighting line and at no time did mutineers either challenge the war or refuse to fight. In spite of the apprehension shown by politicians and Headquarters, the will to fight of the British Army was never undermined. Where it occurred, mutiny was contained by loyal troops. Whilst it might be argued that the use of the Honourable Artillery Company at Etaples was dictated by the fact that its rank and file were drawn from the middle and professional classes, the back-up units were not. As it was, the formidable demonstrations at Etaples were quickly halted by less than 400 men armed with spade handles. At Calais and in London in February 1919, the appearance of clearly unmovable troops was sufficient to stop the disorders, which the Army quite sensibly overlooked, save in the cases of a handful of ringleaders. At the time it was less easy to take a sanguine view of the mutinies thanks to the alarming precedents of unrest in the Russian, French and German forces. From a distance the mutinies appear less than dangerous, merely reminders that civilians turned soldiers were not prepared to be ill-used or, like the sailors in the French Wars, entirely to forfeit their civil rights to humane and honourable treatment.

THIS ILL-CONCEIVED VENTURE:

North Russia, 1918-19

> We had committed the unbelievable folly of landing at
> Archangel with fewer than twelve thousand men ... The
> consequences of this ill-conceived venture were to be
> disastrous both to our prestige and to the fortunes of the
> Russians who supported us. It raised hopes that could
> not be fulfilled. It intensified the civil war and sent
> thousands of Russians to their deaths. Indirectly it was
> responsible for the Terror. To have intervened at all was
> a mistake. To have intervened with hopelessly
> inadequate forces was an example of spineless half-
> measures which, in the circumstances, amounted to a
> crime.
>
> R. Bruce-Lockhart, *Memoirs of a British Secret Agent*

NOT WORTH THE BONES OF A SINGLE BRITISH GRENADIER

In the spring of 1918, the Allied governments committed their
armed forces to the confused affairs of Russia. This involvement
lasted for two years, but was never whole-hearted, with the
Americans pulling out at the beginning of January 1919, to be
followed by other powers during the next twelve months. From
start to finish, the motives and objectives of the governments were

muddled and policies towards what became known as the War of Intervention were liable to sudden change. Yet what appeared fickleness was often the unwilling response to domestic pressure. In Britain, France and the United States there was considerable hostility towards what was seen as an expensive and needless war fought for reasons which did not directly involve national interests. Trade unionists and socialists of all complexions from pink to crimson sympathised with the new Communist government in Moscow and threw their weight behind a 'Hands Off Russia' lobby. Other political parties wondered what benefits would follow the war and concluded that they would be few and worthless. On 3 January 1919, the *Daily Express* insisted 'The frozen plains of Eastern Europe are not worth the bones of a single British grenadier.' It was an opinion which came to be shared by many of the servicemen who found themselves fighting in Russian snows.

It had been easier for Allied governments to justify intervention in Russia before November 1918, when operations against the Communists could be presented as preventive measures to check German ambitions. The treaty of Brest-Litovsk in March had resulted in large areas of western Russia passing under German control, and Turco-German armies continued to advance eastwards towards the Crimea and Caspian Sea, which created the impression that even more Russian land and resources would pass into enemy hands. Before the November 1917 Revolution, the Allies had shipped arms and ammunition to North Russia where large quantities remained, stockpiled at the railheads of Murmansk and Archangel. These dumps were considered to be a tempting target for the Germans and their Finnish allies and so, in April 1918, a detachment of Royal Marines landed at Murmansk. This unit was soon reinforced when the Allies became alarmed at the successes of the anti-Bolshevik Finns under Mannerheim and his German backers. In July further forces disembarked and others were sent to Archangel. These were ordered not only to watch over munitions, but to be ready to help with the proposed evacuation of the 70,000-strong Czech Legion. The Czechs, all former soldiers with the Austro-Hungarian army, had taken over the Trans-Siberian Railway after quarrels with local Bolsheviks. They were needed on the Western Front and the Allies hoped that they could be brought out from Russia either through Archangel or Vladivostok, where United States forces had taken over the port.

Both the Murmansk and Archangel expeditionary forces

extended their control beyond the two ports. Detachments from Murmansk moved southwards along the railway line which eventually led to Petrograd and west towards the frontier with Finland. From Archangel, units penetrated south along the railway line towards Vologda and along the navigable Dvina towards Kotlas and western Siberia. These incursions inevitably ended in collisions with local Bolshevik forces. By December 1918, Major-General Sir Charles Maynard, the Commander-in-Chief of Allied Forces at Murmansk, was in charge of 7,000 British, 3,000 Allied and 15,000 Finnish, Karelian and anti-Bolshevik Russian troops. His opposite number at Archangel, Major-General Sir Edmund Ironside, commanded 6,000 British and Canadians, 4,000 Americans, 1,250 French and various smaller units, including Serbians and 300 Poles – good-quality troops exotically dressed in traditional *czapkas*.[1]

By this date, the war with Germany had ended. The threat of a German occupation of western and central Russian provinces had vanished and, with it, the initial justification for the deployment of close on 40,000 Allied troops in North Russia. Still, the Allied armies remained where they were and so did other troops in Siberia, Vladivostok, southern Russia and on the Russo-Persian border. The reason for maintaining this occupation and operations against the Bolsheviks was the fact that the earlier arrival of troops had given an opportunity for the hitherto dispersed and disarrayed anti-Bolshevik forces to congregate and form administrations and armies. The centres of Allied control in Russia became focal points where the anti-Bolsheviks could receive protection, encouragement and arms. In North Russia, a Provisional Government had been established at Archangel and, drawing on levies from the territory under Allied control, was mustering an army with which to fight the local Bolsheviks. Larger and more formidable armies were concentrating in the east and Siberia under the 'Supreme Ruler', Admiral Kolchak, and in the south under General Denikin. Like other White Russian commanders, both relied heavily on Allied arms and employed Allied officers to train their men. By the winter of 1918-19, the anti-Bolsheviks were making good headway and there seemed a chance that they might defeat the Red Army and overthrow Lenin's regime.

The backing given to the Whites by Allied governments owed something to growing apprehension as to the nature of the Russian Communist government. Moscow had become the powerhouse of

123

global revolution, and from 1918 was generating subversion which led directly to Communist uprisings in Berlin, Munich and Hungary. Assistance was pledged to revolutionary socialists throughout the world. The British Empire was a special target, for, in December 1917, Stalin, the new Commissar for Nationalities, called upon the colonial peoples of the East to 'overthrow the robbers and enslavers'. This appeal drew several Indian nationalists to Moscow during the following year, and Russian propagandists began to concentrate their efforts on China, Persia and India.[2] Post-war disruption and its attendant economic problems in western Europe had led to unrest in several countries, including Britain, and there were official suspicions that this would be exploited by Russia. It soon became habitual to suspect the clandestine activities of Bolshevik agents as the mainspring behind any form of popular protest, including the mutinies amongst demobilised soldiers in Britain and northern France. Government alarms were soon reflected in popular fiction. The 'Webley and Trenchcoat' school of thriller writers in the 1920s quickly exploited anxieties about the underhand conspiracies of 'Bolsheviks' who aimed to foment unrest and overturn the state.

Whilst it was easy to create scares about Bolshevik plotters in Britain, Lloyd George's government found it hard to sell the War of Intervention to the public, especially servicemen. At the end of four years of war, soldiers and public did not want to embark on another for reasons which seemed far from clear. There had been no difficulty, in 1914, in advertising Imperial Germany and its rulers as threats to international peace and stability, but in 1919 an exhausted nation was deaf to claims that Lenin and his supporters were the enemies of civilisation and order. The answer was to limit intervention in Russia and give the Whites all they needed to free their own country. This view was forcefully stated by Winston Churchill, the unswerving champion of intervention, in February 1919:[3]

> If Russia is to be saved, as I pray she may be saved, she must be saved by Russians. It must be by Russian manhood and Russian courage and Russian virtue that the rescue and regeneration of this once mighty nation and famous branch of the European family can alone be achieved. The aid which we can give to these Russian armies ... who are now engaged in fighting against the foul baboonery of Bolshevism – can be given by arms, munitions, equipment, and technical services raised upon a voluntary basis. But Russia must be saved by Russian exertions ...

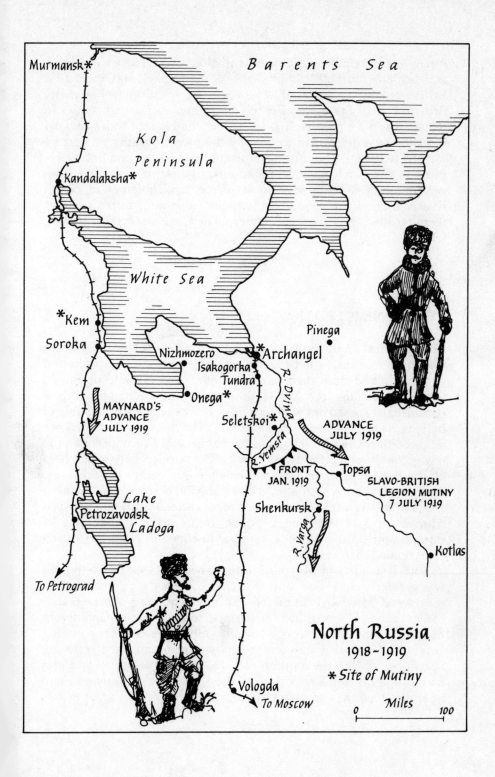

Murmansk ✳

Barents Sea

Kola Peninsula

Kandalaksha ✳

White Sea

✳ Kem

Soroka

Nizhmozero

Isakogorka

Tundra

Onega ✳

✳ Archangel

Pinega

R. Dvina

MAYNARD'S
ADVANCE
JULY 1919

Seletskoi ✳

R. Yemsta

ADVANCE
JULY 1919

FRONT
JAN. 1919

Topsa

SLAVO-BRITISH
LEGION MUTINY
7 JULY 1919

Shenkursk

R. Vatga

Lake Petrozavodsk Ladoga

Kotlas

To Petrograd

North Russia
1918~1919

✳ Site of Mutiny

Vologda

To Moscow

Miles

0 ⊢————————⊣ 100

Allied forces would not fight the anti-Bolsheviks' battles for them, and behind Churchill's flourishes was the implicit statement that British regular forces would eventually be withdrawn. For many British, United States and French forces, this end to their duties in Russia was not a moment too soon. They had fought courageously, but they were perplexed as to why they were fighting and many wanted to get out of uniform, return to their homes and find work, just like their colleagues who had already been demobilised. This consideration did not stop most of the British forces in North Russia from doing their duty without complaint, but, as one of them recalled, over sixty years later, 'There was nowt there to fight for.'[4]

EVERYONE IS FED UP

The political and military architects of the North Russian campaign had their minds set on one objective. Allied armies had to press inland from their bases, conquer territory and defend it, thereby providing the White government in Archangel with a recruiting ground from which to raise a force which was capable of holding its own against the Bolsheviks. The lines of Allied advance followed the railway tracks from Archangel and Murmansk and the navigable course of the River Dvina. The strongpoints which held off the Bolsheviks were defended villages, guarded by blockhouses. A chain of defences had also to be established around the southern rim of the White Sea to guarantee communications between Murmansk and Archangel. Allied fronts were the subject of intermittent Bolshevik raids, bombardments and offensives which were replied to in kind.

Both Ironside and Maynard initially believed that their strength was greater than it was, and that their enemies were weaker than they were. Maynard dismissed his opponents and observed that 'The "Bolshy" was evidently a slack soldier and an indifferent fighter' whom Allied troops 'could whip' whenever they chose.[5] Brigadier-General Finlayson, who had commanded the Dvina operations during the autumn of 1918, was less sanguine and in a memorandum to his superiors in the War Office cautioned them against taking the common view that the Reds were 'a great rabble of men armed with staves, stones and revolvers who rush about foaming at the mouth in search of blood and who are easily turned and broken by a few well directed rifle shots'. His experience showed that they were ably commanded and well organised. Others in the front line shared his views, and one noted that the Bolshevik gunnery was always good.[6]

His quality on the battlefield apart, the Bolshevik was soon recognised as a savage adversary. His forces showed barbaric cruelty to collaborators and POWs, who were tortured and killed, to the horror of British officers.[7] Mindful perhaps of the treatment they meted out to prisoners, captured Bolsheviks expected castration at the hands of their captors.[8] There was some basis for such trepidation, for one British officer, new to the Archangel front, noted that after his White Russian colleagues had taken a prisoner, he was summarily dealt with.[9]

Captain —— held a court martial on him and he was guilty of robbing a peasant and shooting some. He was shot. Not right without GOC's sanction. So we reported he died of wounds.

The British had found themselves in the middle of a merciless civil war of ideology without compassion. It was not, therefore, surprising that one seriously wounded British soldier asked his comrade to shoot him rather than leave him for the Bolsheviks.[10]

The characteristics of the fighting in Russia followed closely those of the final months of the war in northern France and Flanders. In spite of the contempt for the Bolshevik soldier which was felt by some senior officers, both Ironside and Maynard were anxious for as much modern weaponry as could be spared. At their request, two aircraft-carriers were sent from Britain in the spring of 1919 with reinforcements for the squadrons already there, and bombing raids against troop concentrations and strategic targets became common, especially in the final stages of the campaign. Ironside also asked for and got supplies of poison gas. Churchill was willing to accede and commented, 'I should very much like the Bolsheviks to have it', the gas in question being a new formula developed too late for use against the Germans. Gas bombardment on the River Varga front on 28 February 1919 had been a disappointment as a result of the cold, but subsequent employment of it by artillery and aircraft in August on the Dvina proved more effective.[11] For their part the Bolsheviks seem commonly to have used dum-dum bullets.[12]

127

Allied forces not only faced hard fighting against a ruthless enemy, they had also to endure the Arctic winter from late October to the end of April, a period of up to twenty hours of darkness each day and bitter cold. Temperatures fell to minus 40°F so that men on sentry duty could not stay in the open for more than a quarter of an hour without the risk of frostbite. Clothing matched the climate, for, thanks to the advice of the explorer, Sir Ernest Shackleton, the British were dressed in layers of furred and padded kit with at least two pairs of mittens. The detachments serving with the Archangel force fared worse as their supplies had to be transported through Murmansk, which was not frozen up, by train and then for the last part of the journey by sledge. Letters took up to seven weeks to arrive, but food was always adequate, if monotonous. This, together with the knowledge that no further reinforcements or, more important from the viewpoint of British soldiers, replacements, would arrive before the Arctic spring, dulled men's spirits. *The Times* correspondent, who wintered in Archangel, saw the men's mood in their faces. Around him were 'thin-faced men staring intently at nothing, eyes wide open, uncanny in their complete lack of expressions'.[13]

Little cheer could be drawn from the temper of Britain's allies. On 8 November 1918, Ironside had confidentially reported to the War Office that the French 21st Battalion of Colonial Infantry actively shunned fighting, would not engage the enemy in the event of an armistice with Germany, and was openly disaffected. By the following February they had degenerated into what Brigadier-General Finlayson called a 'sullen band of strikers and shirkers' whose obstreperousness infected other soldiers. This was not unexpected since they had been involved in the French army mutinies in 1917, when they had been at Lyons, and had been ordered to Russia to keep them out of further trouble.[14] The 339th United States Infantry were just as bad. Captain Roeber discovered from fellow officers' gossip in October 1918 'that the American troops were rotten attacking Kodish' and how one company 'ran away throwing down rifles even', a sight witnessed by a private of the Royal Scots.[15] Ironside regretted the poor quality of many of the American officers and, on 9 January, he listed for the War Office their defects. These included living with Russian mistresses, selling their men's rations, and embezzlement. There were a few 'stout-hearted' Americans, but most of the talk he heard in messes and clubs was a variation on one, defeatist, theme – 'We've done our bit, why stay and fight for these damn Russians who have always let us down?' The other ranks were, for the most part, Polish and Russian immigrants from industrial Detroit who appeared to have brought with them some sympathy for the Bolsheviks.[16] From these quarters, British soldiers could easily pick up the infection of despair and unrest during the winter of 1918-19, combined with envy, for, in January, President Wilson affirmed his government's intention of pulling out of the Russian campaign.

There had been isolated, but distressing, signs that the morale and will to fight of some British units was decaying fast. On 27 October 1918, the Royal Scots had been ordered to undertake an ill-planned attack against Kuliga which ended in a setback with seventy-seven casualties. Investigating what had happened, Ironside found that the men were 'demoralised to the point of insubordination' and that one man, who threw away his rifle and ammunition, claimed that 'they prevented me from running fast enough'. 'This,' he insisted, 'is not the kind of work for "B" category men to have done and we never expected it.' The Royal Scots recovered quickly and, by 1 November, Ironside reported they were 'in the highest fettle and keen for the fray'. They soon gave proof of their mettle and several companies remained in the front line under hard conditions for the rest of the winter.[17]

Soon after the débâcle at Kuliga and partly, perhaps, as a result of it, a few men from the 2/10th Royal Scots and some RAF mechanics had been discussing amongst themselves a nagging question. Since they all enlisted to fight Germans, why were they now pitted against Bolsheviks with whom the Allies were not officially at war? When Headquarters got wind of this speculation, a severe warning was issued. All officers and men were cautioned against calling into question the motives of the Allied governments, and reminded that talk which might weaken the 'fighting power' of a unit would lead to severe punishment.[18] Such discourse continued unchecked during the long, gloomy hours of the Russian winter when men had little else to do but bemoan their uncomfortable present and uncertain future. 'Matters like the Armistice, demobilisation and general talk of peace have a very depressing effect on [morale],' commented Finlayson in a report to the War Office in February 1919.[19] A hint of what was being said can be found in the diary of Corporal A.E. Thompson, a signaller with the Royal Engineers, who resented the tight censorship of letters. 'We are quite muzzled and can't get the truth out of the country,' he complained, while, in Britain, newspapers assured their readers that the men were all contented. They were not, he concluded: 'Everyone is fed up.' He also disapproved of the presence in Archangel of 'C' Category men, which he considered inexcusable given the climate and the fact that many had been wounded in France. Later, with the coming of spring and summer, his humour improved and he rounded off one day's entry with 'Worked to death as usual but still keeping the old flag flying'. Yet, on 26 June he was reprimanded by his Commanding Officer, 'for writing a letter expressing my doubts on our compulsory retention in this country etc.,' and sourly wondered, 'who said militarism is crushed'.[20] One intelligent soldier's reactions to his predicament were not necessarily those of a whole army, but in the light of events Corporal Thompson's candour was a truthful reflection of the feelings of many of his comrades.

Whilst some British soldiers pondered why they were in Russia, and others hoped that they would be sent away, their enemies were busy contriving propaganda to answer their questions and deepen their misgivings about the war. From the beginning of the campaign, officers and men came face to face with Bolshevik subversion, in the form of either sabotage or the circulation of literature which aimed at weakening morale. In December 1918, the Consul-General in Archangel reported that local Bolsheviks pinned leaflets to trees, although by July more sophisticated methods of distribution had been adopted and showers of handbills in English and Russian were dropped from aircraft.[21]

The material in English was written for British, Canadian and American servicemen. According to the Consul-General, the 'most poisonous and least honest' was from the pen of Mr Phillips-Rice, who called himself the *Manchester Guardian*'s Russian correspondent; also persuasive was Arthur Ransome's open letter to President Wilson which, with a preface by Radek, circulated amongst US troops.[22] In essence most of the propaganda emphasised two closely connected points. Allied soldiers were playing the part of blacklegs and were waging a war against the working class. On Boxing Day 1918, the *Commune* wished servicemen the season's greetings and then exhorted the 'English worker soldiers' to recognise 'all the lies, all the hypocrisy of their Lloyd Georges, Northcliffes, Masseys and other lords and capitalists' for whom they were fighting. When they went into battle against 'Revolutionary and Socialistic Russia, they murder at the same time the work of their own working class, the work of its liberation from exploitation and slavery.' The *Commune* also claimed that American troops had no heart for the war, for they 'never want to fight with these rogues of the White Army'. *The Call*, which said that it spoke for all English-speaking Bolsheviks, expanded on the theme of the war as a means of re-instating the detested *ancien régime* of Imperial Russia.

> You have been used as the tools of your capitalists who are working here in close unity with the agents of bloodstained Tzarism for the overthrow of the first Socialist Republic, and the re-establishment of the former reign of oppression ... Be honourable men. Remain loyal to your class, refuse to be accomplices of a great crime. Refuse to do the dirty work of your master.

Its issue of 2 April 1919 contained an extravagant report of the mutiny at the Kinmel Park camp, and an address to all Allied soldiers from the French sailors who had just mutinied against the war at Odessa. They demanded an end to the 'ignominious attempt on the life and freedom of the working class to which we belong'.[23]

The Bolsheviks thought that they were doing a good job with such appeals. A double-agent revealed to Major-General Maynard that a planned Bolshevik *coup* to seize Murmansk on the night of 22-23 March depended for its success on the imagined sympathies of Allied troops there, including the British. The Bolshevik command supposed that, once Allied Headquarters had been overrun, the rank and file would desert and join the insurgents. This was most disturbing for Maynard, who took the implications against the loyalty of his forces seriously. On 22 March he told his officers the news that the Bolsheviks had taken for granted that disaffected British soldiers would co-operate with them. In his view this was because the men were 'fed up' and believed that the British Labour Party was all but converted to the views of the Bolsheviks. There was, Maynard acknowledged, 'a feeling of discontent amongst our men, which is fostered by a pernicious and ignorant press [in Britain], and they feel themselves entitled to rather more than the average grouse which is characteristic of the British soldiers.' Matters had been made worse by the 'unwise talk' of a handful of officers about conditions in Britain, which, in his opinion, encouraged the Bolsheviks to think that the British soldiers would cave in. After a long exposition about the moaning and the best

131

antidote for it, Maynard suggested that his officers should say a few words to the men on the subject of the connection between Bolshevism and the Labour Party. They were to explain that the Bolsheviks stood for 'the nationalisation of women' and that no 'decent Britisher' would, for a moment, imagine that this was Labour policy![24] Not all Bolshevik propaganda could be so easily brushed aside. Seaman R. Jowett, serving aboard the seaplane carrier, HMS *Pegasus*, read one leaflet which fell from an aeroplane. It was 'asking us why we are fighting them, when we ought to be at home celebrating Peace etc., after five years of war. Strange to say, that is what we all want to know.'[25]

Ironside discounted the effect of the Bolshevik propaganda on his own forces with the argument that since they were British, they possessed an inbuilt and implacable contempt for all foreigners which extended to their writings. The Consul-General in Archangel took much the same view and observed that the British soldier was not taking the paper war very seriously.[26] Certainly, appeals for class solidarity fell upon deaf ears, for, in Murmansk, former train drivers serving in the British Army were quite happy to take over the jobs of Russians who were on strike.[27] Yet there was one area where the Bolsheviks' propaganda may have struck the right note with British soldiers and that was when it asked them why they were in Russia. The same question was raised by the anti-war press in Britain, which was also read by the troops, as Maynard bitterly regretted, and worked on the soldiers' feelings. It was hard to do one's duty in an unkind country in the knowledge that many of your countrymen were uncertain whether it was worth doing at all.

NO MORE FIGHTING

The Bolsheviks' unfounded belief that British forces in Murmansk might not actively resist their *coup* may well have owed something to knowledge of a mutiny which had occurred at Seletskoi at the end of February 1919. In the previous month, the Bolsheviks had launched a powerful offensive against British positions near Shred and reinforcements were needed to hold the line. On 2 February the 13th Battalion of the Yorkshire Regiment was ordered to entrain at Murmansk for Soroka and from there travel by sledge to

Seletskoi, where they would take over from a battalion of the King's (Liverpool) Regiment. Most of the men had reached Seletskoi by 22 February. There were then about 1,000 men billeted in the small town, most from the Liverpools, who were about to leave, and the Yorkshires, with smaller units of the RAMC, ASC and Machine Gun Corps. What happened when the Yorkshires took over their billets was described by Private Riley Rudd, who was serving with the RAMC.[28]

[Saturday 22 February] All have gone on strike – held meetings in IM hut last night and passed resolutions that they must be withdrawn from Russia immediately. Others to the effect that censorship be removed from letters in order that the people in England may get to know the true state of affair out here and that a cable be sent to L. George demanding the immediate withdrawal of all troops in Russia. They all positively decline to go up the line or to obey any orders but are conducting themselves in an orderly manner.

It was not a complete stoppage, for on the following day a patrol was sent out to investigate firing which had been heard nearby. Major-General Ironside was immediately sent for and he reached Seletskoi on 24 February, deeply perturbed by what he had heard. According to Riley, he met the men and, after listening to him, they agreed to move forward towards Shred, where Bolshevik forces were believed to be concentrating. The following day, the 25th, marked the end of the mutiny with an announcement by Ironside that all the men would return to Britain once the thaw had set in and that there would be 'no more fighting'.

In his version of the event, Ironside described the receipt of the news of the mutiny from the 13th Yorkshires' newly appointed commander, Colonel Lavie, whom he subsequently spoke with when he arrived in Seletskoi. Lavie told him that he had been astounded by his adjudant's news that the men had refused to leave their billets and parade. Lavie went to their huts and ordered the mutineers to fall in without their arms. They complied and once the battalion was drawn up, two sergeants stepped forward and said, on behalf of the men, that they would do no more fighting. Lavie then marched to the right of the lines, commanded a corporal to take a file of men and fetch rifles. When the armed file returned, Lavie ordered the corporal to arrest the two sergeants, which he did, and they were taken into custody. There they were interviewed

133

by Ironside who found them nervous and dejected; they were ex-Pay Corps men who had been seconded to the Yorkshires in March 1918 and may well not have expected to have been called upon to fight, particularly once the war with Germany had ended. One other NCO and thirty men from the Yorkshires, the ASC and the Machine Gun Corps were subsequently tried by court martial and several were sentenced to be shot. The death sentences were commuted to terms of imprisonment by Ironside, who later attributed his clemency to 'secret orders' from George V, who, it must be assumed, had asked Ironside not to carry out executions for military offences during the Russian campaign. This leniency did not extend to India where a mutineer was shot in 1920. Ironside had the news of the Yorkshires' mutiny sent by wireless to the War Office on 23 February and that of the RAMC and ASC men three days later.[29]

A third and intriguing account of the Seletskoi mutiny was set down by the White Russian general, V.V. Maruchevsky, whose account of the North Russian campaign was published in 1927.[30]

Towards the end of March extensive preparations were carried out for the Pinega operation. Around this time the situation on all fronts had already begun to calm down and the threatened region around Seletskoi was being reinforced again by the Yorkshire regiments of British infantry from Murmansk.

During the movement of these forces from Murmansk to Onega, via Chekuyevo-Obozevskiy along the wintry highway, not everything went well. The Yorkshires were travelling on sledges and were provided with many luxuries, but nonetheless, whilst passing through the region of Chekuyevo, they organised a mutiny and, it seems, this developed into a strong wish to stop fighting. The English have concealed all this very thoroughly, but I came to know of this episode through a despatch from Colonel Micheva, who, at the request of the local British command, positioned machine-guns on the road in case of open riot by the British.

In view of these events, General Ironside decided to deal a crushing blow to the Reds, in order to give them an impression of our strength and, on the other hand, to secure a success in order to smooth over the sensitive losses of Shenkursk and Turchasovo.

The date is, of course, mistaken, even allowing for Maruchevsky's use of the traditional Julian calendar, but his references to the deployment of the Yorkshires and Ironside's subsequent efforts to keep hidden the news of the mutiny are substantially correct. The absence of court-martial papers and the complete lack of any mention of the incident in the unit's war diary make it impossible to produce an exact account of what happened at Seletskoi on 22-25 February 1919. Nonetheless the three versions coincide on certain essential points.

Towards the end of their journey to Seletskoi, some NCOs and men of the 13th Yorkshires decided that they would refuse to leave the base for active service in the line. On their arrival, they made their views known to their officers and quickly found that men from the Liverpools and the base units were sympathetic. Everyone involved wanted to get out of Russia, an end to British involvement there and the opportunity to tell people in Britain what was really happening to them. Ironside was able to calm the men with a promise of demobilisation once the weather permitted, and with what must be interpreted as a promise of no further offensive operations. It was impossible, given the fact that the Bolsheviks were probing Allied positions in force, for this last pledge to be honoured. Just over a fortnight later, E Company of the 13th Yorkshires took part in the successful capture of Kholmogor, and other units from the battalion were in action during April. Ironside attributed the successful suppression of the mutiny to the purposefulness of Colonel Lavie and the instinctive loyalty of some of the men in his battalion, and made no mention of the coercive machine-guns manned by White Russians. Ironside's reticence when he published his account of the incident in 1953 is understandable, since knowledge that foreign troops had been deployed to overawe British soldiers with a not altogether unjustifiable grievance was likely to arouse public disquiet, the more so since Churchill, the enthusiastic patron of the campaign, was Prime Minister and at the height of his popularity. Yet Maruchevsky's description of the events stated that the machine-guns were set up along a road, which may indicate that they were there in readiness after the mutiny had collapsed and the battalion was preparing to move out of Seletskoi. If this was so, then Ironside and Lavie were clearly taking no chances with the men's loyalty.

The Seletskoi mutiny was serious and its repercussions were grave. In spite of efforts to hush up what had occurred, news of the incident spread, although it was kept out of British newspapers. Local rumours may well have encouraged the already restless French troops in the region to follow suit. On 23 February, a

French ski company refused to move to the relief of a detachment at Segesha on the grounds that they did not want to be shelled. Their officers caved in and, five days after, the men were transferred to garrison duties, which must have cheered them greatly. In Archangel, a French battalion disobeyed orders to entrain from the front. Their feelings were summed up by a stout corporal, who informed an officer, '*Je me fiche bien de ce qu'on pense de nous! Faites du pis que vous pourrez! Assez de cette guerre contre les bolshevistes!*'[31] The French command again turned to appeasement and the mutineers were placed under a guard of *marins*, shepherded aboard the cruiser, *Gueydon*, and later shipped back to France. News of all this was sent to Churchill, who, on 1 April, wrote to Clemenceau and asked him to order the evacuation of his troops who 'have to a large extent lost heart and discipline'.

Churchill also knew that this might equally have been said of some of the British units, for he warned Lloyd George that all was not well in North Russia, as 'we have had four or five unpleasant incidents'. He had been informed of these by Ironside who, at least a month before the mutiny at Seletskoi, had been fearful that something of that sort would occur. He had voiced his anxieties to the Chief of the Imperial General Staff, Sir Henry Wilson, who from January pressed the Cabinet to send reinforcements. After the Seletskoi mutiny, Ironside took comfort from the fact that front-line units were in good heart, but suspected that overall, 'we were drawing terribly near to the end of our tether as an efficient fighting unit'.[32] His apprehension was shared by the Director of Military Operations, Major-General Radcliffe, who warned the Cabinet about the 'unreliable state of the troops' in North Russia. What he, Ironside and the soldiers all wanted was a clear lead from the government as to what their future was. Would the men who had endured the Arctic winter be replaced? Would the operations be extended or curtailed?

Churchill sent messages to put the heart back into the men, who, on 4 April, were encouraged to:[33]

Carry on like Britons fighting for dear life and dearer honour, and set an example in these difficult circumstances to the troops of every other country. Reinforcement and relief are on the way.

There was more fighting to come but, Churchill reassured the men, 'You will be back home in time to see this year's harvest gathered in.' Major-General Maynard also did his bit to cheer his men.

Officers were ordered to take more pains about ensuring the comfort and welfare of their men, to cement close links with their NCOs and so be better able to judge the mood of their men, and they were to explain that they were all now helping the Russians, who had assisted Britain in the war against Germany. This extension of service would not, Maynard insisted, jeopardise the soldiers' future chances of finding work in Britain.

The most cheering news was that help was on the way. The Cabinet, strongly urged by Churchill and Curzon, had devised a new strategy for the Russian campaign which included the evacuation of detachments which were there and their replacement by new units. The changeover would begin when the White Sea ice broke up, and so men in North Russia could expect to be shipped home during the summer.

By the beginning of March new plans for the campaign were beginning to take shape in Whitehall. Two brigades of volunteers, tempted by a £30 bounty, were created under Brigadier-Generals Sadleir-Jackson and Grogan, and this force of 3,500 was to form the spearhead of an advance down the River Dvina as far as the Red Army base at Kotlas. What Churchill called 'these fine, war-hardened soldiers' were to be backed by a Royal Navy flotilla of gunboats and monitors, RAF bombers, RNAS sea-planes, and gas units. The objective of their summer offensive was to join the right wing of Kolchak's White Russian army which was poised to move westwards from Siberia towards Moscow. At Kotlas, the British would meet General Gaida's army whilst, behind the line of advance, the Provisional Government in Archangel would be busy drafting peasants into its army. This would, in the autumn, take over the conduct of the war from the British forces, which would withdraw. The plan, drafted by the War Office on 15 April, was approved by the Cabinet and conveyed to Ironside on 4 May. Maynard's forces at Murmansk were ordered to undertake a secondary offensive which would push their line forward to the shores of Lake Onega and put further pressure on the local Bolsheviks.

The key to this strategy's success was the progress made by the 50,000 men of Kolchak's army. On 17 June the right wing of his forces, under Gaida, was beaten and fell back, leaving the Red Army still in occupation of Kotlas and its environs. There appeared no further point in pressing south along the Dvina, and, in an emergency War Cabinet session the day after Gaida's defeat,

Curzon and Sir Austen Chamberlain pressed for the abandonment of the advance on Kotlas. Churchill stuck by the original strategy, but shifted his ground in defending it. There was still, he argued, a need to strike a heavy blow against the Red Army's base at Kotlas which, if successful, would prevent close harassment of the British withdrawal and offer a breathing space for the White Russians in Archangel. Backed by the General Staff, Churchill overcame the doubters and on 27 June Ironside was ordered to press on with his offensive.

Unaware of the shifts in strategy, the British forces in North Russia continued to do their duty. Yet the unrest, which had broken surface in February, did not disappear completely and there were two further mutinies amongst the British forces which formed part of the relief force. The first involved the crew of the China River gunboat, HMS *Cicala*, which was one of the flotilla of shallow-draught warships which had been ordered to Archangel in March for service against the Russian squadron on the upper Dvina.

According to Commander Edwards, in his account of the naval unrest which culminated in the Invergordon mutiny, there was a mutiny on board the *Cicala* in June 1919. When orders had been received to steam up the Dvina and engage Russian shore batteries, her crew refused to sail. They did not think that their thinly armoured vessel with its two 6-inch guns was suited to play the part of a monitor, and were dissatisfied with the standard of their rations.[34] On hearing of this defiance, the Senior Naval Officer, Rear-Admiral Sir Walter Cowan, a noted disciplinarian, sent an officer on board with a warning that *Cicala* would be shelled by other ships in the British squadron unless her crew did their duty. They did and the *Cicala* weighed anchor. *Cicala*'s log says nothing about this incident, although six hours before she proceeded up the Dvina on 27 May, three ratings were sent, under arrest, to HMS *Fox* for detention and *Cicala* was made fast to the tender *Bacchus*.[35] On 29 May, *Cicala* engaged enemy guns on the Dvina and with her consort, the *Cockchafer*, came under fire and faced the peril of mines. Her tour of duty ended on 9 June when she re-berthed at Archangel. She sailed up river again on 20 June, without incident, and stayed on duty on the Dvina for ten days. *Cicala* was in action again during August when she was holed by Russian fire. Whatever the precise date of the trouble on board, her crew performed their duties with courage although, as Cowan later pointed out, many of the crews of warships serving in Russian waters possessed a strong 'desire to know why we are out here'. Far away in London, the First Sea Lord assured the Cabinet that everything was well, since 'The Naval ratings who would take part in the expedition were not conscripts, but ordinary long-service men, and absolutely to be trusted.[36]

Sailors and soldiers at Archangel may well have been trustworthy, but they were becoming disturbed by the precarious loyalty of their anti-Bolshevik Russian allies. This showed itself, intermittently, during June and July when there was a series of mutinies among Russian troops which left a bitter taste in the mouths of many British servicemen. One, aboard HMS *Pegasus*, set down his exasperation.[37]

> Truly we are doing a wise thing! Fighting the battles of a people who do not want us, and who turn on us at every opportunity. Probably the Russian troops at Archangel will mutiny next and then there will be some fun. And if a ship were sunk in the fairway of Berezovi Channel, we should be locked in here so securely as rats in a trap. What a wise Government is ours!!

Just a week before, on 17 July, in the wake of the news of a mutiny of the Slavo-British Legion, British sailors attacked Russian troops in the Archangel Park and the 'Russians suffered a severe battering by Jack Tar'.[38]

This mood of disillusion, intensified by the knowledge that offensive operations were merely a prelude for a general withdrawal, infected the 6th Battalion of the Royal Marine Light Infantry which had disembarked at Murmansk on 9 August. They were mainly young soldiers whose hearts were not in the forlorn Russian venture, but in action they fought gallantly, often against heavy odds. In one action they were ambushed and betrayed by their 'guide', who turned out to be a Bolshevik agent. Supplies failed to reach the men and they were exhausted after combat. As a consequence of one ill-starred action on 8 September, over a hundred marines were court-martialed for mutiny, the gravamen of the charges being that they had refused orders to continue fighting. Thirteen were sentenced to death and the rest were given terms of imprisonment. No executions occurred and all the sentences were considerably reduced. Nevertheless the condemned men had to face the ordeal of having their sentences read aloud and their badges ripped off whilst they stood in the middle of a hollow square formed by the rest of the battalion. General Rawlinson then addressed them, laying the blame on their officers.[39] One, a veteran of proven worth, was cashiered (and later joined the Black and Tans as an undercover agent) and others were censured. This strange business was raised in the Commons by a Conservative MP, Lieutenant-Commander Kenworthy, and Walter Long, the First Lord of the Admiralty, pledged clemency on grounds of the youth of the convicted men. None served more than eight months.[40]

The misfortunes of the Marines were uncharacteristic, and the unavoidable consequence of the infirmity of purpose of the British government. It had never made up its mind whether Britain was at war with the Bolsheviks or whether its armed forces were merely offering short-term assistance to their adversaries. This irresolution left British servicemen in the field unclear as to why they were there and what they were supposed to be doing. This bewilderment, which appears, at times, to have been shared by those officers accused of being critical of the venture, led to much demoralisation and two of the rarest of mutinies, in which British soldiers showed an unwillingness to go into action. When it became clear that the Cabinet was prepared to impose a period on British involvement in North Russia, those there quickly became aware of the hopelessness of their position, especially when it was clear that the Whites would not fight. In the summer of 1919, British sailors and soldiers were called upon to fulfil Churchill's promise to hit the Bolsheviks hard and then withdraw, leaving operations in the hands of soldiers who were bound to be beaten. The fruits of this decision were two mutinies in which sailors and marines refused to co-operate in such a futile exercise. At each stage in this dismal tale, many of the fighting men were all but ignorant of what they were fighting for and, when the decision had been taken to evacuate them, little effort was made to inform the men of the timetable of their withdrawal. Seldom had any war been so mismanaged, or a British government behaved so irresponsibly towards its soldiers and sailors.

BETTER THAN ANYTHING THE
BOLSHEVIKS COULD PRODUCE

The creation of a native Russian army with which the Archangel Provisional Government could defend itself had been the primary objective of Allied operations since the autumn of 1918. The scheme floundered, wrecked by the deliberate neutrality of the mass of the local, peasant population and the barely concealed hostility of the working classes of Murmansk and Archangel, who were known to be sympathetic to the Bolsheviks. The soldiers conscripted from this material served with two simple aims, survival and a desire to be on the winning side. Even the *bourgeoisie* in the region, often refugees of the official, landowning and commercial classes, were pessimistic. Some took the bizarre expedient of having bogus announcements made of their deaths which were followed by fake funerals, after which the 'officially' dead man or woman reappeared under a different and humbler identity. By this means, it was hoped, the contriver of the hoax might avoid the inevitable attentions of the Bolsheviks. Others, lacking such resources and forced to serve with the White Army, found their insurance either in desertion to the Bolsheviks or in mutiny or, sometimes, a combination of both.

In the two ports and in the villages of the countryside, there was an abundance of Bolshevik agitators and spies who spread the message of revolution and encouraged conscript soldiers to mutiny. In January 1919, Headquarters Intelligence at Murmansk and Archangel was conscious that both towns contained sailors and workers who would throw in their lot with the Bolsheviks once the Allies had withdrawn, a fact which was recognised by British servicemen.[41] French intelligence sources in Stockholm in December 1918 had wind of Bolshevik plans to infiltrate the White Armies with agents posing as 'deserters' who would spread unrest and encourage mutiny.[42] This information was forwarded to the Foreign Office and was presumably known by senior officers in Archangel and Murmansk. Counter-measures were taken by the Allies but, as events showed, they were not effective. Following the revelation of the plot to take over Murmansk in March 1919 and various acts of sabotage on the railway, Bolshevik suspects in the Soroka region were rounded up and driven off towards enemy lines. In Archangel, the White Governor-General, Miller, supervised the detection, arrest, summary trials and executions of suspected Bolsheviks. Their bodies were dropped into the harbour through holes in the ice, according to the *Times* correspondent.[43] The daily methods of Miller's operatives were remarked on by Corporal Thompson.[44]

> Four Bolshevik leaders were shot dead in the Street today in broad daylight as they were walking along. The officer who recognised them didn't want to ask any questions.

The White conscript lived and fought between the chilling alternatives of the White and Red Terrors. The Red seemed, from his vantage point, to be more frightening since all that prevented it from being unleashed was the presence of Allied armies. The Russians therefore watched carefully the progress of these armies for, as both Ironside and Maynard appreciated, battlefield reverses or faltering morale indicated the possible success of the Bolsheviks. Faced with this, it was natural that local Russians thought about their own safety and how to come to terms with the eventual victors.

Russian officers had a very different view of the question of loyalty. The Bolsheviks' past record and present practice showed that they could expect no mercy if they were taken and, for this reason, many chose to keep as far away from the fighting as possible, much to the disgust of their British colleagues.[45] There was, however, often little to recommend some of the officers who had been sent out from Britain for training and liaison duties. Ironside classed some he encountered in October 1918 as 'the scum of the officers in England' and four, whom he met on the boat to Archangel, he ordered home again on account of their drunkenness.[46] Not that this would have disconcerted the Russians for, as Prince Marusi sadly noted, many of his brothers-in-arms were notorious for 'the abuse of spiritous liquors'. Two of these 'behaved in an indecorous manner in the lodging of the Sisters of Mercy' and when they were thrown out, they fired their revolvers. Such mayhem, reminiscent perhaps of the high spirits of young Czarist subalterns, reflected the hankering by many Russian officers for the days of the *ancien régime*. The temper and ideals of the old Imperial Army were still dominant in the minds of a great number of the officers who proffered their swords to the Archangel Provisional Government. Ironside guessed this on his arrival in Archangel in October 1918, and was sensitive enough to what had happened and was happening in Russia to realise that former Czarist officers, whose thinking and methods were entirely shaped by their previous experiences, would be useless for his purpose.

On a popular level, the two revolutions of 1917 had overthrown all the forms of traditional authority, whether exercised by officers, civil servants, landlords, employers or policemen. It no longer carried any weight with those classes whose duty in life had been obedience, and they commonly took violent revenge on their former masters. Yet this fact was often ignored completely by many White Officers who openly proclaimed their attachment to the *ancien régime* and their ardent hopes for its restoration. When, during exuberant celebrations in a mess in south Russia, officers of the White Army broke into the words of the old Imperial anthem ('God save Czar Nicholas, ruler and guide ...'), their British counterparts were dismayed.[47] The old order had gone for ever, and it was courting disaster to fight for its restoration.

In Archangel, the new order clashed noisily with the old on 29 October 1918. A company of locally recruited infantrymen refused to come on parade for an inspection by the Governor-General. The atmosphere in the barracks approximated to that which had obtained in countless other barracks and camps during 1917. The soldiers held meetings, passed resolutions and tried to form a soviet. When addressed by officers, they shouted, 'We want more food!', 'Our hours are too long!' and 'We don't want to be under foreigners!' When the local White Army's Chief of Staff, Colonel Samarine, spoke to them, the soldiers addressed him as 'Tovaritch' in the accustomed classless, Bolshevik manner. He had seen it all before when he had served as a military adviser to Kerensky in 1917 and gave up his new post and joined the Foreign Legion.[98]

The soldiers were eventually quietened. Their new commander, General V.V. Murachevsky, was a man who had no truck with what Ironside called the 'tovaritch' methods of command, for he 'had had bitter experience of mutinies in France and fully expected to meet some of his old delinquents in North Russia'.[49] Murachevsky had presumably witnessed the mutiny of the Russian battalions in France during the summer of 1917 and he soon gave notice of his willingness to use the same strict methods which had been used to quell those disorders. On 11 December, large numbers of Russian recruits and their NCOs stayed in their barracks, fired shots in the air and flourished Red Flags. The demonstration was a protest against a penny-pinching order which had come from

143

London and relegated all Russian troops to half rations. However, the Red Flags suggested that this grievance was being exploited by political agitators amongst the troops. Murachevsky immediately brought up Lewis guns, crewed by NCOs, and called on the mutineers to leave the barracks. Their refusal led him to summon up two Stokes mortars manned by officers which were trained on the barracks' roof. The first shot went wide and killed a civilian passer-by, but the next two struck the roof and persuaded the mutineers to surrender. When they had fallen in, thirteen ringleaders, all NCOs and older men who had been POWs in Germany, were arrested. They were tried by a Russian court martial, sentenced to death and shot.[50] The incident was vividly recalled by Corporal Thompson.[51]

> [23 December 1918] There was a mutiny at Sonombula Barracks some days ago. A regt of Russkies barricaded themselves in and declared war, so we turned machine-guns on them. They threw up the sponge after we had thrown Mills bombs through the windows. All guards in Archangel were doubled, a rising was anticipated. About twenty rebels were shot next morning and all was quiet again.

Two mutinies in six weeks was a less than heartening start to the formation of the North Russian national army. The executions, the first of many, were a sign that Ironside and his Russian counterparts were determined to deal firmly with all forms of mutiny by the new recruits.

Some of the men who had taken part in these mutinies were ex-prisoners, repatriated from Germany, who had no wish to carry on soldiering. They wished to follow the path already trodden by Russian soldiers during the past two years which led to home and land, now freed from the landlords' grasp. Others may have been enlisted locally from the refugee population, among whom Ironside had discovered the 'worst imaginable type, the very riff-raff of the revolution'. Both types may very well have contained men who actively supported the Bolsheviks and their programme. However fallible they later turned out to be, the promises of the Bolsheviks offered more to the mass of Russians than did the programme adopted by the divided White leaders, which were often twisted by their opponents into no more than schemes for turning the clock back. The peasants of the villages which were toured by the recruiting officers probably did not comprehend the subtleties of the contending ideologies, although they resented the conscription law of the White government which took away young men, and the Commissars from the Red Army who commandeered food for their soldiers. It is also unlikely that the men ordered away to barracks in Archangel cared much about what they were fighting for, even if they understood, but they were anxious to stay alive, which meant watching to see which side was winning. As they trained, there were plenty of men who urged them to take their chances with their brothers in the Red Army.

The growing armies in the north were a target for Bolshevik subversion. Following the unsuccessful *coup* in Murmansk on 22-23 March 1919, the Bolsheviks turned their attention towards the troops which were guarding the railway line to Vologda. On 30 March, a loyal Finnish officer reported to Headquarters at Murmansk that his battalion was ready to mutiny on 6 April and destroy two railway bridges before making south to join the Bolsheviks. They anticipated that the Karelian Regiment at Kem, where a pro-Bolshevik officer had been stirring up the men, would join forces with them. Forewarned, Maynard quickly moved loyal troops down the line, including marines from the *Glory* and *Sussex* with machine-gun detachments. Once the Finns were aware that their plan had been scotched, they offered no resistance and pledged loyalty in the future, a promise they kept until their regiment was disbanded in August.[52]

The Bolsheviks had more success in the vicinity of Archangel where there were a number of mutinies from April to July amongst the conscripts of the North Russian Rifles (NRR). The 2/3rd NRR, which had been formed on 11 March, had been ordered to garrison Toulgas, on the west bank of the Dvina, which had been held during the previous winter by the Royal Scots. Soon after taking up their new positions in the village, 300 men rose up, surrounded the HQ billet and murdered nine Russian officers. There seems to have been some collusion with local Bolshevik forces, for they were immediately ready to enter the village and join up with the mutineers. The attached Russian artillery unit remained loyal and was able to land a few shells on the mutineers, before retiring seven miles to the Allied lines at Shushega. One $4\frac{1}{2}$-inch howitzer had had to be abandoned because of poor roads. Aircraft were quickly summoned, and the mutineers and the Bolsheviks in Toulgas were bombed. The village was later recovered by a force made up of the US 339th Infantry, the Royal Scots and the North Russian

Dragoon Squadron.[53] The incident served as a warning, for it showed the extent to which a Russian battalion could be subverted, unknown to its officers, and the way in which the Bolsheviks could take advantage of a well-prepared mutiny to gain their opponents' position. This pattern of mutiny was soon to be repeated.

The coincidence of a wave of mutinies during July 1919 with Ironside's advance south towards Kotlas cannot be accidental. The offensive was designed as a heavy blow which would temporarily unnerve and damage the local Bolshevik forces so that they would be unable to take immediate advantage of the British evacuation. Yet the knowledge that the withdrawal had been scheduled for the autumn did little to reassure the White Russians about their future or encourage their soldiers, who were in danger of finding themselves on the losing side. This consideration alone must have convinced many of the need to shake off their associations with the Whites and accommodate themselves with the Bolsheviks. The Bolsheviks, who intensified their propaganda campaign, deliberately exploited the trepidation of the White soldiers. Leaflets dropped by aircraft towards the end of May warned deserters and traitors that their families would suffer. British and Russian officers were sensitive to this propaganda and maintained a careful look-out for signs of its circulation amongst their men.[54]

The Bolshevik command was also taking active measures to subvert the White Russian soldiers through infiltrators and agents. The first target was Onega, a small town of wooden houses and a fort, which lay astride the overland route between Archangel and the Murmansk-Petrozavodsk railway. On 20 July, in the early hours of the morning, men from the 5th North Russian Rifles and the Archangel Regiment murdered their officers, an uprising which coincided with the entry into the town by a small Bolshevik detachment. British intelligence expected more Bolsheviks to arrive by sea. A smaller mutiny occurred nearby at Cheknevo and three British officers were taken prisoner. They escaped to a monitor, which was lying off the coast, after its gunfire had scared off their guards.

The Onega mutineers had at first shown themselves lukewarm to the Bolsheviks for, according to a Russian warrant officer who had escaped on 24 July, a hundred of them, who were still in the town, were disinclined to accept offers to join the Red Army. An unknown number had taken the first opportunity to desert and had made for the woods surrounding the town in the first stage of their journey home. Those who stayed had their minds made up for them when Onega was attacked by White Russian forces, supported by British artillery, on 30 July. The assailants found the town well defended by 600 mutineers, who fought alongside the Bolsheviks in a struggle which lasted nine hours. Other mutineers had joined a second Bolshevik unit, which attacked Nizhmozero, along the coast to the north, where the defenders discovered that their adversaries were 'using people who know our position well'. The Onega mutineers also attempted to suborn a small detachment which was guarding a blockhouse on the Archangel-Vologda railway line to the east. Some of the messages were intercepted and a detachment of Polish troops arrived in time to disarm the would-be mutineers. Two, both sergeants, ran for the woods, but were shot and killed. They were suspected to be the ringleaders. Further south, at Seletskoi, Colonel Lavie of the 13th Yorkshires took the precaution of disarming a Russian company which had shown signs of disaffection. The situation had stabilised by 1 August with the retaking of Onega, but the incidents had caused a bout of jitters in Archangel, where all British personnel were ordered to carry arms in anticipation of a general uprising in the port.[55]

Archangel was already in a state of unease following the news from the Dvina column that the 1st Battalion of the Slavo-British Legion (SBL) had mutinied on 7 July and many of its men had defected to the Bolsheviks. In psychological terms news of this calamity was the most damaging to general morale, both British and White Russian. The SBL had acquired the status of an élite unit and was seen as the most efficient and loyal of the locally raised Russian forces. It was a formidable force which numbered, on 1 July, 4,340 men, including thirty British officers and fifty-seven British NCOs, although a quarter of the rank and file served in labour and railway corps.

The SBL had been born during the first weeks of the British occupation of Archangel and the midwife had been Major-General Poole, then local commander.[56]

I was able to interfere in a local riot and save the life of a Commissar of the Red Guard ——, who was about to be murdered by his men. He promptly enlisted to ensure his own safety and started to obtain results for me.

Of the volunteers that came forward, some were ex-Czarist officers, and there were 200 sailors from the cruiser *Askold*, whose crew had, in June 1918, mutinied and murdered their officers. By the time Ironside took over the Archangel command, the Legion numbered 500 men. He was impressed by what he saw and decided that the Legion was to be expanded. One source of recruits was the local gaol, where prisoners were being held without charge, and another, possibly the largest, was the growing body of Bolshevik POWs and deserters. Many of these were interviewed personally by Ironside, for he was conscious of Bolshevik schemes to infiltrate White forces. The Whites were sceptical of what Ironside later called this 'experiment'; Prince Marusi thought that the SBL was no more than a collection of 'gangsters', and the Provisional Government wanted many of its men to be shipped to an offshore island camp. The answers to such criticism lay, so the Legion's defenders claimed, in the quality of British officers and the discipline they implanted into these apparently recalcitrant recruits. The formation and training of the Legion became an exercise in local British prestige.

Faith in the fighting qualities of the SBL was quickly vindicated. The 1st Battalion (or Dyer's, after Lieutenant Dyer, its first commander and instructor) performed well during heavy fighting in January 1919 when one sergeant and nine men held a blockhouse to the last man. Three platoons attached to the King's Liverpools during the attack on Kodish in February gained one Distinguished Conduct Medal and four Military Medals. The continuing courage of the unit and its devotion to service were rewarded on 1 June (George V's birthday), when Ironside presented Dyer's battalion with its Colours at a public ceremony in Archangel.

The presentation was a prelude to the battalion's service with Grogan's column at the end of June. Official inquiries undertaken after the mutiny insisted that the men were all in good heart, 'showed no disloyalty' and were glad of the chance to fight shoulder-to-shoulder with British Regulars. Yet there were undercurrents of doubt among some of the battalion's officers, which were revealed by their conversations with the *Times* correspondent during the cruise up the Dvina a few days before the mutiny. Captain Barr informed the journalist that the Legion's commanding officer, Colonel Barrington-Wells, had just got rid of two troublemakers. 'You had them shot?' inquired the *Times* man. 'Fancy asking me that,' replied Barr. He and the other officers

The Nore Delegates: Isaac Cruikshank's contemporary cartoon of the ruffianly crew, covert Jacobins to a man. Under the table, Charles James Fox and sundry Whigs and Radicals admit their part in the Mutiny.

An oil painting by Francis Holman of HMS *Sandwich* getting to grips with the French in happier days before she was the centre of the Nore mutiny.

RICHARD PARKER.

Richard Parker: the leader of the Nore mutineers gives warning to others of his fate.

Injustice and oppression – two common causes of uprisings. Some naval officers scarcely needed an excuse to flog a sailor. In 1797, the crew of *La Nymphe* wrote 'we are kept more like convicts than free-born Britons. Flogging is carried on to extremes . . .' A cartoon by George Cruikshank.

HMS *Hermione* lying at anchor off La Guira. Nicholas Pocock's oil painting shows the successful night action to retake her in 1798.

A youthful Viscount Bridport; his tact and good sense did much to bring the Spithead mutiny to a peaceful end. This portrait in oils was painted by Sir Joshua Reynolds in 1764.

'In the early days of the War our men were like crusaders; chivalrous, confident in the justice of our cause, and ready and willing for sacrifice . . .'

Mounted Military Policemen, *c.* 1917: At Etaples the MPs' heavy-handedness did much to provoke the first outbreak of the mutiny.

Etaples Base Camp, *c.* 1917: the tented Infantry Base Depots are in the background. In the foreground are the railway tracks which separate the military quarters from the town. The bridges over the lines were the main focal points for mutineers who wished to cross into Etaples.

OUT OF BOUNDS
TO
ALL TROOPS
BY ORDER

Looking for trouble: Assistant Provost-Marshal on the lookout for men in an out-of-bounds house in a northern French town, 1918.

Demob men from the RAF and Army. The end of the war brought on a series of 'strikes' among soldiers, largely in protest at the inefficiency and injustices of the demobilisation scheme.

Back to Blighty: RAMC men setting off for demobilisation, 1919. There seems to be little transport available.

A Slavo-British Legion camp somewhere in the forest region south of Archangel; present are a Russian officer, a British and a woman in uniform. The alliance was an uneasy one, and spawned several bouts of unrest and mutiny.

Russian manhood: volunteers, including schoolboys, for the North Russian Rifles and Slavo-British Legion, with British and Russian officers, Archangel, 1919.

Reds: captured Bolshevik prisoners at Archangel in 1919. They are being interviewed prior to enlistment in the Slavo-British Legion.

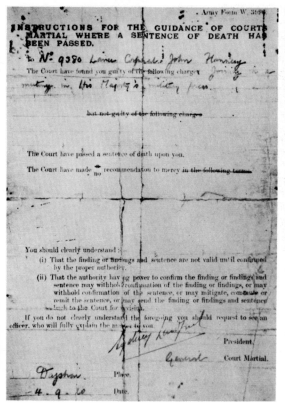

The notification of sentence of death given to Corporal Flannery in 1920. Altogether, fourteen soldiers of the Connaught Rangers were sentenced to death. In the event, thirteen, including Flannery, were reprieved.

Private Jim Daly of the Connaught Rangers – the last soldier in a British regiment to be executed for mutiny. He is shown here wearing the ribbons of the Victory and General Service medals awarded for active service in the First World War.

A firing squad executing Indian mutineers in Singapore, 1915: the mutineers, of the 5th Light Infantry, were shot by a squad drawn from various European volunteer units which had suffered losses during the uprising. A misunderstanding led an officer to open fire prematurely and several volleys had to be fired. These did not prove effective and police had to shoot several mutineers with revolvers.

Keeping the men in the trenches supplied: Chinese Labour Corps dockers unloading forage at Boulogne docks, 1917. There were several revolts among frightened and resentful Chinese and Egyptian labourers working in the French Channel ports in 1917 and 1918.

The West Indies help the Empire: men from the West Indies Regiment in camp, France, 1918: many saw no fighting, but were forced to work on the lines of communication.

seemed in good heart, although afterwards it was admitted that they and their colleagues had been keeping their eyes open for signs of the circulation of Bolshevik propaganda.

On 4 July, soon before taking up their positions on the west bank of the Dvina, the SBL was inspected and everything was found to be most satisfactory with no signs of restlessness. B and C Companies were placed in a village, Tuisamnika, close by the river bank, whilst the rest were in adjacent villages inland. At 2.00 a.m. Lieutenant Komarov inspected the lines and found everything quiet. Half an hour later, eight men, led by Corporal Nuchev and Private Leuchenko, approached the two-roomed hut where several British and Russian officers were sleeping. Nuchev shot dead Captain Finch through a window and the others shot and killed two British and four Russian officers and three orderlies. The killing of the two companies' commanders was a signal for the start of the mutiny. The sound of the firing roused all the men of B and C Companies whom the ringleaders rallied with threats and told to desert to the Bolsheviks. 150 chose to do so, much to the subsequent disgust of the author of the official report, who commented, 'It only shows the sheep-like nature of the ordinary Russian, one propagandist can make them do anything.' While some of the men were running off to the enemy's lines, their Russian officers were stupefied. 'Many simply ran away and deserted their posts', and, according to the official report, were still, several hours later, 'in a state of panic, and quite useless for any military purpose'. One, a lieutenant, was suspected of complicity in the mutiny and was tried by a court martial on 15 July, but was found not guilty. Of the surviving British officers, Captain Barr, though fatally wounded, managed to escape by swimming to a monitor anchored 500 yards off the shore. Others were able to restore order finally and one, Lieutenant Beavan, was later awarded the Military Cross for his courage and presence of mind.[56]

At the same time as the SBL mutiny, there was an uprising by 200 men of the 4th North Russian Rifles, who were stationed close by at Troitsa. Two British officers and the HQ Company servants were disarmed and locked up in the village bath-house whilst the mutineers, who included a machine-gun company, took over the position.

Rifle and Lewis-gun fire between 2.30 and 3.00 a.m. alerted nearby units which were soon informed of the two mutinies. Once it was clear what had taken place, artillery fire was directed against mutineers, probably from the 4th NRR, who were picketed out on a hillside. Half a dozen shells drove them for cover in adjacent woods. Ironside was immediately sent for and, when he arrived by launch from Ossinovo with reinforcements from the 45th Royal Fusiliers, an attempt was made to round up those mutineers who were still loitering in the woods. They were surrounded by a pincer movement and rounded up after a skirmish in which three were killed and two ringleaders were wounded. Other companies of the 4th NRR were reluctantly involved in this engagement against their former colleagues and they suffered twenty casualties, including ten self-inflicted wounds. Eleven of the mutineers were shot on 14 July after they had been found guilty by a court martial of British and Russian officers. Others were given terms of imprisonment. The *Daily Mail* reported that the executions had been by machine-gun fire, which it was alleged was a Russian military tradition. The captured mutineers whom *The Times* correspondent encountered 'were arrogant in their bearing'.[57]

An immediate and unavoidable consequence of Dyer's battalion's mutiny was the disarming of all other detachments of the Slavo-British Legion on 16 July. The astonishing surprise which the mutineers had achieved made vigilance imperative and, as a result of the wariness of British officers, plans for a mutiny by two companies of an SBL Labour battalion were soon revealed. The two companies were employed digging sand and loading it on to trucks at Tundra on the Archangel-to-Vologda railway line. The men had been silent when their rifles had been taken away from them and six had deserted, circumstances which aroused their commanding officer's suspicions.

On 18 July, an interpreter who had been called to investigate the desertions was able to uncover signs that men from the unit were contemplating a mutiny. A company sergeant-major revealed that a deserter had been overheard boasting that he would soon murder all the officers and railway workers. Another man was discovered to have said much the same to the station-master at Tundra. The memory of the SBL mutiny less than a fortnight ago was too fresh for this information to be ignored, so the detachment's British commander commandeered an engine and travelled to Archangel the next morning. His fears were appreciated by HQ, which ordered an officer with twenty British soldiers and a Lewis gun to move down the line to Tundra. On their arrival, they posted sentries, and Russians living nearby were warned that anyone who tried to escape would be shot.

With Tundra in quarantine, intelligence officers started investigations which soon revealed that 60 rounds of ammunition had been secreted by two Russian privates. Later, a British intelligence officer arrived and when all the information was collated, thirteen Russians were arrested. Two Russians, both deeply involved in the conspiracy, had already deserted, and it was revealed that messages from the Bolsheviks were being passed by women. Accordingly all women travelling on the morning train to Isakogorka were searched. Two letters were found; one incriminated a Russian medical orderly and another, intended for publication, was filled with Bolshevik sentiments.

The unit's commanding officer was by now convinced that a plot had been contrived which involved his men and Bolsheviks. Two deserters, who had been implicated, had been arrested at Kholmogor station further south, presumably as they were travelling towards the safety of the Bolshevik lines. They were brought back to Tundra the same day and were examined by their CO that evening. He had already been empowered to try them, and after his examination, he found them guilty of desertion. Death sentences were passed and were carried out the same evening by a firing squad of five men. The men were chosen from the Penal Battalion, and each issued with a rifle and one round. Both deserters stood to attention, and one shouted out: 'Hurrah for the Bolsheviks and long live the Russian Revolution!', leaving no doubt that he had been a Bolshevik agent. Neither man was killed outright, so that the final *coup* had to be given by an officer. Vigilance and careful intelligence work had frustrated a serious mutiny which, if it had succeeded, would have cut the rail link between Archangel and the front to the south. Its nearness in time and place to the mutinies in and around Onega, the evidence for external encouragement, and the deep involvement of one man who was a dedicated Bolshevik, suggest that it had been planned as part of an attempt to distract British forces and create panic behind the lines.

The two mutinies of the Slavo-British Legion dismayed the White Russians. One of them, an officer, told a journalist that the fault lay with the British: 'You blame us for harshness, but that is the only way to deal with these people. These people do not understand kindness; and what they don't understand they suspect.' The SBL had been wearing British uniforms, and, in Russian eyes, seemed to be a British unit. Its disintegration appeared to many anti-Bolsheviks the beginning of the end. This view was taken by Ironside, whose immediate reaction was despair: 'I felt a distinct urge to extricate myself and my troops as quickly as I could.' His subordinate officers 'were disgusted at having to put down mutinies', and Sadleir-Jackson expressed mistrust of all Russian units.

The post-mortem on the mutiny of the SBL explained it as the result of a 'most carefully arranged plot' by the Bolsheviks. The eight ringleaders who had escaped had given no hint of what they were up to and the battalion's commander, Colonel Barrington-Wells, admitted that the 'worst and most dangerous were those who seemed the best disciplined'. It was conjectured that Nuchev and Luechenko, whilst they claimed to be deserters from the Bolsheviks on enlistment, were in fact Red Army officers sent to subvert the Legion. (The British authorities were naturally anxious to get their hands on them and other mutineers, and in September 1920 GHQ of the Allied Control Commission at Danzig reported that the ringleaders were now POWs, taken by the Poles after the campaign outside Warsaw. It appeared that after the mutiny they had served with the 18th Division of the Red Army and were being held prisoner in camps at Parchim and Prenslau. Further investigations revealed that by the beginning of November most of the mutineers had left Parchim. Amongst the prisoners and refugees there were two former officers of the SBL – Kropatkin, an ex-sailor, and Togkin, an ex-electrician – both of whom expressed a wish to join Ironside in Persia. The mutineers were, officially, in the custody of the German government, and, without precise information as to their identity and whereabouts, it was considered unwise to plunge into a legal and diplomatic wrangle to secure their extradition. By January 1921 the trail had gone cold and the matter was forgotten.[58]) Some of the mutineers from the 4th NRR appeared among Bolshevik forces during the fighting on the Dvina in August 1919.

The July mutinies had dealt a blow to Churchill's credibility. He had accepted Ironside's opinion that the White Russian recruits were 'better than anything the Bolsheviks could produce' and had publicly expanded on this assertion to reassure both the Cabinet and the Commons. For him the news of the July mutinies was distressing, and he attempted to deflect his colleagues' criticism by slurs on the White Russians who, he claimed, had 'no real leaders of character and determination and their subordinates are a hopeless lot'.[59] By 23 July, Churchill resigned himself to the inevitable, which had been bluntly put to him by Lloyd George, who, on hearing of the mutinies, observed, 'I told you so.' 15 October was the date set for the final stage of the evacuation of North Russia by the 18,000 British forces. As for the 37,000 Russian troops who were left behind, Churchill faced the sour truth: 'The state of Russian troops was such that efforts to consolidate the Russian army must now be regarded as a failure.'[60] Those who wished to escape the Bolshevik murder squads were offered a free passage with the retiring British forces.

There were lessons to be learned. British soldiers and sailors during the war against Germany had been highly interested in how the war was going and were always hungry for news. A doctor, serving aboard a battleship, had noticed that during the long hours of inactivity, the sailors complained about being kept in the dark about what was happening. Men with some education resented being kept in ignorance by their superiors; those in Russia felt this resentment most keenly. Many thought themselves qualified for demobilisation, and all were mystified as to why they were in Russia fighting the Bolsheviks. During the Arctic winter, there was the more immediate concern about when, if at all, the soldiers were to be sent home. These misgivings and their forceful expression by mutiny did little to encourage those native Russians who had, for whatever reason, been drawn into the White Army. Many were in uniform against their will and better judgement and would have preferred to have sat on the fence and then joined the successful side. Such sentiments may also have infected many men in the Red Army, for, in December 1918, British intelligence picked up news of a mutiny by the 3rd Battalion of the 3rd Vologda Regiment, in which the men revolted in protest against inadequate clothing and bad rations. It was believed that one in three men from the battalion had been shot. The flood of Bolshevik deserters during the summer of 1919 also said something about conditions in the Red Army. Yet the Bolsheviks appeared to be winning and, through fear and the exposition of the cause for which they were fighting, were able to foment mutinies. Britain could create and train crack units like the Slavo-British Legion, but its officers could not give the men who served in them a cause to fight for. Neither could the White Russians. The pattern of the North Russian campaign, in which British politicians and general believed that they could shore up the ideologically bankrupt with men and arms, was repeated over fifty

153

years later by the United States in South-East Asia. The evacuation of Archangel and Murmansk forecast that of Saigon. As one British officer remarked, 'One didn't want to get caught by the Reds, one didn't want to lay down one's life for Holy Russia.'

TO INVERGORDON AND BEYOND:

Mutinies, 1919-46

AIRING THEIR GRIEVANCE

The naval mutiny at Invergordon in September 1931 is the best-known modern mutiny. This demonstration by 12,000 sailors occurred in peacetime during the middle of an unprecedented economic crisis, which it worsened, and then, and after, became the subject of much investigation.[1] The events at Invergordon were the culmination of over twenty years of intermittent agitation and restlessness amongst naval ratings. The question at issue was whether the Admiralty and ships' commanders should abandon the traditional ban on collective action by sailors. Since the early 1900s, a mass movement had been started by seamen which manifested itself in the growth of lower-deck societies. At one level these groups were the sea-going equivalent of the working man's Benefit and Friendly Societies, but the concerns of their members extended beyond matters of welfare. The lower-deck societies interested themselves in pay and conditions of service, and so seemed to be developing as embryonic trade unions.

The new societies were encouraged by the activities of a former rating, James Woods, who wrote under the name of Lionel Yexley. He was a lobbyist and journalist who spoke for the lower deck through his magazine *The Fleet*, which first appeared in 1905. Yexley's business was to expose abuses and injustices aboard warships, and his campaigning secured him and his supporters some success. Before 1914, his activities had contributed toward slight increases in pay, the end of flogging as a punishment for junior seamen, and improvements in canteens. He had also helped to implant in the minds of sailors the belief that if they joined together they could do something to improve their lot. Whereas before sailors relied solely upon individual petitions to their officers or the Admiralty, now they were beginning to realise that collective requests carried more clout. Yexley's campaigns had also demonstrated that the weight of public opinion, coloured by Imperial sentiment about the Army and Navy, was behind them.

The outbreak of war in 1914 continued this process. New men arrived in the Navy who brought with them habits of thought learned in factories and mines, and gave sailors the opportunity to compare their own wages and conditions with those which obtained on land. They also discovered the benefits which trade unions could secure for their members. The impact of what can be called trade-union thinking was greatest on skilled artificers, whose work was closest to that of civilians, and they soon came to think in terms of 'rates for the job' in much the same way as some of their opposite numbers in army workshops and transport depots. Wartime inflation gave an edge to sailors' discontent for, whilst their own pay was held down, that of civilians rose. The lower deck felt cheated and their feelings were expressed in one of the new societies' magazines, the *Naval Warrant Officers Journal* of February 1919.[2]

> Whilst Mrs Jack Tar or Mrs Tommy Atkins have found it a tight squeeze to stretch the money far enough to cover ordinary necessities, Mrs Noveau-Riche of munitions fame, and Mrs Dockyard Matey have been able to indulge in finery that never came their way before.

Comparisons with rates of pay of United States and Dominion sailors added to the sailors' sense of being deprived of what was rightfully theirs.

Memberships of the lower-deck societies grew during the war, and by 1917 these groups were making co-ordinated demands for increased pay. Meetings and delegations smacked of trade unionism and were contrary to the Naval Discipline Act, but when the agitation reached a peak in the autumn of 1917, the Cabinet decided to make concessions. Two petty officers, found guilty of circulating letters about lower-deck activities on board HMS *Resolution*, were

156

treated leniently by a court martial. Neither the Admiralty nor senior officers wanted a head-on collision with the ratings, although Admiral Beatty, for one, was apprehensive about what seemed to be the unchecked growth of covert organisations below decks. Not only was a fundamental principle of naval discipline infringed, but the eventual outcome of the sailors' movement would be the emergence of naval trade unionism in which sailors sat down and bargained with their officers and the Admiralty, like workers and bosses.

Something much like this happened in January 1919 when the Cabinet, seriously alarmed by the growth of agitation for higher pay in the Navy during the previous months, agreed to a committee of inquiry into the matter. When the Jerram Committee first met on 7 January, its members found themselves face to face with delegates chosen from the lower-deck societies and armed with resolutions drawn up by their members. The sailors' mood was intransigent and the committee was well aware of external circumstances which made their task a delicate one. Hitches and muddles in the demobilisation programme troubled the Navy as they did the Army. On 27 January, the commander at Rosyth was forced to discharge a hundred ratings from the *Cyclops* immediately rather than risk disorder.[3] The crews of the many fishing drifters, pressed into service as patrol boats and minesweepers, were anxious to get out of the Navy and, 'under the impression they are being treated unfairly', were becoming restive.[4] On 13 January a mutiny occurred on the patrol boat *Kilbride*, which was stationed at Milford Haven. The crew asked for additional pay for two extra watches and were turned down by their commander. The men then disobeyed his order to put to sea and hauled down the White Ensign and hoisted the Red Flag. Eight of the thirty-nine crew were tried for mutiny, and the evidence at their trial suggested that pay was not the only cause of the trouble. One temporary lieutenant threatened the crew that 'in the Merchant service he had broken the hearts of niggers and he would do the same to them'. The mutineers were given between 70 days' and two years' imprisonment.[5]

The Jerram Committee listened to evidence against this background of indiscipline, which was mirrored by the disorders which were simultaneously disturbing the Army. The government therefore considered it judicious to announce an interim pay award of 1s 6d. a day to sailors at the same time as the pay increases for the Army and Air Force were made public on 29 January. The Jerram Committee's decision to allow 4 shillings a day as the seaman's basic rate was announced in May. The welcome increase vindicated the sailors' efforts and showed what collective action could achieve. The view from the bridge was less happy, as one officer remembered:[6]

> The men of the lower deck were given opportunity of airing their views without fear of incurring displeasure or more serious charges of insubordination, disaffection, mutiny or the preferment of 'frivolous requests'.

There were further signs that discipline was being undermined, but it came from a different quarter. Like the soldiers who had been drafted to Russia in 1919, the sailors on duty in the Baltic were unhappy about the war which they had been ordered to fight. A squadron of six light cruisers and ten destroyers were on duty there to give assistance to anti-Bolsheviks in Finland and the newly created Baltic republics of Esthonia, Latvia and Lithuania. They were operating in waters which were mined, were open to attack by the Russian navy, which included two battleships, and also faced the bizarre hazard of Bolshevik agents masquerading as food-sellers, who hid bombs amongst their wares.[7] The local commander, Rear-Admiral Sir Walter Cowan, was unsure about his duties and ignorant about his rules of engagement with the enemy. On 4 July, in response to his inquiry, the Chief of Naval Staff asked the Cabinet, 'Were we, or were we not at war with the Bolsheviks?' Lloyd George answered that we were, and added, 'our Naval forces in Russian waters should be authorised to engage the enemy on land and sea when necessary'.[8] This was puzzling for the sailors in the Baltic, for, officially, no war pensions were to be given to the dependants of men killed or wounded in any action with the Russians.

This anomaly led to a mutiny on board the newly commissioned cruiser, *Delhi*, the flagship of the squadron, in November 1919. She had sailed for the Baltic the previous June and had engaged Bolshevik shore batteries on 14 and 27 October. The crew protested that they wished only to perform peacetime duties and locked themselves in the recreation room. They were brought back to obedience by Captain Mackworth who, it was alleged, threatened to blow up the ship. One man was singled out and charged with sedition and mutinous assembly, and given 18 months in prison.[9] On 9 November, the whole crew was addressed by Rear-Admiral Cowan, who explained why they were in the Baltic and promised that their grievances were being investigated by the Admiralty.

There had just been another mutiny aboard the aircraft-carrier *Vindictive*. Like other sailors serving in the Baltic, the crew of the *Vindictive* found the opportunities for recreation and leave sparse and largely confined to the delights of Copenhagen. These proved very popular, although the crew of the cruiser *Caledon* had protested that orders to be back on board at 9.30 p.m. detracted from their pleasures at the time when the fun was just beginning. Rear-Admiral Cowan agreed and extended the period of leave.[10] The *Vindictive*'s company had no such luck, for in September their leave in Copenhagen was stopped, which led to a mass demonstration on the quarter-deck in which the men shouted, 'No leave, no work.' When an order was given for the ship to change anchorage, some stokers attempted to immobilise it by cutting off the steam fans, but were frustrated by an engineer officer brandishing a spanner. Two were later arrested, tried and given five years each.[11]

The unpopularity of the Baltic station led to mutinies in Britain among sailors who had just returned or were about to be posted there. These occurred during October 1919 and were no doubt encouraged by the news that the Army was being taken out of Russia. Disorderly behaviour by returning marines at Portsmouth helped to persuade forty sailors, all about to join the Baltic squadron, to break ship and make for London. London was also the destination of forty-four sailors, part of a group of ninety who had deserted from the destroyers *Velox, Venerable* and *Wryneck*, all at Rosyth and under orders to sail for the Baltic. The men were all arrested on King's Cross Station, as they formed up for a march to the Admiralty, where they intended to present their objections to Russian service.

All were long-service men, the very kind whom the First Sea Lord, Lord Beatty, had assured the Cabinet in June were 'absolutely to be trusted'.[12] Beatty, who had the task of sorting out the problems of the Baltic squadron, had little sympathy for the men and he turned down demands for additional pay for active service on the grounds that it was only allowed by the Army for 'colonial' campaigns. The men were promised seven days' leave and deceitfully assured of a Baltic Service bar for the Naval General

Service Medal.[13] Meanwhile Rear-Admiral Cowan did his best to explain the purpose of the campaign and announced, on 29 October, that the men-o'-war would remain in the Baltic until 'stable and humane' governments were set up on its southern shores. This was interpreted by sailors as 'Policing the ruddy Finn', a task to which few warmed. Their mood was exploited by the Bolsheviks, who sent out radio messages which exhorted the British sailors to mutiny like the French in Odessa and the Americans in Archangel.

These unfortunate operations were terminated at the end of 1919, but they left behind them an uncomfortable impression that a restive mood existed below decks in the post-war Navy.

One reason why the Baltic and Russian campaigns had been concluded was the awareness that Britain could not afford to act as the policeman of the world. 1920 saw the beginning of a period of financial constraint in which successive governments were faced with the necessity of balancing their books. The exercise was seen as best achieved through cuts in public expenditure from which the armed services were not immune. Total spending on defence dropped from £766 million in 1919 to £102 million in 1932. The Admiralty, anxious to maintain maritime supremacy, had to face wrangles with the Treasury as to the size of its budget as well as decide the best way to divide its dwindling resources. The most favoured arguments always supported building new and better ships, but what was available for those was inevitably reduced by the wages bill. The rates of pay awarded by the Jerram Committee in 1919 saddled the Admiralty with a burden which it and the Treasury would have been happy to shed.

Whilst there was a temptation to tamper with the pay rates, it was always resisted on the grounds that the sailors would object. Hints that reductions were under consideration in 1924 breathed new life into the welfare committees, although the scare vanished after Labour's victory in the General Election, for Ramsay MacDonald had pledged support for the 1919 pay settlement. A year later, the Conservatives came back to power and, in response to the Treasury's demands for cheeseparing, reduced levels of pay were introduced for all men who joined *after* 1925.

The sailors, aware of the government's keenness to cut costs, knew that their pay was always in jeopardy and might have to be defended collectively. The revolutionary left saw an opportunity for gaining converts among the sailors by playing on their fears and grievances. This was part of a wider strategy during the inter-war years, since, in the view of a former Communist Party member, Douglas Hyde, soldiers and sailors 'were expected to be used against us sooner or later if we did not win them first'.[14] Canvassing of servicemen took place at naval ports, parades and tattoos, and was a perilous business. The government was ready to take vigorous action against subversives. In 1920 Sylvia Pankhurst was given six months' imprisonment for sedition after the publication of her article 'Discontent on the Lower Deck' in *Worker's Dreadnought*. A collaborator, C.J.L'e. Malone, Labour MP for East Leyton and a former naval aviator, was also imprisoned after security investigators found that he had taken £300 from Russian sources for subversion in the forces. The pair were discovered to have made contacts with leaders of sailors' welfare committees at Chatham. Revelations of this kind reinforced official fears of Russian-inspired sedition being spread amongst sailors and led to close intelligence surveillance of Communists. The British Communist Party went out of its way to offer a programme designed for servicemen which included the abolition of church parades, courts martial and saluting, and made capital out of the discrepancies in pay and treatment between officers and other ranks. Wal Hannington, organiser of the National Unemployed Workers Union, wrote in 1932 that he hoped that his organisation would implant revolutionary awareness in those unemployed men who enlisted. Such men 'will enter with their eyes open, knowing how to say Invergordon and knowing to do other things besides obeying orders'.[15]

Officers were on the look-out for such men. One, Able Seaman Len Fagg, a Communist Party member since 1921, was discovered on board the cruiser *Dragon*, where he played a leading part in running the ship's welfare committee. His exposure came in 1923 after he had, understandably but tactlessly, objected to his commander's proposal that the lower-deck welfare fund should be mulcted of £25 as a contribution to a wedding present for Princess Mary and Viscount Lascelles.[16] This earned Fagg a discharge and added to the Navy's suspicions that the welfare committees were just focal points of agitation. The Communist Party's campaign to draw members from the forces was a flop. What mattered was not so much its success, but the anxiety it caused the government, which took the whole business very seriously. This made it willing to believe any evidence which pointed towards the Invergordon mutiny as the result of a conspiracy hatched by Communists and their allies.

From the standpoint of those naval officers who blamed what happened at Invergordon on lax discipline, the later mutiny had been foreshadowed by the trouble on the submarine depot ship, *Lucia*, in January 1931. A mutiny had occurred after the sudden announcement of the cancellation of leave. This provoked thirty ratings to refuse to fall in for painting duties and then retire to the mess deck. They were arrested, taken under armed escort to Portsmouth barracks and tried. The trials and a subsequent official inquiry revealed that in the past months *Lucia* had been plagued by a number of disciplinary incidents and much of the fault lay with her commander, Captain O.E. Hallifax, and his executive officer, Lieutenant-Commander Hoskyns. This was the view of the First Lord of the Admiralty, A.V. Alexander, who censured the two officers' 'want of tact and consideration' in a statement to the Commons. The Labour Cabinet decided to quash the sentences on the mutineers, a move which left the officers publicly discredited and 'quite broken', according to Admiral Lord Keyes. In his opinion, the Admiralty had shown a lack of 'guts' and laid the Navy open to further trouble of this kind. Behind his anger there was a feeling amongst officers that the Labour Party would always incline towards the other ranks and take their part against officers.[18] Tolerance towards the 'strikers' on the *Lucia* was not forgotten by the men at Invergordon.

In 1931, three-quarters of the men serving with the Navy were still being paid at the 1919 rates; some of the older, long-service men had taken part in the agitation which had led up to their adoption. Subsequent inflation meant that married men with families were facing difficulties in making ends meet. When such men rejoined the Atlantic Fleet after their seven-week summer leave, they came back to their ships well aware of domestic problems in balancing the budget. They also knew that the government was also having a hard task in balancing its books in the face of a national economic crisis. It had placed some of its hopes in a committee, chaired by a former insurance man, Sir George May, which was instructed to investigate ways in which government money could be saved. Its report was submitted on 31 July and urged severe cuts in government wages and salaries.

Servicemen were expected to take their share in the pay reductions, for, it concluded with astonishing insensitivity, 'No officer or man serving His Majesty has any legal claim to a particular rate of pay.' The message was clear enough, but what the sailors did not know was how much they would have to forfeit.

When the sailors returned to their ships on 7-8 September, common rumour asserted that the cuts would be 25 per cent. This tale was never denied and caused deep anguish, especially to married men. In two cases, quoted by Commander Edwards in his account of the mutiny, the reductions caused particularly grim hardship.[19] An able seaman, married with one child and another expected, would have his weekly pay cut from 31s 6d. a week to 25s 1d., and a stoker, married with one child and supporting his wife's invalid parents, would expect to receive 32s 8d. instead of 38s 6d. In the latter case the man was already burdened with unpaid doctors' bills. Many sailors who lived in rented accommodation and were paying hire-purchase instalments anticipated that their families would be evicted or that they might be sued for debt. What their future position would be was not made clear by the Admiralty, and so they were forced to find out what they could from newspapers and BBC bulletins.

Once the fleet had anchored at Invergordon on 11 September, there was the first of a number of meetings at canteens on shore. The Sunday papers, delivered on 13 September, confirmed the sailors' worst fears, for they contained news that 25 per cent wage cuts were in line for all of them, that officers faced an 11 per cent cut and that soldiers were less harshly hit. During the meetings in the shore canteens on 13 and 14 September, many men spoke of their apprehensions about the loss of their property, impounded by bailiffs, the hardships faced by their children and the possibility that their wives would be forced into prostitution. There was, however, some amusement when the men read that George V had braced himself for sacrifice and remitted £50,000 of his allowance to the government. The mood of the shore meetings was such that the men agreed to hold a strike the following day, a gesture with which to remind the Admiralty of its responsibilities to them, and to press for allowances for cases of hardship. Aware of what was going on, the shore patrols did not intervene, although one officer who warned the men was treated to a tirade about 'brass-hatted buggers' at the Admiralty, and withdrew after barracking.

The mutiny began at six the following morning, 15 September, a fine, clear day on which the fleet was scheduled to sail for the next stage in its exercises. The key ship was the *Valiant*, which was anchored to seaward of the line-of-battle ships and was therefore the first to make steam and weigh anchor. The response from her crew was not wholehearted at first, but there was sufficient absenteeism and shirking to make it impossible for the battleship to be ready by eight. Staying off duty and lurking was the pattern on the other battleships and the cruisers, so the Fleet's commander, Rear-Admiral Tomkinson, rescinded his orders. He had had, the previous evening, some intimation of what would happen, but then and later he chose to show forbearance and avoid any precipitate action which might have led to a clash and bloodshed. Like many other officers, he understood his men's position and he chose to seek guidance from the Admiralty.

The news of what was officially called 'unrest among a proportion of ratings' caused consternation in London and amazement throughout the country, for it was broadcast by the BBC on the evening of 15 September. The new First Lord of the Admiralty, Sir Austen Chamberlain, immediately ordered the dispersal of the fleet, and promised action which would be aimed at alleviating any hardship. To this end, special committees were formed to listen to cases when the ships returned to their home ports, Chatham and Portsmouth. The measures satisfied the sailors and after some initial wavering (the *Nelson* was markedly obdurate and some of its crew sang 'The Red Flag'), the ships' companies returned to their duties and the fleet sailed from Invergordon on 16 February. On the following day, Chamberlain promised an amnesty.

On the surface, the mutiny seemed to be at an end, but the Admiralty feared otherwise. It moved swiftly to discover whether what had just taken place was the result of a deeply laid conspiracy, fabricated by agitators of the left, who, after all, were known to have been busy for years trying to subvert sailors. Naval Intelligence and MI5 agents, helped by local police, moved to Chatham and Portsmouth on 18 September, briefed to find out what was really happening. In the following few days they produced a chilling dossier of hearsay evidence which pointed towards a conspiracy. What was worse was that the evidence suggested that further disturbances were likely and the first, in the dockyard ports, was due for 22 September, two days after the mutinous ships had tied up. The Sea Lords and Major Sam Basset of the Royal Marines, who had been seconded to MI5, presented their findings to the Prime Minister and the Cabinet of the National Government on the morning of the 21st. They predicted that the lower deck was tightly organised, had the sympathy of most petty officers and intended to protest against the cuts by walking off their ships and demonstrating in the ports. Communist agitators were making capital out of their grievances, and there was the possibility that civilians would join in the protests which the marines might not be able or willing to contain. The Sea Lords favoured concessions as the only means to avoid clashes. Ramsay MacDonald and his coalition agreed and, the same afternoon, the Prime Minister announced to the Commons that the cuts were to be reduced to 10 per cent.[20] The sailors had successfully defended their 1919 rates of pay, not so much by the mutiny itself, but by showing a determination which scared the government.

The post-Invergordon intelligence summary which frightened the ministers appears to have been an overstatement. The strength of the seamen's organisation was over-estimated as indeed was extent of Communist subversion, although this was not easy to perceive when overhearing dockyard and pub gossip. What appeared to matter was that the Invergordon mutiny, which had already wounded Britain's financial standing, might be followed by more unrest. This, whether serious or not, would inflict further damage which a government, already faced with a financial crisis and rising unemployment, could not afford. The concession was therefore judicious and best made quickly.

There was further trouble, but it was isolated. There was a mutiny on board the cruiser *Durban* on Christmas Day 1931, when it was anchored off Port Stanley. There had been further mass disobedience on board the *Delhi* at New Brunswick, but the men were calmed by the commander of the West Indies station, Rear-Admiral Sir Vernon Haggard. The crew of the *Durban* had already threatened to refuse to sail for Chatham when they heard the news of the Invergordon mutiny, and so it was thought wisest to dismiss twenty of the mutineers. In spite of the promise to the contrary by Chamberlain, twenty-four men were sacked from the Atlantic Fleet. Their discharges were defended on the grounds that the dismissed men had persisted in agitation and were suspected of links with the Communist Party. Two, Fred Copeman and Len Wincott, did become Communists (Wincott later went to live in Russia), but they later denied that their party had played any part in the Invergordon mutiny. This disclaiming of Communist influences was, in part, supported by the evidence of several captains of ships involved, who had found it difficult to pinpoint the men who were behind the unrest. Still, the Admiralty remained very jumpy and continued with the policy of weeding out men who combined extreme left views with activities as sea lawyers.

Members of the Labour Party who had parted company with Ramsay MacDonald and opposed his National Government in the General Election of October 1931, adopted the Invergordon mutiny for their campaign. A poster proclaimed, 'The British Navy at Jutland in 1916 beat the ex-Kaiser, and at Invergordon in 1931 it beat Mr Montagu Norman.' Norman was the Governor of the Bank of England and was widely seen in some circles as a sinister *éminence grise* behind policies of retrenchment. The Tories were furious about the poster, the more so since its message was not too far from the truth.

The Navy was distressed and frightened by the mutiny. Its prestige was tarnished and it was feared that a gulf had been opened up between officers and other ranks which it would take some time to bridge. There was a strong feeling that senior officers, especially the executive officers of the ships involved, who might have been considered responsible for the mutiny, had indelible black marks on their records which could count against their promotion.[21] In 1935 the old pay rates were restored, although the able seaman's weekly wage remained low, comparable to that of a farm labourer.

One extraordinary consequence of the Invergordon mutiny was the Admiralty's proposal to spend £340,000 on the building of four fully rigged sailing barques which were to be employed for the training of young sailors. It was seriously believed that a reversion to the exercises of Nelson's navy would breed better morale and a keener spirit.[22] The mentality of the senior officers who promoted this scheme may best be judged by the fact that they allocated £5,000 for the alleviation of financial hardships suffered by sailors' families. This atavism was stopped in 1935 when Lord Chatfield became First Sea Lord, but the notion behind it has since enjoyed wide acceptance, so that today picturesque sailing craft cruise around the oceans crewed by various kinds of people thought to be in need of moral regeneration. What is perhaps most revealing is that one official reaction to Invergordon was an attempt to escape back to the methods of Nelson's time in the hope that indiscipline would somehow be corrected.

A TRAGEDY OF ERRORS

At one level, the Invergordon mutiny was an echo of the wider social disharmony which marked British society during the years of the Depression. When war with Germany broke out in September 1939, the government had to call upon all members of what was still a divided and sometimes a demoralised society to join together to wage a mass war. Men and women were again asked to forgo civilian rights and habits, put themselves into uniform, and enter a world which was based upon unquestioning obedience to orders and the suppression of individualism. In 1914 the demand had been backed by appeals to pure patriotism, but the experience of the First World War had debased that ideal. Twenty-five years later men and women were asked to roll up their sleeves and throw themselves into what quickly became a struggle for survival which could only be won by common exertion and sacrifice. 'Let us go forward together' was the call to duty in 1940, a slogan far different from 'Your Country Needs You'.

Morale was soon identified as the key which would open the door to victory. Considerable official energy and personnel were concentrated on the measurement of morale and the concoction of ways in which it could be raised and directed. The armed services had learned some lessons about morale from the last war, in particular the years 1917-19 which had been marked by waves of unrest among soldiers and sailors who had thought themselves unjustly treated. There was no repetition of this kind of unrest during the Second World War. British naval and military authorities faced only two mutinies, one at the Salerno beach-head in September 1943, and the other in Malaya in August 1946. Both were the consequence of purely service misunderstandings and neither was marked by any violence. A third mutiny occurred in April 1944 in Egypt when units of the Greek army and navy, attached to the Middle East Command, rebelled. The root of the trouble lay in Greek politics, but it fell to British officers and units to handle the unrest.

One reason why there were so few mutinies was that the Army had learned how to treat with greater sensitivity the civilians who were now entering its ranks. Studies made just after 1918 acknowledged the existence of shell-shock, battle hysteria and battle fatigue, and the Army's selection procedures were more precise, so that the emotionally and psychologically unfit could be turned down and sent to other war work. When symptoms showed themselves which suggested that a soldier, sailor or airman might not measure up to stress, he was medically discharged. In 1918 the Army Education Corps had been formed, and in 1940 it came into its own when every battalion commander was ordered to designate an education officer (often a former schoolmaster) for his unit. One of his duties was to show the men 'how the British Empire stands for the essential factors of a new and better life'.[23] This instruction from the Education Corps's commander, Lieutenant-General Hanning, possessed the curious quality of embracing both the traditional theme of Empire and the novel one of fighting for a better life. The latter loomed larger as the war progressed. In 1941 the Army Bureau of Current Affairs was set up to promote both instruction and discussion, both of which tended to focus on the future. Its recurrent theme of what sort of Britain would emerge after the war was one which aroused deep interest amongst the soldiers, and with good reason. The mendacious electoral pledges of Lloyd George and his followers in 1918 had passed into popular folklore in the wretched years which followed. 'This plan for social security makes me laugh,' commented one soldier in 1942, 'I don't forget the Land Fit for Heroes of the last war.'[24]

Yet the Army Bureau for Current Affairs went ahead with stimulating the interest of soldiers in the future of Britain. On one level this kept soldiers busy and on another it made them think. As part of the programme in the Western Desert, a sergeant from the Royal Tank Corps addressed men from other squadrons on the Russian campaign. This was not to the taste of a major who barracked the talk, and was further irritated when the speaker ended by singing 'The Red Flag'.* The major commented to a captain, 'My goodness, I seem to have got the Bolshie squadron in this battalion.' The reply – 'It isn't just this battalion, sir, the whole of the Eighth Army thinks the same way' – could not cheered him.[25] Anecdotes like this, coupled with the fact that nearly a third of all servicemen read the *Daily Mirror* (probably as much for 'Jane' as for the political comment), have given rise to the suggestion that the Army's lessons in political thinking helped the Labour Party win the election in the summer of 1945. Over one and a half million men

* On some RAF camps a man who even hummed the tune was liable to a charge, at least before Russia entered the war.

did vote, and most of them plumped for Labour, but their numbers only gave weight to the general landslide. Civilian Labour voters were enough to secure an outright victory.[26] Still, as the Army's Morale Committee reported in August 1945, there was 'considerable satisfaction' with the Labour victory amongst men serving in India and the Far East.[27] This was a result of 'a widespread feeling that they [the Labour government] would produce some new and magic methods of solving problems of reconstruction'. By contrast, servicemen had been all but prevented from casting their votes in November 1918.

Churchill had been uneasy about the way in which soldiers were learning about politics and he personally banned one poster. It showed a dismal slum yard in which a child, infected with rickets, was playing. On the walls were written 'Disease' and 'Neglect' and the caption announced: 'Your Britain – For it was'. Another poster, permitted for use, showed two sides of a building. One, in shadow, was a derelict terrace of old houses, the other, brightly lit, showed an airy, modernistic block of flats built 'for workers' by London County Council in 1936. The message was 'Your Britain – Fight for it now'. Men were left in no doubt as to what they were fighting for and that victory would bring with it what soon came to called 'social justice'.

The soldiers' reaction to this sort of material and much else was carefully monitored through reports from various theatres, which were collated and presented by the Welfare Committee of the Adjutant-General's Department. The reports need to be treated carefully since they were attempts to present an overall picture from each front, and the complexity and variableness of the reactions of hundreds of thousands of soldiers often defied generalisation. For instance, during the summer of 1943, the censors' reports suggested scant interest in the proposals of the Beveridge Report, a conclusion which would have been challenged by others in close contact with soldiers at the time.[29] What the reports do highlight is a predictable range of grievances and sources of unease. Absence Without Leave (AWOL) was the commonest offence amongst men serving in Britain, usually prompted by soldiers hearing disquieting news about their families' circumstances.

The value of such information was that it gave the Army authorities the chance to deal with problems which, ignored, could sap morale. Between October 1942 and May 1943, Lieutenant-

Colonel T.F. Main of the Army Psychiatry Unit toured depot camps in the Middle East and investigated those factors which lowered men's morale. Two-thirds of the 3.6 million men in the Army were serving overseas, often for long periods. Regularity of mail from home, the quality of entertainment, especially wireless broadcasts, and the effective handling of difficulties which might arise for their families in Britain were the major concerns of men on overseas postings. What Main saw as the 'corrective and tonic' effect of films and broadcasts assumed a considerable importance in the Army's efforts to overcome the inevitable boredom of routine life and to raise spirits. Great care was taken with training films (camera shots from behind guns were preferable to those in which the audience faced guns!) and those general-release movies which passed to the troops were written with an eye to presenting commonplace problems and showing how they could be overcome. Army psychiatrists advised the scriptwriters of *The Way Ahead*, in which David Niven portrays the *beau idéal* of the junior officer intimately concerned with the personal problems of his men. He mingled compassion and understanding with the traditional martial virtue of leadership in a film which dealt realistically with a platoon's life, from enlistment through to combat. The army recognised, during the unrest in 1919, the value of cinema as a form of escapism and an antidote to boredom and restlessness. It also came to appreciate that films encouraged recruitment. In 1946 men in the Middle East were treated to *Forty Thousand Horsemen* (which told the story of the Australian Light Horse in Palestine in 1918) and *Eight Graves to Cairo* (in which Rommel, played by Eric von Stroheim, is checked) in the hope that the National Servicemen amongst them would elect to become full-time soldiers.[30]

As in the First World War, all fighting men were deeply concerned to discover what was happening to them as well as to know what was going on in other theatres of war. The Army was often not very obliging; in the late 1930s, men serving on the North-West Frontier had to rely on what they could pick up from the wireless to know exactly what they were up to. In keeping with the overall strategy of working for a community of endeavour, Montgomery in the Western Desert, and Eisenhower and his associate commanders before D-Day, visited, cheered up and addressed men of as many units as it was possible to visit. Yet a feeling often persisted that men were being kept in the dark, not only about the nature of their own duties and what they would do next, but about the wider issues of the war. This was felt particularly strongly at the beginning of 1942 (after the Japanese victories in the Far East) when there was a strong body of opinion amongst soldiers that 'the country could be trusted' and would 'stand being told the truth'. They were probably right, but, as always in war, the question remained of how much to tell the men about future operations in which they were to be involved. Security obviously intruded in this area, and it was usually thought wiser that men should remain in the dark.

Misinformation was one of the two factors which caused the Salerno mutiny. The other was the Army's stress on unit loyalty and pride which was rightly seen as an important ingredient in fighting efficiency. This emphasis was nowhere more pronounced than in the Eighth Army. Major-General D.N. Wimberley, the commander of the 51st Highland Division, had told his men, 'If wounded etc., and separated from your own units, do not allow yourselves to get drafted to other battalions, but see that you come back to us.' The sentiments stemmed from an honourable tradition in the British Army, which extended back to the county regiments established in 1881 and embraced the 'Pals' battalions of the First World War. Very commonly, men in the same unit came from the same town or region and might well have known one another in civilian life. This was undoubtedly true of many Territorial battalions in 1939 and remained so throughout the war.

The 51st Division had, in 1943, a fine reputation built up during the Desert campaigns. Equally high was the standing of the 50th Division, which drew heavily from the Tyne and Tees region. Both were part of the army which invaded and conquered Sicily in July and August 1943 and, at the end of that campaign, they were withdrawn from action. In the coming months the two divisions were taken back to Britain for training prior to their attachment to the 21st Army Group for the D-Day landings. Fifteen hundred men from these divisions who had been wounded in the Sicilian campaign were evacuated for treatment and convalescence to the Libyan port of Tripoli. Here they were ordered, on 15 September, to embark on three cruisers, and the following day they were put ashore at the Salerno beach-head.

The Allied landings at Salerno on 8 September had met with much initial success, thanks to surprise, but after six days of fighting the Germans still clung to positions inland which made a breakthrough and advance to Naples impossible. The Commander-in-

Chief in Italy, General Alexander, had ordered up reinforcements which were to be carried in haste from Philippeville on the Algerian coast. There had been a blunder, and the ships had embarked the convalescents of the 51st and 50th Divisions, some of them still with unhealed wounds, from Tripoli. The men from the 50th and 51st were unaware of this blunder and, as they crossed the Mediterranean, were encouraged to think that they would shortly rejoin their old units. This was claimed by the men when they later defended themselves against charges of mutiny, but the allegation that they had been misled has since been officially and privately denied.

The upshot was that these men suddenly and unexpectedly found themselves on the beach at Salerno as part of the reinforcements, although for the next four days they were left to mill about without any clear orders. On 20 September, the detachment was ordered to move inland and join the 46th Division, and about 1,200 men obeyed and set off. Three hundred stayed behind and were placed under a guard of Military Policemen. They were remembered by Mr A. Roberts, who had come to the beach to collect ammunition for his battery.[31]

> I saw a huge group of men sat on the sand and, being a nosey-parker, I asked an MP what was happening. He said they were on strike, which of course amazed me. Just at that moment General McCreery arrived and of course we were shooed away. The next time I went down they had been herded into a kind of compound – there were about 500-600 of them. To make matters worse there was a compound of German POWs next to them, they were catcalling, then booing and hissing. It was disgraceful.

After Gunner Roberts and other onlookers had been moved away, Lieutenant-General Sir Richard McCreery, commandier of X Corps, spoke to the men. He admitted a mistake had been made, promised it would be rectified, but still insisted that the men move off to join 46th Division, which was part of his corps. All but 191 did.

Those who stayed were placed under arrest in a compound which had been made ready for German prisoners and was unfortunately near one already filled with POWs. These men were told that they would be charged with mutiny and would be shipped back to Constantine to face trial. As for those who had witnessed the scenes on the beach, 'a couple of days later we were warned that it was a subject that wasn't to be talked about and any who did would be put on a charge'.

The 191 who were taken to a camp near Constantine were confident that their behaviour on the beach would be justified, and, once the full details were known, would be endorsed by a senior officer. They considered themselves victims of an official muddle which would be cleared up once the authorities realised their mistake. In the camp where they awaited their trial, all the men charged maintained a strict military discipline and stuck to the highest standards of soldierly conduct. When tried, they were found guilty; three sergeants were sentenced to death, the corporals to ten years in prison and the privates to seven. The sentences were immediately suspended and the men were informed that they would be sent straight away to the battle-line. A senior field officer warned that any misdemeanour by the men would mean that their sentences for mutiny would fall due.

At the time of their trials, the men were examined by Lieutenant-Colonel T.F. Main, the Army psychiatrist, who later attested that, save for a few shirkers, all were courageous men, veterans who wanted to get back to their familiar unit and fight alongside men they knew. It has been pointed out that both the 50th and 51st Divisions were rumoured to be due for posting back to Britain, and that this had become known to the men in their rest camps. This was indeed so, although a return to Britain in fact meant the beginning of training for the D-Day landings in Normandy. Yet, Colonel Main insisted that the mutiny was the consequence of a 'tragedy of errors', which was more or less the opinion of Montgomery. Certainly the authorities had handled the business clumsily, and one unexpected outcome was that many men, burdened by the heavy punishments hanging over them, deserted. The case was reviewed in 1947 by a civilian, the Solicitor-General, who discovered no injustices in the way the trials were conducted. In a written House of Lords reply, given in March 1982, the Minister of State for Defence Procurement, Lord Trenchard, insisted the men called to the beach at Salerno were all capable of fighting. A check of available records confirmed that the reinforcements came from a transit camp which contained men who were waiting and ready for active service; those who had been wounded earlier had already completed a period of con- valescence. As fresh and rested infantrymen, they would have been used to the maximum extent to relieve battle-worn troops. For their part, the survivors insist that many who were sent were unwell.

Purely service misunderstandings were the only cause of the mutiny of the 13th (Lancashire) Parachute Battalion at Muar in Malaya in May 1946. The battalion had just been withdrawn from Java, where it had been part of an Anglo-Indian contingent which had been ordered to reimpose Dutch colonial government on the Indonesians. There was a new CO, and a new RSM who seems to have been little liked by some of the men, who later accused him of black marketeering and being involved in the procurement of women. The battalion's new quarters were most unsuitable and soon aroused angry complaints. One present remembered conditions and discipline:

> Men with dirty boots were put on charge by the RSM sometimes getting 7 to 14 days. You had only to walk outside your tent and your boots were thick with mud. As for an RSM drill parade now and again – we had one every day. We got up at 6 o'clock and had to have a wash, shave, make beds up, draw a rifle from the stores and be on parade for RSM drill by 6.40 and to do all this there was only one tap between 200 men – Then they started to teach us to clean a rifle and this with chaps of 3 to 7 years in the army, and men who were 60 miles in front of any troops in Germany and noted as the finest fighting men in the army.

Sick parades were inspected and men with malaria could find themselves on small charges. Questions about conditions were rhetorical, as one man found out when he told an officer that he wished to complain about the food and got 7 days confined to barracks. There were none of the recreational facilities which had been promised, there were only two baths for 120 men of C Company, and nearly every tent leaked. Against this background of unrelenting petty irritation there was a canteen meeting on 13 May in which pledges were made for a 'strike' the following day. There was heavy rain on the night of 13-14 May, in which tents were again flooded with between four and six inches of water, a common enough condition at Muar and one which must have stiffened the men's resolve.

The first protest came at dawn on 15 May, and immediately the CO, Lieutenant-Colonel Layland, warned the men that he could not countenance a 'collective' expression of grievances.[32] The men's obduracy led to their arrest by a hastily summoned battalion of the Devonshires (who had been deceived into thinking that they had been called out to handle unrest amongst Chinese). The trial of the

258 men was held in an aircraft hangar at Kluang and was reported by the press. The men appeared, manacled and handcuffed, and their defence was to place the blame for what occurred on the shoulders of their NCOs and officers whom they presented as negligent in their duties. One lieutenant was said to have have had a waterproof tent whilst his men's leaked. Public disquiet was aroused by the news of all this, particularly the fact that the men lacked any right of appeal. All were found guilty, but their sentences of imprisonment were immediately suspended by the C-in-C South East Asia Command, Lieutenant-General Sir Montague Stopford. In the end, the Labour government quashed all the sentences and, to ward off future trouble of this kind, instigated Army Welfare Committees in March 1947 which were empowered to make collective complaints on behalf of the men.

Not long before this outbreak, there had been restlessness, insubordination and a strike amongst RAF personnel at various bases in India. The trouble was about pay, gratuities, and slow demobilisation, and it led to a number of 'strikes' at Dum Dum and elsewhere in January 1946.[33] Something of the kind had been in the wind for some time, as Lieutenant-General Sir Francis Tuker recalled. In December 1945 he had been told by an RAF officer that the morale of men on ground installations was decaying. 'They looked upon themselves far too much as factory hands and far too little as men of a great fighting service admired by the whole world and to which it was an honour to belong.' After the strike had ended, intelligence officers rightly identified a trade union spirit abroad, and during March 1946 checked lists for any 'who would be identified with the Labour, Communist, Trade Union and progressive movements'. Various of those later charged with involvement had connections with unionism and Communism, and some had links with the Indian Communist Party. When tried, they claimed, not surprisingly, that they had been victimised. Since the defeat of Germany and Japan, many men serving overseas felt that there was no longer any 'obvious purpose' in their remaining abroad. Some regarded 'a shorter tour of duty overseas and speedy release' as 'inalienable rights'. Another 'recognised right' which many soldiers thought they possessed was the writing of letters to their MPs, a habit which had become common during 1945 and which the Army decided not to check.[34]

The mutinies at Invergordon, Salerno and in Malaya all had their origins in British service conditions. Together, they belonged to a tradition in which men rebelled when they saw that there was no alternative available to them to secure what they considered justice, or to defend imperilled rights. On a smaller scale, there was a mutiny of this kind by men from the 1st Battalion of the Mauritius Regiment at Orangea in December 1943, when there was a mass refusal to do PT. Officially the men were said to 'browned off' (hardly an efficacious phrase) and angered about their removal from Mauritius. Four ringleaders were tried and found guilty and two death sentences were passed but later annulled. In temper, such protests reflected a spirit of the times which was a product of nearly a hundred years of political change. Trade unionism and the emergence of the Labour Party with its doctrines of class politics had created a new awareness that working people possessed rights and the collective power to assert them. The Naval unrest between 1917 and 1931, like that in the Army during 1919, were by-products of this consciousness. The sympathy given to the mutineers from the *Lucia* in 1931 and the paratroopers in 1946 showed that when Labour was in power, it was willing to go some way towards supporting the claims of service protestors against those of the naval and military authorities.

This was not an approach which pleased all officers. After the trouble in India in 1946, Eastern Command officially stated that the word 'strike' was not to be used for indiscipline. Mutiny was mutiny in the Army no matter what it was called elsewhere. It was to be nipped in the bud if it started, force at once used and the ringleaders arrested and heavily punished by summary court martial. The essential quality of the treatment of the disease was that it was to be dealt with speedily, quietly and without temporising, from first to last.[35] Preventive medicine had of course been used throughout the war. The naval, military and air force authorities had gone a long way towards meeting the problems of civilians turned servicemen, and the measures taken to improve and shape morale during the Second World War showed a concern for the individual and his difficulties. Boredom and grumbling did not disappear, they were and still are the constants of war. 'They don't train you to fight, they train you for the parade ground', 'I bet they don't have all this bullshit in the German Army', 'Silly old bugger, thinks it's the Boers he's fighting' were a random selection of comments from one RAF unit during February 1941, but the spirit behind them is timeless.[36]

The old type of mutiny had not disappeared. In June 1940 four men in a forward post at Mersa Matruh locked up an NCO and assaulted their CO when he visited them. The ringleader's drunkenness saved him from a death sentence. Another mutineer, travelling on a train in Egypt in December 1942, was able to persuade fellow travellers not to obey an NCO and tie him up after obstreperous behaviour. Disagreements between drinkers from the Royal Fusiliers and the authorities over closing time in a canteen on a base in Egypt in 1948 led to brawling, an attack on the guardroom and charges of mutiny. A sergeants' mess party led to bottles being thrown at officers, a near riot and damage to military vehicles at Singapore in May 1948. Ten men from the Royal Pioneer Corps (Ceylon) were subsequently charged with mutiny. There were several other charges against other men from this unit during the year.

A PACK OF FOREIGNERS WHO WERE MAKING A NUISANCE OF THEMSELVES

In scale and violence, the mutiny of Greek army and naval units in Egypt in April 1944 was the most serious faced by the British authorities during the Second World War.[37] The uprisings came like a bolt from the blue and were an annoying embarrassment to commanders and politicians alike. The origins of the mutiny were wholly political. The Greek soldiers and sailors involved were part of the forces which had been evacuated from Greece after it had been invaded and overrun by the Germans in June 1941. Since then, the Greek units had served under British command in North Africa and the Mediterranean and, at the time of the mutiny, the Greek armoured brigade was in readiness for transfer to the Italian front.

Inside Greece, occupation by German and Bulgarian forces was opposed by local resistance groups which, as elsewhere in Europe, coalesced around pre-war political parties. EAM (National Popular Liberation Front) was a left-wing coalition with an energetic Communist element which projected itself as the spearhead of resistance to the Germans and their quisling administration. EAM's fighting section was ELAS (National Popular Liberation Army) which received some British logistical help. By the end of 1943, it was clear that the days of German rule in Greece were numbered, and EAM turned towards political consolidation, creating an administration in those areas abandoned by the Germans and their allies. Relations between ELAS and other resistance groups deteriorated, and by the spring of 1944 internecine war had broken out.

The British government had a deep concern for the future of Greece and in particular the political sympathies of its post-war government. Britain's position was plainly expressed by Harold Macmillan in a conversation with Giorgis Papandreou in October 1944, when he asserted, 'It is a British interest that Greece should be a fortress guarding the Imperial route.'[38] This was in line with Churchill's plans for the restoration of British political and military influence in the western Mediterranean, which, in turn, would buttress the security of the Suez Canal. This was a traditional, imperial policy and one on which the Americans looked askance. What Churchill feared, in 1944 and later, was the steady advance of Russian power in this region, which followed the Red Army's conquest of Bulgaria and Rumania, and the establishment in these countries of puppet, pro-Soviet governments. 'Partly Communists and partly bandits', according to Macmillan, EAM threatened to turn itself into a successor government to the German-backed regime which was crumbling. If EAM succeeded, then British interests would be severely, possibly fatally, injured.

At the beginning of 1944 British diplomats were seeking to establish the framework for a strong and benevolent Greek government to rule after the war. There already existed the government-in-exile of King George II which, under the Prime Minister Tsouderos, operated from Cairo. It was difficult to judge what level of support it enjoyed within Greece, and the British, knowing of the unpopularity of the monarchy, were anxious to keep the King in the background until a plebiscite had been held to make clear how the Greeks felt about a royal restoration. In Greece, EAM opposed the return of the King and was keen to press its own claims for inclusion in any successor government. Demands for control over the ministries of justice, the armed forces and the interior made in 1943 indicated the extent of EAM's ambitions and aroused British suspicions.

For some time before the mutiny, EAM supporters and agents had been at work amongst Greek soldiers and sailors in Egypt. At the time, British intelligence in Cairo was convinced that three

German agents were also involved in this subversion, posing as EAM men. By the beginning of April 1944, EAM had secured widespread sympathy amongst sailors in the Greek fleet and soldiers in the Greek armoured brigade. Signs of unrest had appeared in the 2nd Greek Regiment and mutiny was anticipated on 4 April, when the unit was split between camps at Qassassin and Beni Yusef under British guard. Elsewhere there seemed nothing to fear. According to the report of the British liaison officer with another Greek brigade, 'morale was so high that personnel in the Brigade would themselves shoot troublemakers'.

Trouble amongst the Greek warships in Alexandria Harbour began on 4 April. Some of the ships' companies included ex-merchant-seamen and were under the influence of a former union organiser, and they, with their sympathisers, were able to take over their ships and imprison the officers. Five ships in all were involved, and a few days later the discontent spread to the antique cruiser *Averof* and the submarine *Papanicolis*, both of which were in Port Said.* Four days after the outbreak, Admiral Sir Henry Harwood, Commander-in-Chief in the Mediterranean, reported to the Admiralty that the 'subversive movement appears widespread and well organised and the mutineers are prepared to resist with gun armament and small arms'. At the same time as the ships' crew mutinied, there was a mutiny of the Greek armoured brigade at their camp thirty miles south of Cairo.

The objective of the mutinies was made clear soon after the outbreak. On 4 April, a deputation of officers saw Tsouderos in Cairo and demanded his resignation as Prime Minister. He gave way the following day, leaving the British in the position of having to cobble together a new Greek government. This was only part of what the mutineers wanted, for they also demanded that any coalition which might be formed had to include EAM members.

When the destroyer *Crete* had refused to obey an operational order, the position of the British authorities was made clear. The Greek ships were under Royal Navy command and their crews had to abide by British naval law, which forbade collective demands and mutinous assemblies. On this point, Admiral Harwood was unwavering, but, whilst he admitted that he hated 'pandering to mutinies', he decided to postpone using force as long as a chance

* The *Averof* is still afloat. In 1985 plans were in hand to move her from Poros to Phaleron Harbour. She was built in 1910.

remained that the mutineers might be persuaded to return to their obedience. When he wrote this, on 10 April, there appeared to be a hope that the affair would be settled peacefully, for he had received messages which indicated that the crew of the *Apostilis* was anxious to return to duty. By this stage Churchill had been alerted to the state of affairs in Alexandria and he had instructed Harwood to: 'Make sure you have ample forces available in Alexandria to enforce discipline upon the mutinous Greek ships.' Taking a practical interest, he urged a concentration of artillery on the dockside and precautions against the destroyers loosing off torpedoes in the harbour.

A state of siege now obtained in Alexandria, with the Greek ships cut off from the mainland. On land, the armoured brigade's camp was also under a blockade, although later some of the mutineers were able to get food from the Beduin, and intercept and loot a supply train. The official policy was, according to Macmillan, 'to starve them into reason' at the same time as creating a new Greek government which would satisfy some at least of the mutineers. On 12 April there was a conference of the men directly responsible for bringing the mutiny to an end – Admiral Harwood, Sir Bernard Paget, Commander-in-Chief of Land Forces in the Middle East, Lord Killearn, the British Ambassador to Egypt, and Lord Moyne, the Deputy Minister of State at Cairo. They agreed that if the mutineers continued to disobey orders, an ultimatum would be issued to them. Suppression of the mutiny by force was a last resort and one which, it was considered, would lead to a 'lasting ill-effect on Anglo-Greek relations, the probability of very bitter criticism in America and Russia', loss of Egyptian lives, and damage to property in Alexandria. Yet the hard-line EAM supporters made up less than a third of the mutineers in both the army and the navy, and so measures were put in hand to isolate them through propaganda. Aircraft dropped leaflets and broadcasts were directed at the camp and ships to weaken the mutineers' resolve.

There had been indications of wavering in the mutineers' ranks. On the 14th and 15th, a number of loyal men had stolen out of the army camps in spite of small-arms fire from their colleagues. They brought with them news that four-fifths of the mutineers were fed up and that the militants had had to set up a 'reign of terror' in order to maintain solidarity. The news, conveyed by reports and handbills, that a new government was being formed under Sophocles Venizelos had divided the army mutineers, some of whom wanted to leave the camp and negotiate with the new administration. This information justified British policy; on the one hand the Greeks' political demands were being met and on the other their defiance was being faced with firmness. The extreme element was also facing isolation and revealing their hand more openly. On 20 April intelligence sources revealed that a former Communist deputy had made approaches to a Russian agent with a request for the Greek units to be transferred to the Balkan front for service alongside the Red Army.

By 22 April, the British military and naval authorities sensed that the mutineers' will was faltering and a slight push from the outside would bring a complete collapse of the mutinies. Churchill advised that a few ranging shots against the batteries holding the perimeter of the camps might do the trick. The First Sea Lord suggested that a motor torpedo boat attack on the notoriously militant submarine depot ship *Hephaistos* would persuade other ships' crews to throw in the sponge. Harwood disagreed. He did not want to endanger British lives 'in bringing mutinous Greeks to their senses', and he was uncomfortable about 'the capricious behaviour of torpedoes in shallow water'. The need for such forces was disappearing fast. The Greek naval training school and barracks surrendered on 22 April and the Commander-in-Chief of the Greek Navy, Admiral Voulgaris, was on hand in Alexandria with orders from the new government which empowered him to suppress the mutinies. In the early morning of 23 April parties of loyal sailors boarded the most irresolute ships, the destroyer *Ierax* and the corvettes *Apostolis* and *Saktouris*. After an exchange of machine-gun and small-arms fire, the ships were carried and the mutineers surrendered. There were twenty casualties. The mutineers on the remaining ships were vexed by searchlights and smoke and, seeing that their cause was hopeless, surrendered on the night of 23-25 April. Admiral Voulgaris announced, 'Greek warships have returned to the path of honour and duty to their country.' What was more important politically was that they had been made to do so by fellow Greeks.

It was not considered wise to deploy Greek troops against the armoured brigade camp, on practical grounds. Its defended perimeter had since 13 April been surrounded by a British force, which included the 8th Royal Tank Regiment, the 104th Battery of the Royal Horse Artillery and battalions of the Royal Welch and the Durham Light Infantry. General Paget had issued his ultimatum to the mutineers at six on the evening of 23 April, which insisted on an unconditional surrender the next morning. The imminence of an attack on the camp had disturbed the Greeks and the besieging forces noticed a flurry of activity within the compounds. At first, the mood of the mutineers was challenging and there were threats to shoot at aircraft which overflew the camp and dropped leaflets. Churchill had placed responsibility for suppressing the mutiny on Paget ('Act as you think best') and Paget, thinking that the news of the surrender of the ships would further weaken the mutineers' resolution, postponed his attack for twenty-four hours.

The operation was undertaken in conditions of secrecy. Kenneth Matthews, the BBC's Middle East correspondent, was permitted to watch the preparations. For the British troops commanded to take the camp, 'the Greeks were simply a pack of foreigners who were making a nuisance of themselves'.[39] The plan adopted involved ejecting the Greeks from their forward positions and then laying a smokescreen under which loyal men could escape from the camp. The Greeks needed no urging to pull back, although a handful of them, firing wildly as they drove back to the camp, shot and killed a British officer. They surrendered the following morning without any further trouble.

The collapse of the two major mutinies did not signal an end to unrest amongst Greek forces. During the first days of the mutiny there had been an attempt to extend it to other Greeks serving elsewhere in the Middle East. On 12 April, after the corvette *Pindos* arrived in Valetta, members of her crew went aboard the *Corinthia* and persuaded her company to set up a Pan-Hellenic committee. Further trouble of this kind was anticipated by Admiral Harwood on 1 May when he ordered all Greek warships on duty in the central and western Mediterranean to stay away from Alexandria. Numbers of agitators were still at large there and, in consequence, there had been a handful of limited disturbances. Over 600 Greeks at the Elli training camp began a campaign of passive resistance on 1 May, and there had been isolated incidents at Qassassin on 29-30 April, where the 2nd Greek Field Company had refused to obey orders, but their own officers had quietened them down.

The naval mutineers had been disarmed and sent to POW camps in Malta after the collapse of their mutiny, but they were by no means pacified and, for a time, it was feared they would rebel again. The 2,300 mutineers from the army, whom the authorities

182

feared could not be trusted, were sent under armed guard to a camp at Bardia over the border in Libya. The 2,500 loyal men were moved to another camp. That so many many men were judged to be mutineers and potentially disloyal may have indicated that the Greek and British authorities were extremely cautious about taking risks, or that earlier estimates of support for the mutiny in the army had been far too low.

In political terms, the mutinies had forced the hand of the British government, which was compelled to permit EAM representatives to come to Cairo and join talks about the formation of a broadly based Greek government. The administration formed by Venizelos survived the end of the mutinies by two days and was replaced, following a conference in the Lebanon, by another under the social democrat Giorgis Papandreou. EAM members joined his cabinet and threw themselves wholeheartedly into the plotting and manipulation which was the hallmark of wartime Greek politics. In October 1944 the centre of political activity shifted from the bar at Shepheard's Hotel in Cairo to Greece, which was being liberated by British forces. Two months later, the Communists attempted an armed *coup*, but were checked by British forces. The uprising in Athens marked the first stage of a civil war which lasted another five years. Through the mutinies, EAM and its Communist adherents had gained a temporary advantage, recognition, and admission into what Britain hoped would be the official government of Greece. The authorities in Egypt had in both political and military terms showed considerable good sense. The mixture of political concession and military resolution secured a felicitous end to an awkward crisis with very little bloodshed.

RED COAT AND GREEN FLAG:

Irish Mutinies, 1798-1920

Though I evidently did not regard myself as a slave, and had a pride in my loyal subordination, did I not consider the free soil of America as in every way preferable to that of Ireland? He said that, for his part, he had seen so many unpleasant sights amidst the grandeur and pageantry of the rich in Dublin City that the total impression was one pain and horror. Such hosts of street beggars, such troops of poverty-stricken children, such a mass of degraded poor people!

... I informed him that, though he might consider it a depravity in me, I would in all events remain loyal to the King to whom I had sworn allegiance.

Robert Graves, *Proceed, Sergeant Lamb*

INFERNAL DESIGN

Between late summer and early winter of 1798, the British public, already perturbed by news of uprisings in Ireland and Bonaparte's expedition to Egypt, were further alarmed by the revelation of a series of conspiracies aboard men-o'-war of the Channel Fleet. Cabals of sailors on three line-of-battle ships, the *Caesar*, *Captain* and *Glory*, had planned to murder their officers, take over the ships and sail them to French ports.[1] Two dozen seamen on another capital ship, the *Defiance*, cherished similar designs, but they were

185

checked before their plans had been developed. All the accused men were Irish and the evidence against them showed plainly that their mutinies were designed to assist their fellow countrymen who had been in revolt throughout the summer. Behind both the mutinies and the mischief in Ireland was the French Republic, which again had shown its desire to cripple Britain's war effort through domestic subversion.

Since the start of the war, five years earlier, Ireland had been expected to play its proper part in Britain's war effort. The census of 1801 was to show that Ireland had an adult male population of 2.6 million, compared to 4.4 million in England and Wales, and so Irish manpower was crucial in the creation of a mass army and navy. Yet efforts to tap this supply of recruits had met with resistance in the form of anti-militia riots in 1793 and the formation of secret associations of young men who swore never to join Britain's armed forces. These disturbances, like the rebellion of 1798 and the naval mutinies in the same year, were a warning that the mass of Gaelic-speaking, Catholic Irish was either indifferent or hostile towards Britain's war with revolutionary France. The mood of Ireland was not new. Edmund Spenser had recognised it in the last decade of the sixteenth century when he observed that the native Irish 'have their ears upright, waiting when the watchword shall come that they should all rise generally into rebellion, and cast away the English subjection'.

Spenser had also noted that when the Irish 'are brought down to extreme wretchedness, then they creep a little perhaps, and sue for grace, till they have gotten some breath and recovered their strength again'. For most of the eighteenth century, the Gaelic Irish had been creeping, reduced to abjectness by the settlement imposed after they had thrown in their lot with the deposed James II in 1689. The Catholic faith had been all but outlawed, and political power was concentrated in the hands of an English administration which ruled from Dublin Castle and was upheld by the Protestant minority. There had been some enlightenment during this period of gloom and it enabled the Irish to gather their strength again. Many Irishmen from the landowning and professional classes, both Catholic and Protestant, sensed that Ireland's needs could never be satisfied by an administration whose policies were largely dictated by England's interests. This feeling was deepened by two external events – the success of the American colonists in 1783 and the French Revolution of 1789. Irishmen could learn many lessons from these upheavals, for each demonstrated what could be achieved by men who loved liberty and were determined to fight against tyranny and injustice. The ideas which blew from Paris made the deepest impression and were transmitted to every level of society, even if they were not always completely understood. 'The common people of this country,' reported a Meath magistrate in 1793, 'have been deluded by [and] possessed with an idea that liberty and equality should only govern in the future.' ... 'The *first law* is the General Will,' asserted the Belfast Volunteers, in spite of their oath to George III. In the same city, men who sympathised with the French Revolution formed clubs in imitation of the Paris Jacobins, spread radical ideas and even subscribed to funds for bolstering the French war effort.

The ferment of new ideas meant that many Irishmen in the Navy possessed some political education and were willing to broadcast it to their shipmates. Illicit political clubs met in the galley of the *Captain* and pamphlets were circulated amongst the sympathetic on *Defiance*, although a few recipients were illiterate. There were meetings here as well, where Irish politics were discussed in simple terms, usually accompanied by rum drinking. One sailor spoke for many, on board ships as well as in Ireland, when he asserted, 'they should have Equality and freedom in Ireland, why should they not have it there as well as other parts?' Words and slogans remembered on land were defiantly repeated on ship. In April 1799, Robert Powell, a seaman on the *Repulse* cried out: '*Vive la République, bogre le Roy!*' during an address by his captain. On examination, it was found that he commonly shouted '*Vive la République*', 'Damn the King!' and 'Success to the French!' and was a United Irishman. He was given 100 lashes, delivered before all the ships in his squadron.[2]

In the Navy – where all sailors were repeatedly warned that all forms of clubs and oath-swearing were outlawed – and in Ireland, the authorities took a firm stand against the expression of radical, seditious ideas. In Dublin, the Viceroy responded to the seething unrest by reaching for the instruments of coercion. From 1796 Ireland suffered an official 'terror' in which regular forces, militia and yeoman cavalry scoured the countryside in search of arms dumps and suspected agitators and dissidents. This campaign intensified in 1797 and reached its peak during and after the 1798 rebellion. The intimidatory hangings, tar-cappings, floggings and looting added to the stock of Irish grievances and deepened bitterness. What was happening was known to many Irish seamen through their own experiences, letters from home and newspapers. David Reed, a ringleader aboard the *Defiance*, had bruised himself trying to enlist converts to the United Irishmen and one, Laurence Carrol, later turned evidence against him. Reed cross-examined the turncoat: 'Did you tell me that your Brother was amongst the Rebels and that you was writing this letter home that nothing may be against you on board the Defiance?' Carrol's memory failed him and he said that he thought that this might have been so, but trade was bad at home and his brother must have been forced to join the rebellion. While *Defiance* was at anchor in Cawsand Bay, reports in a newspaper of events in Ireland stirred Thomas Darbyshire to rage. 'With a pipe in his mouth, much the worse for liquor, he expressed the words, there has been Injustice done to my country, I will be revenged for it if it cost me my life.'

Since its foundation by Wolfe Tone in 1791, the Society of United Irishmen had been widely seen as the instrument by which Irishmen might secure their revenge. Vengeance had not been the first purpose of the organisation. Tone had dreamed of a body of men, both Protestant and Catholic, who would secure liberty and freedom for an Ireland released from English control, and ruled by its own elected government. Yet, in spite of the great numbers of Irishmen who took the oath and pledged themselves to the United Irishmen, the society was never strong enough to take on the government in Dublin with its troops and spy system. Driven underground, many of the leaders, like Tone, took themselves to France and badgered the Republic for assistance. In 1796 the Directory gave its approval in principle for the liberation of Ireland, and troops had been mustered for the invasion army. But the enterprise was stillborn. Irish hopes were raised again in 1797, when, at the conclusion of the campaign in Italy, a powerful army of veterans under Napoleon Bonaparte was released for service elsewhere. Britain, now alone, still defied the Republic, and a blow was needed which would force its government to come to terms with France. Tone wanted this blow to be struck in Ireland, where, he assured Napoleon, half a million patriots would rise up the moment the first French soldiers stepped ashore. Tone recalled that Napoleon was frosty but polite. His mind was in fact elsewhere, dreaming of conquest in the East. When he and other revolutionary generals waged wars, they made them pay for themselves. In Italy, the Rhineland and the Low Countries, French armies lived off the land and stuffed their war chests with levies imposed on conquered cities and provinces. Nothing like this would have been possible during a campaign to liberate Ireland. The deliverance of Ireland possessed some superficial attractiveness as an idealistic venture, but it was not the sort of war which appealed to professional soldiers like Napoleon.

Napoleon, as he admitted later, 'was full of dreams', in which he imagined himself 'founding a religion, marching into Asia, riding an elephant, a turban on my head'. Ireland was not the stage where Napoleon could play Alexander the Great; the Middle East was. A blow struck at Egypt and the Levant would be more damaging to Britain's commercial interests than one delivered against Ireland, and it offered the possibility of the fulfilment of Napoleon's fantasy of an invasion of India. In February 1798 the Director gave in to Napoleon and, on 19 May, the French invasion force sailed from Toulon for Egypt. In the same week Irish peasants began their uprising and many fondly looked to the western seas for the expected French fleet and its transports filled with soldiers.

Irishmen in the Royal Navy knew nothing of Napoleon's strategy and the vainglory which was its mainspring. Like their fellow countrymen, the Irish seaman looked to Napoleon and the French as allies and liberators. Bartholomew Duff, a ringleader on board the *Caesar*, promised his shipmates aid from Napoleon and claimed that he possessed letters from France, although none were ever discovered. The *Defiance* Irishmen regularly raised their tankards in toasts to the French and a single, very bold, United Irishman, Patrick Townsend of the *St George*, received 300 lashes for publicly toasting Napoleon.[3] Standing up for Bonaparte and the French inevitably led to arguments below decks with English seamen whose patriotism was offended. One was recalled by a sailor from the *Caesar*.

Me and my messmates were saying among each other that no Frenchman should govern us. Alexander Matthews replied, 'Well behaved, my Briton.' The prisoner, Divine, was unlashing his hammock at the same time and made reply, that he was no Briton but a true Irishman and that he was a true Catholic and repeated I am no heretic. I replied, 'I am no heretic but a true Protestant.' Divine then said, 'By the Holy Ghost, I never will be easy but I've washed my hands in their blood.'

On another occasion, the sturdy patriotism of an English seaman (which would have pleased Gillray) clashed with the disappointed resentment of an Irish sailor. The ship's quartermaster recalled:

> I was walking on the Poop on the starboard side with Corporal Dean and I remarked to Corporal Dean what a comfortable thing it was, the taking of the frigates off Ireland with 30,000 stand of guns on them.* Corporal Dean replied it was so, James Climey, the prisoner, came up immediately and said, 'I wish to God in Heaven that they had landed with a hundred thousand instead of thirty and I wish to the Lord in Heaven that I could join them. The Irish have been under the crown of Great Britain long enough and that they would be under the crown of Great Britain no longer.' I went to Climey and said to him, 'You villain, what do you mean by this, you're fighting for your King and Country.' He made answer to me, 'I would sooner kill an Englishman than a Frenchman.'

Rash words of this kind angered English sailors and aroused their suspicions. When the Irish mutineers stood their trial, there were plenty of English seamen willing to testify against them with accounts of seditious conversations either engaged in or overheard.

News of the events in Ireland during the summer of 1798 excited the Irish sailors and made many desperate to play some part in them. The idea that Irish sailors might be able to strike a blow for their country was of comparatively recent currency. The exiled United Irishmen in Paris had contemplated plans to kindle mutinies in the Royal Navy, but the project had been fitfully pursued. It had been proposed that when warships engaged in battle, Irish sailors could create panic and, at the moment of boarding, switch sides. This may have been one of the suggestions carried by Christopher Carey, a United Irishman and French agent, who secretly visited naval ports in the south-west during the autumn of 1796.[4] Whatever else Carey may have achieved by his contacts with disaffected sailors, he gave no indications to his masters of the intensity of lower-deck discontent which erupted into the mutinies at Spithead and the Nore a few months later.

Like the French, the United Irishmen, both in Paris and Ireland, were astounded by the news of the mutinies. Once they recovered

---

* This was the action off Tory Island on 12 October 1798 in which Commodore Sir Borlase Warren's squadron intercepted and successfully engaged a French squadron under Commodore Bompart. The French ships were carrying 3,000 soldiers and arms for the Irish insurgents. None reached their destination, to the sorrow of the Irish.

from their amazement, the United Irishmen swiftly realised the potential of mutiny as a weapon with which to advance their cause. What they failed to understand was that the sailors were not in revolt against the government, its war or its policy in Ireland, but were seeking the redress of shipboard grievances. Still, at some country fairs, sympathisers with the United Irishmen were induced to contribute money for the mutineers. In Belfast, on 23 April 1797, Sir Edward Newenham sent a cautionary letter to Lord Spencer in which he claimed to have heard that rebels sent by the courts to the Navy were well pleased with their sentences. They claimed that 'they would be of more service to the *cause* on board a man-of-war than they could be at present on land, for they immediately would form clubs and swear every man to be true to each other'.[5] Between the first breaking of the news of the Spithead mutiny at the end of April and the collapse of that at the Nore in June, 1,200 Irishmen volunteered for the Navy in what must have been a bewildering spasm of uncharacteristic patriotism. This process of infiltration was unwittingly assisted by the application of the 1796 Insurrection Act which had given magistrates the power to draft suspected United Irishmen to the Navy and so keep them from making trouble at home. By the beginning of 1798 it was estimated that there were 15,000 Irishmen serving on British men-o'-war, in all 15 per cent of the Navy's manpower. Many were Defenders – a Catholic underground movement dedicated to nocturnal terrorism against tithe-collectors and landlords – or United Irishmen, and were, therefore, well schooled in the arts of covert conspiracy, the administering of oaths and the formation of clandestine cells. Together, such men hoped that they could make mutiny a weapon in their country's coming struggle against Britain.

On no ships where mutiny was planned were the United Irishmen more than a small minority. There were twenty-two men charged from the *Caesar*, twenty-four from the *Defiance*, twelve from the *Captain*, and twenty-two from the *Glory*, although the witnesses against them suggested that there were plenty of seamen who were prepared to listen to their arguments and even be tempted by them. Yet the plotters had a disadvantage in that their grievances, unlike those in 1797, were purely Irish and unlikely to win any support from English, Scottish or Welsh seamen. Indeed, they were invariably unconcerned or actively hostile. At no stage could any of the ringleaders claim to have anything approaching unanimity as to their aims from their shipmates. It was soon found that agreement from their fellow Irishmen was hard enough to achieve. Whatever their private feelings, Irish sailors were often sceptical of the chances of mutiny, or, for that matter, the rebellion in Ireland. John McKenna, an officer's servant on board the *Captain*, was told about the united Irishmen on his ship by two ringleaders, who explained their intentions over drinks at a friend's house and a Portsmouth pub. 'I did not like it,' recalled McKenna, who later turned evidence against them. On board *Defiance*, Thomas Jourdain, a ringleader, asked a fellow countryman whether he thought the United Irishmen would succeed and was told, 'that one disciplined man was better than two or three others'. In the light of the fighting in Ireland during the summer this was true enough, for the Irish rebels, lacking firearms and artillery, were inevitably at a disadvantage in open engagements with the Army and militia.

On board *Glory*, Dennis Mahoney, a would-be mutineer, was confident of widespread support or so he suggested to a ship's corporal who had told him to be quiet. Mahoney asserted, 'that if any Protestant or any Person offered to molest him, he would in one Minute raise Fifty or Sixty Men who would go through the ship.' This was just before the time appointed for the seizure of the ship, 3 August 1798, when the mutineers had agreed to get arms, take control of the gratings, throw the officers of the watch overboard and then sail the ship from Torbay to France. The uprising was, however, postponed until 3 September. Various devices had been used to secure support for the mutiny, including rumours and the promise of reward. Patrick Murphy obtained a paper which, he alleged, contained stories which told how the *Queen Charlotte* had run aground at Cork and her crew had unloaded guns and stores for the rebels. The *Ramillies* was also said to have gone aground at Dublin and that her crew had murdered their captain before going ashore to join the rebels in Wicklow. The support of other ships from the Channel Fleet was promised by Bartholomew Duff of the *Caesar*, who claimed to have exchanged letters with like-minded men aboard them when the squadron had been anchored at Torbay in May. A month later, plotters on the *Captain*, which had returned from the Mediterranean Station, alleged that they had been in contact with sympathisers on an unnamed ship.

Supposed affirmations of solidarity from other ships were not enough to convince the lukewarm. Patrick Murphy promised that, when the *Glory* was in the French service, all the mutineers would be given commissions and 'be made Gentlemen for ever'. Edward

McLaughlin, heartened by tales of 24,000 Irish rebels under arms and camped at the Bog of Allen, speculated that he might be made a captain. A fellow mutineer on the *Defiance*, William Lyndsey, tempted the faint-hearted with the promise that every renegade would receive £1,000 in prize money when the 74-gun ship was handed over to the French at Brest.

Such arguments were advanced to enlist men and bind them to the United Irishmen by an oath. On board the *Caesar*, this appears to have been quite simple, for all who were drawn into the plot swore 'to be United Irishmen equal to their Brethren in Ireland and to have nothing to do with the King or his Government'. The surgeon's mate on *Defiance* repeated a more elaborate version.

I swear to be true to the free and United Irishmen who are now fighting our cause against Tyrants and Oppressors, and to defend their rights to the last Drop of my Blood and to keep all secret and I do agree to carry the ship into Brest the next time the ship looks out ahead at sea and to kill every officer and man that shall hinder us except the Master and to hoist a Green Ensign with a Harp on it and afterwards to kill and destroy the Protestants.

The Master, who was never implicated in the conspiracy, was presumably to be kept alive in order to steer the ship into the Brest roads.

The vengeance specified for the Protestants showed that the men on *Defiance* shared the feelings of their countrymen. From the first uprisings in May, and in spite, in some cases, of Protestant leadership, the Gaelic peasantry used the rebellion as a means of paying off old scores and murdering as many Protestants as they could find. This mindless, rural *jacquerie* was not what Tone had wanted and it did much to drive his Protestant sympathisers away from the United Irishmen. William Lyndsey, on the *Defiance*, understood perhaps that religious disunity would handicap the rebellion and approached Daniel Lynch for his support. 'Knowing me to be a Protestant,' Lynch recalled, he said, 'Daniel Lynch, there are many Jacobin Protestants in the ship who to get free of their Slavery and Confinement will as soon go there [Brest] as any where else to get quit of the service.' This appeal to Lynch's desire to desert was fruitless. Lynch, like many other sailors on *Defiance*, must have been well aware of the feelings of the Catholic mutineers towards Protestants, for they were freely and frequently voiced.

John Hopkins's 'damn and bugger all Protestants' was a view shared by most of his fellow plotters.

Outbursts like this were commonly heard during meetings held by the mutineers, which were usually noisy and drunken. John McKenner, a wardroom steward, attended one in the forecastle when the *Defiance* was cruising off the Irish coast in June. The men were 'talking about the Irish and the French' and insisted that 'they were upon a just good cause and damn the dog who would not die for it'. Shipboard grievances soon intruded into the talk and one mutineer swore:

> By his holy Ghost, if he went to the yardarm for it he would be the first man who would step forward and he would himself give the Captain a bloody neck; they all got up and joined hands and gave three huzzas and expressed over and over again that they would commit bloody Murder and they would have Equality in the ship and take the ship to France.

Another boasted 'he would be a greater Man next cruise than Lieutenant Williams', and another swore he would cut 'from Ear to Ear' the throats of all those who could not speak Irish. Defenders' songs were sung and some thought, not very serious, was given to forming a committee. The Irish on board *Glory* behaved in much the same manner and were remembered by the ship's lieutenant as being 'riotous and disorderly in the extreme' so that he was forced to carry a brace of loaded pistols whenever he went on deck.

Many who witnessed these routs and listened to the boasting kept quiet out of fear. 'They [the ringleaders on *Defiance*] carried the sway a great deal in the ship and as I did my Duty with them, they would do me some injury in the night' was the reason why one who disapproved of their behaviour kept silent. The men concerned were indeed a harum-scarum lot. James Mason, a coloured seaman, had the misfortune to have his hammock close to where the mutineers often assembled for drinking bouts. 'They would wake me and call me black Buggar,' he remembered, and one night one of his tormentors, Thomas Laffin, tried to get into his hammock, but another Irishman, perhaps shocked at his intent, dragged him off. John Howard, whom a fellow sailor described as 'a good man because he was a civil, quiet man who would not say anything to hurt anyone', was vexed by one ringleader, John Brady, who was in debt to him. Brady assured Howard one night that 'he would have the pleasure of walking in my blood', and when reprimanded, threatened to eat his creditor's liver. 'If you had some Captains you would often be flogged,' interjected one sailor, which suggests that many appreciated the check which flogging kept on bullies. Later, Brady, talking of religion to the man in the next hammock, said that, 'he would think nothing of turning out at 12 o'clock at night to cut a Presbyterian Throat'.

It is hard to imagine what men like this could have achieved in their proposed mutinies. They had set their stakes on the seizure of men-o'-war manned by between six and eight hundred sailors, most of whom, including many of their fellow countrymen, wanted no part in their enterprise. The organisation of the mutinies was shaky, and whilst threats of action were abundant, none was attempted. The tolerance towards the plotters and their wild language may well have owed much to the fact that few of the listeners took their claims seriously. Leadership was drawn from the ranks of ordinary seamen, in contrast to the rebellion in Ireland itself, where the insurgents followed their priests and some local gentry. Exposure of the plots was easy and witnesses were readily forthcoming, not a few perhaps anxious to exculpate themselves from association with the ringleaders. On board *Caesar*, William Oliver, the captain of the forecastle, revealed the plot on behalf of the 'most respectable men in the ship', for which he later suffered some inconvenience.* Captain Aylmer of the *Captain*, informed of unrest, took it upon himself to investigate what had been happening, and on *Glory* the mutineers' boastings were eventually revealed to the captain.

All on trial strenuously denied the charges. The seven ringleaders on *Glory* abhorred the 'horrid plot' of which they had been accused and avowed their determination to 'defend King and glorious Constitution against all Enemies foreign and domestic'. The twenty-seven men sentenced on *Defiance* protested their innocence of the 'Infernal Design or Horrid Conspiracy' alleged against them, but twelve were hanged and seven transported to the Australian penal settlement at Botany Bay. Their indiscretion and courage inspired one imitator, Patrick Townsend of the *St George*, who on 7 January 1799 was sentenced for making the toast: 'The Tree of Liberty, liberty to all United Irishmen and Damnation to all that are Enemies thereto'.[6] By this time the Tree of Liberty had been uprooted in Ireland and the government was back firmly in

* See pages 50-1

the saddle. Two years later, Pitt's government introduced the Act of Union which removed the last traces of Irish independence and brought Ireland more closely under British control.

The mutinies, kindled but not ignited by the United Irishmen in the Channel Fleet in 1798, were overshadowed by the larger rebellion in Ireland which they had hoped to assist. Yet, unlike many of the rebel leaders, the would-be mutineers were, by and large, ignored in the compilation of later nationalist martyrologies. Without cohesion and with indecisive leadership, the Irish sailors had planned their mutinies under a misconception. They mistakenly believed that an underground organisation, like the United Irishmen, which had flourished in the sympathetic environment of the Irish towns and villages would also thrive on board British men-o'-war. They also thought that the mutinies at Spithead and the Nore were indications of a deeper dissatisfaction among seamen which they might have exploited. In fact, non-Irish and many Irish sailors were reluctant to risk mutiny, especially when the ringleaders made no secret of their attachment to France. After the discovery of these conspiracies, there were no further attempts by Irish sailors to stir up mutinies. They realised, like their countrymen at home, the hopelessness of challenging a government which would crush rebellion ruthlessly. Irishmen were left to gather their strength for the next campaign.

AN ENGLISH OR AN IRISH SOLDIER?

The Act of Union did not, as its architects intended, bind Ireland more closely to Britain, rather its termination became the focus of a hundred and twenty years of political agitation. Ireland, in fact, moved further away from Britain, for whereas after 1850 violence gradually ceased to be a feature of British political life, its use increased in Ireland. All the major movements in Irish politics, for Catholic Emancipation, for tenants rights and for Home Rule, were marked by considerable disorders which reached their peaks during the land war of the 1880s and the 'troubles' of 1919 to 1922. One consequence was the emergence of the persistent cartoonists' image of the Irishman as a simian-featured ruffian who was a stranger to reason and ever looking for a fight. Yet, if the Irishman was always reaching for his cudgel in his quarrels with the British government, his pugnacity was, at times, a national asset. Nineteenth-century Ireland was a reservoir of manpower for the British Army and, in the opinion of many of its commanders, yielded tough, reckless fighters whose only shortcomings were a cheerful addiction to insubordination and intemperance.

Before the 1845-7 famine, the Irish population had grown at much the same rate as the rest of Britain's, but whilst the surplus on the mainland was absorbed by the swift expansion of building, mining and manufacturing, in Ireland little such work was available. Ireland remained predominantly an agrarian country, but with an agriculture which was incapable of supporting its people. Unattached young men were therefore forced to look to soldiering as a means of livelihood. In 1830, 43 per cent of Britain's soldiers were Irish, either recruited in Ireland or from the immigrants who had come to Britain in search of unskilled work. By the early 1860s the proportion had fallen to just under a third, and on the outbreak of the First World War only one-tenth of British soldiers were Irish. The potato famine and consequent emigration to the United States led Ireland's share of the population of the United Kingdom to fall from a third to a tenth in seventy years.

The Irish recruit came from a country which was periodically convulsed by agitation for independence and the terrorism of underground groups which waged hit-and-run warfare against landlords and the police. Once he was in the Army, he was cut off from the sources of discontent of his homeland and beyond the reach of the men who exploited them. Like other soldiers, he discovered new loyalties to battalion, comrades and officers. It was, however, impossible for the War Office to keep the Irish soldier insulated from the unrest of his country. Ireland required a garrison, which, at times of crisis, needed topping up. As long as the Irish rejected the customary, but for them ineffective, British political methods of negotiation and compromise, and instead chose military answers to their problems in the form of terrorism and rebellion, British forces had to be concentrated in the island. When these forces were Irish, there was a clash of loyalties.

Irish nationalists had, in 1798, realised the possibility of appeals to Irish servicemen to place country before duty, but the results had been unpromising. A further attempt to suborn British forces was made in the early 1860s by agents of the Irish Republican

197

Brotherhood, a nationalist underground organisation known then and later as the Fenians. The rebel scheme for recruitment amongst British forces stationed in Ireland appeared, at first, to meet with some success and at various stages the men responsible claimed to have converted several thousand soldiers in different regiments. The programme had been undertaken by a number of agents who buttonholed off-duty soldiers in streets, alleyways, pubs and the back rooms of bars. John O'Leary claimed to have talked one soldier on sentry duty into taking the Fenian oath. The Fenian line was to tell the soldier of the distress of his countrymen and to show how he suffered from landlords and the bloodsucking Anglican Church.

This canvassing was a risky business, for the Fenians were often under police surveillance and the soldiers themselves, whilst quite happy to drink beer paid for by Fenians, often proved unreliable converts. Not all were co-operative and it was one, from the 25th Regiment, who brought about O'Leary's downfall. O'Leary had approached this soldier on the bridge at Athlone and offered him porter, asking whether he wished to be an English or an Irish soldier. If he chose the latter and could make a further ninety converts, the Irish private was assured of a captaincy in the Fenian army. This was not enough, and the soldier fetched three comrades and a constable, who arrested O'Leary. He was sentenced to seven years' imprisonment at Mullingar Assizes in March 1865. It was clear to men like the private of the 25th that close involvement with the Fenians was a perilous business. In February 1864 Sergeant Thomas Darragh of the 2nd Regiment had been sentenced to be shot by a court martial which had found him guilty of mutinous conduct in joining the Fenians. Soon after, a private in the Royal Artillery received two years' hard labour for traitorous language, and a private in the Buffs a similar sentence for sending a treacherous letter to the Fenian journal, the *Irish People*.[7] Such punishments did not deter completely, for, in 1866, a police raid on a Fenian cell led to arrests of ten soldiers who were present. The Commander-in-Chief in Ireland, the Crimean veteran, Sir George Brown, had been dismissive of Fenian penetration of the Army, since he was convinced that 'it was impossible that the British uniform could cover a traitor'. The Indian Mutiny experience of his successor, Sir Hugh Rose, made him take the problem of infiltration more seriously and instigate courts martial of suspected Fenians.

Two of the men suspected, both from the 32nd Regiment, were

convinced that most of their comrades at the Curragh Camp were Fenians, but this claim, like those of the Fenians, was unsubstantiated. An oath sworn over a pot of ale did not make a soldier into a potential mutineer. Moreover the lack of any organisation within barracks, and the likelihood that battalions would be moved to other postings, made it impossible for the Fenians to put down deep roots in the Army. It was less than clear just how the Fenians intended to employ their alleged converts in the Army, for at the time they were canvassing soldiers there was no exact timetable for an Irish revolution. As it was, the isolated insurrections during the winter of 1866-7 were fiascos, and when Army detachments were used to assist the police, all proved completely loyal. Fenian ineptitude and the exemplary punishments handed out soldiers who had dabbled with Fenianism saw to that.

The failure of the Fenian uprising was followed by a temporary eclipse of revolutionary nationalism. From the late 1870s, Irish nationalism worked through the British parliament with constitutional methods which excluded political violence (save in debate) and the subversion of the Army. In 1912 these methods bore fruit and the Home Rule Bill was passed which gave Ireland its own elected legislature. The Bill was due to become law in the autumn of 1914. Its passage marked the beginning of a new Irish crisis in which the Army soon became deeply embroiled. Protestant objections to Home Rule led, during 1913, to the formation of the Ulster Volunteer Force of over 10,000 men, armed with smuggled Mausers and machine-guns, all sworn to fight against the new form of Irish government. In response, the southern Irish upholders of Home Rule began to muster their own armies, the Irish Volunteers and the Citizens' Army, which contained many ex-soldiers and trained with the British Army's infantry drill-book. The Irish had again turned their back on the norms of political behaviour and looked towards an armed struggle as the only answer to their problems.

At the beginning of 1914, Asquith's Cabinet faced its responsibilities for keeping the peace in Ireland and the possibility of having to deploy the garrison there to disarm the Ulstermen, or at least deter them from some rash action. Such action was distasteful to many officers. Those who were politically Conservative shared that party's partisanship for the Ulster Unionists and were anxious not to become involved in any kind of action designed to make them knuckle under Home Rule. They certainly did not want to have any part in operations which might trigger off a war with the Ulstermen. The government may well have had in mind a gesture, such as the reinforcement of military depots in Ulster which would, in effect, test the Volunteers' mettle. Disquiet about these possibilities was strongest amongst officers of the 3rd Cavalry Brigade, stationed at the Curragh, and through their commander, Brigadier-General Hubert Gough, they presented their misgivings to the War Office. Their intention was to force the government's hand. Their action was not mutinous, but it was a warning to the Cabinet that they would not be willing to obey hypothetical orders which might order them to intervene in Ulster. These exchanges are sometimes known as the Curragh Mutiny, but there was no mutiny since at no time during the crisis did any officer actually disobey an order. None in fact ever came, for the Cabinet shrank from putting the issue to the test. Their anxiety was deepened by rumblings from naval officers of the squadron which lay at anchor off Lamlash. This squadron was there, so it was widely believed, to steam to Belfast and scare the Ulstermen. Not all Army officers were apprehensive about leading their men in support of the government in Ulster; Major-General Macready, who had been designated as commander in Belfast, was more than willing to bring its inhabitants to heel. This duty was denied him and, safe from Army interference, the Ulstermen were free to smuggle in more guns during April and June 1914.

The outbreak of war in August 1914 put on one side the question of the enforcement of Home Rule and what, if any, part the Army might play in it. Whilst Redmond, the leader of the Home Rule Party, called on his countrymen to take up their share of the war effort, the struggle with Germany did not arouse the same enthusiasm in Ireland as it did elsewhere in the United Kingdom. In some areas there was sullenness and indifference, and in Wicklow Colonel de Montmorency remembered a heckler who interrupted a recruiting rally with, ''Tis the English who are our enemies and always will be; to Hell with them!' There was, not surprisingly, some wonderment at the discrepancy between Britain's championship of Belgium and its treatment of another 'small nation', Ireland. One who volunteered in 1914 and six years later was a ringleader in the mutiny of the Connaught Rangers, recalled sourly that, 'they told us we were going to fight for the liberation of small nations'.[8] Yet during the war there were no signs

200

of serious or widespread restlessness among Irish troops in the British Army. At the same time the government thought it wise not to impose conscription on Ireland, which remained exempt from the Acts of 1916 and 1918.

As in 1798, a section of nationalists saw Britain's war as a historic chance for Ireland to secure its independence. This was the view of a former diplomat, Sir Roger Casement, who dreamed of the creation of an Irish Legion from amongst Irish POWs in German camps. His suggestion was warmly endorsed by the German High Command when Casement came to them in November 1914. He was given facilities to address Irish POWs, who were taken from their several camps and brought to Limburg with promises of better treatment. From then on the whole business was a bungled flop. Casement and his German backers had little that was attractive for the Irish soldiers, all of whom were either Regulars or Territorials. The proposed Irish Legion would either fight in Ireland, presumably as part of an insurrection against British rule, or, incongruously, in Egypt. Here they would fight for the liberation of the Egyptians, presumably alongside troops from the Turkish army. If, at the end of the war, Irish independence had not been gained, the Legionaries would be given a free passage to the United States. In all, fifty POWs accepted these terms, all latterly claiming that they had done so to procure a better standard of living. Their excuse was accepted by the British Army, which took no action against them on their repatriation in 1918-9. Faced with the failure of this scheme, Casement turned to gun-running for Sinn Fein and, in 1916, was arrested, tried and executed for treason. Among the witnesses against him were twelve soldiers from the Limburg camp who had later been exchanged by the Germans.

What Casement had failed to understand was that the POWs whom he hoped to subvert had little real hatred for England and no love for Germany. The Munsters had lost half their strength in fighting at Etreux, and the Irish Guards had suffered severe loss at Villers-Cotterêts. None of the prisoners had any reason to feel gratitude to the Germans for their treatment in POW camps, and there was much affection for British soldiers with whom they had recently fought. Even the events during and after the Easter Rising in 1916 did not weaken the loyalty of Irish troops, although a handful of men serving with the Royal Navy's armoured-car squadron in Russia had to be sent home after they had become restless on hearing reports from Dublin. There was no reason for

Irish soldiers and sailors to consider renouncing their loyalty since Home Rule was only postponed by the war and would be introduced once it had ended.

TROOPS OUT

The end of the First World War marked the start of a new and savage phase in Anglo-Irish relations which included a large-scale mutiny by Irish soldiers. The old Home Rule party had passed away and in its place was Sinn Fein which swept the polls in the December 1918 election. The following January, the Sinn Fein MPs held their own parliament, the Dáil, in Dublin and declared a republic. The British government's reaction was ambivalent. The Cabinet saw a measure of Irish self-government as unavoidable, even welcome, but was unwilling to surrender Ireland to rebels. What was adopted was a policy which swung from rhetorical bombast, in which Lloyd George and others pledged themselves to inertia in the annihilation of terrorists, and to an unwillingness to fight terrorism with the full rigour of martial law. After a year in which outrages by the Irish Republican Army multiplied, and control of the country gradually slipped out of Dublin Castle's hands, the policies of 1798 were revived. The Viceroy, Lord French, began to recruit ex-NCOs and officers from Kitchener's Army as additional policemen. This *gendarmerie* soon became known as the Black and Tans, and gained a reputation for ferocious reprisals against Republicans and their suspected well-willers. 1920 therefore saw the intensification of barbarism by both sides.

The new counter-insurgency war had, as one of its consequences, the mutiny of the first battalion of the Connaught Rangers, stationed at Jullundur in the Punjab. Since 1917, the War Office had kept Irish battalions out of Ireland after indications that some of the men in them were susceptible to Sinn Fein propaganda and infiltration. In India, the Connaughts were at the centre of a province which had been convulsed by unrest during the previous year. In March 1919, Gandhi's *hartal*, a form of general strike and mass non-co-operation by Indians, had triggered off widespread disturbances. At Amritsar, a hundred miles from Jullundur, over 300 demonstrators had been shot by Indian Army troops after several days of rioting. Two months after, in May, there had been an invasion of the North-West Frontier Province by the Afghans. Whilst this war had ended the previous autumn, operations against the Wazirs were still in hand throughout 1920.

In their attempts to calm the mutineers and deflect them from their purposes, several British officers pointed out the precariousness of British rule in India at the time.[11] Colonel Deacon warned his men that they were on active service, that India was in an explosive state, and recalled to their memories the bogey of the Indian Mutiny, which had recently been invoked to justify the measures taken at Amritsar. British women and children would be endangered, he argued, if the Connaught men did not return to their duty. The same fears were expressed by the commanding officer at Jullundur, Colonel Leeds, who asked the mutineers what would happen in the event of native uprising. The mutineers assured him that they would never allow their rifles to get into Indian hands.

In reminding the Connaught Rangers that they were, in effect, an army of occupation in a potentially restless country, the two colonels unwittingly drew attention to a paradox. It had been recognised by Private Joseph Hawes, who had served with the regiment since 1914, during discussions held in a 'Boozing School' on the evening of 27 June. Irish soldiers in India had the same job to do as British soldiers in Ireland; both were instruments of alien oppression. This observation had led on from angry talk about the news from home. Hawes, whilst on embarkation leave, had been driven from a hurling match at bayonet point; another man's father had been thrown from his sick bed into the night by Black and Tans and had subsequently died, whilst another soldier claimed his sister had been shot by the Tans. The upshot of these exchanges was that the five soldiers pledged themselves to give up soldiering until the British left Ireland.

It was not an easy gesture to make. Hawes was told by a corporal that his action would be interpreted as cowardice and that he would be shot for it, and a ringleader, William Daly, asked, 'What can *you* do against the British Army?' The five men went ahead and presented themselves at the guardroom: 'In protest against British atrocities in Ireland, we refuse to soldier any longer in the service of the King.' The sergeant was unmoved and ordered them on their way – 'What do they think we're running here – a Home of Rest?' The men persisted and were locked up. News of the incident passed through the lines.

On the morning of 29 June, when C Company paraded, Private

Tommy Moran demanded to be locked up with the five men 'for Ireland's cause'. Major Payne warned him and others of the penalties which would follow such recklessness and appealed to their regimental loyalty. 'You and I, Moran, fought together in the trenches. You're a damned good soldier, and I'm proud to be one of your officers. Don't let me and the regiment down.' Moran was unswayed and twenty-nine others joined him at once. They joined the five in the guard room where they sang 'The Boys of Wexford', 'The Wearin' o' the Green', and shouted 'Up the Republic!'

Colonel Deacon hoped that the incident could be contained, and so the thirty-five men were released and spoken to. They emerged and, after an address, were joined by men from B Company. In reply to their colonel, one remarked, 'All those honours on Connaught's flag were for England. Not one of them was for poor Old Ireland. But there's going to be one added today, and it'll be the greatest honour of them all.' Without any obviously reliable men to call upon, the Colonel, officers and NCOs withdrew, leaving the mutineers and their supporters free to hold a meeting at midday. It was held in the Royal Army Temperance Association hut. The leaders insisted that the men should conduct themselves correctly and dismissed calls for paying off grudges against NCOs. The objective was to protest against the policies of the British government and call for freedom to be granted to Ireland. The mutineers then gave public affirmation of their republicanism by hoisting the green, white and orange tricolour, and many pinned Sinn Fein rosettes, made from cloth bought in the bazaar, on their uniforms.

The mutineers also agreed to send messengers to A Company, which was stationed at Solon, twenty miles off in the hills (the temperature at Jullundur in June seldom went below 100°). The man they were to contact was Jim Daly, a keen Republican, who it was thought would organise a similar protest. Daly did indeed take charge of the mutiny at Solon. He held a meeting, called the men to attention and presented the officers with a statement that they were going to do no more work until British troops were taken out of Ireland. Afterwards they marched to the railway station, where they had hoped to get a train to Jullundur, and then back. Sinn Fein songs were sung until midnight.

The following day, 1 July, it was clear to the men at Solon that troops from outside would soon arrive to arrest them. A fatigue party under a company sergeant-major was ordered to prepare the gymnasium for the detachment. He was warned that his party might be attacked, and found two men breaking into the arms store. At this stage the Catholic padre, Father Baker, intervened, and it took him three hours to dissuade the men from keeping the weapons, which included a Lewis gun. An armed guard was placed over the store of officers, two sergeants, two corporals and fourteen English bandsmen. At the orders of a major, they were issued with 50 rounds apiece and told to fire to kill to keep the arms from the mutineers.

At 9.15, Daly and three other mutineers approached the store but ran off when a lieutenant approached. Soon after, the guardroom gong sounded, followed by shouts of 'Fall in', and twenty-five files approached the magazine from three different directions. Many of the mutineers were carrying drawn bayonets. The officers fired three or four shots and some mutineers scattered, but more came forward and there was more firing. Two mutineers were killed and one was wounded. Father Baker again intervened and rushed among the men calling on them to stop in God's name. Daly, armed with an unsheathed bayonet, challenged the guards to a fight and called to them, 'If you want to know who the leader is, it is Private So and So Daly from Mullingar, County Westmeath, Ireland.' Calmed by the priest, the men withdrew to their bungalows. The next morning, 2 July, detachments from the Suffolks and the South Wales Borderers arrived by train, and the mutineers, including Daly, were arrested.

A Sinn Fein flag was flying over one of the bungalows and at least one mutineer was wearing a Sinn Fein cockade. At the meeting on 30 June, Daly had assured listeners that 'similar and simultaneous action' would be taken 'by all Irish regiments in the British Army and that the news would appear in every paper in the United Kingdom'. Later he told an officer that he and the other mutineers 'refused to do any more parades until the British dogs were withdrawn from Ireland'. The cause, as with that of the men of B and C Companies at Jullundur, was clear, although there is no evidence to suggest that other regiments were likely to imitate the Connaught's behaviour.

The Solon men also, when aware that loyal troops were on their way, prepared to use force to defend themselves. They were turned from this course by their courageous chaplain who seemed clearer than they of the Army's likely response. During the attack on the arms store, one mutineer shouted 'Let us charge them, it is only blank they are firing', and another tore open his shirt and exposed his chest to the guards, although 'he appeared to be drunk' according to one bystander. The background to the attack was recalled by some who were present and had heard rumours that English troops had machine-gunned the men at Jullundur (hints of another Amritsar) and that the Royal Sussex Regiment was on its way.* It may say much for the mood of the times and feelings after the disorders of the previous year, in both Ireland and India, that the Solon mutineers genuinely feared some kind of murderous reprisal against them and their colleagues.

The Jullundur mutineers were disarmed without incident by the South Wales Borderers and the Suffolks, and taken to a barbed-wire compound outside the town. Ringleaders were singled out, and there was an incident in which it was alleged that Major Payne, who had previously tried to reason with the men, threatened to order the SWB to fire into the mutineers. Later they were joined by the Solon men. All appear to have been questioned by an Irish staff officer who wanted to know whether the ringleaders had been spending heavily or whether they had been secretly encouraged by foreign, particularly Russian, influences. He was assured that Bolshevism had played no part in the mutiny, and that the mutineers did not intend to harm British interests and security in India. They believed that other units would fulfil their obligations during the 'strike'.

Seventy-five mutineers were taken to Dagshai Military Prison, all manacled, and were tried between 23 August and 10 September 1920. Although a Republican, Daly recognised the court's jurisdiction, but was not cross-examined. He and thirteen others were found guilty and sentenced to death, some were acquitted and the rest received terms in prison ranging between one and twenty years. Daly's death sentence was confirmed and he was shot: the other men under sentence of death were reprieved and given life sentences. The decision to execute Daly may well have been the consequence of his encouragement of the attack on the magazine in which two of his followers had been killed, and the fact that he and other assailants had carried arms. Two privates of the Royal Welch Fusiliers, who had been found guilty of mutiny at Ranikhet in July 1920, were also given death sentences, but these were reduced to

* Forty men from this Regiment had been in Amritsar at the time of the suppression of the riots in 1919.

five years. A further argument against leniency towards Daly* was the possibility of further trouble amongst other Irish regiments in India. This did not materialise and, in March 1921, detachments from the Leinsters were in action against the Moplahs during the short rebellion in western India; this was the last campaign fought by soldiers from a Southern Irish regiment in the British Army.

Given the nature of the war being waged in Ireland in 1920 and the reports of it which were reaching the Connaught men in India, some kind of disturbance was inevitable. Daly and many like him had joined the regiment within the past year, were strong Republicans, and had enlisted as a consequence of a shortage of work in western Ireland. What is interesting about the Connaughts' reaction to the news of the brutality of the Black and Tans was their own unenviable reputation in India, as recorded by Frank Richards.[12]

> The Connaughts were strong believers in the saying that what had been conquered by the sword must be kept by the sword: but not being issued with swords they used their boots and fists to such purpose that they were more respected and feared by the natives than any other British unit in India.

In fairness, Richards's impressions had been gathered a dozen or so years before and, as he later remarked, other regiments, 'though perhaps not so brutal in their methods, handled the natives in the same manner'.

During the trials of the Connaught mutineers no evidence was offered to suggest direct involvement by Sinn Fein, nor of any efforts to contact other Irish regiments. The mutineers had hoped that when news of the incidents at Solon and Jullundur spread, it would stimulate other mutinies amongst other Irish regiments in India. This thought troubled the War Office and prompted the decision to disband all the Southern Irish battalions after the signing of the Anglo-Irish Treaty in December 1921. The new Free State Government requested an amnesty for the mutineers and, after some cavilling from the War Office, they were released from the English prisons to which they had been sent. One retired senior officer regretted the end of the Irish regiments which was 'a sore

---

* It was said that Daly was shot by a squad of Irishmen from the Royal Fusiliers; this was not so, at least one English survivor from the squad is still alive. (I am indebted to Dr Charles Kightly for this point.)

fighting loss to our army', but it was more than redressed by the many thousands of men from Eire who joined Britain's forces between 1939 and 1945.

SHADOW OF MEERUT:

Mutinies in the Indian Army, 1915-1946

WARRIORS OF THE RAJ: THE INDIAN ARMY AFTER 1858

'The sepoy is a child in simplicity and biddableness, if you make him understand his orders, if you treat him justly and *don't* pet him overmuch.' The advice was Lord Dalhousie's, delivered shortly before he relinquished his Governor-Generalship of India, and on the eve of the Indian Mutiny of 1857. Nearly sixty years later, Field-Marshal Lord Roberts, who had helped put down the mutiny and later commanded the army in India, emphasised that the Indian soldier was nothing without his British officers. 'With British officers they fight splendidly, without them they will not do much. I can recall many occasions during the Indian Mutiny when a handful of British soldiers, a couple of guns, and some volunteer British Cavalry we defeated large bodies of rebels because they had no one to lead them.'[1] It had not been as easy as that. The campaign had lasted over a year and even while it lasted was being transformed into a Victorian epic which exercised a powerful hold over the imagination of Roberts's countrymen, both in Britain and India.

The sudden outbreak of the mutiny, the betrayal of trust, the massacres, particularly of women and children, deeply shocked Victorian Britain. The sequel, with the frequently indiscriminate but always fearsome vengeance, was a direct reflection of public

209

outrage. Order and faith had been broken, and those given the task of repairing them behaved as if they were the agents of divine retribution. As in all epics, there were lessons to be learned. There had been crassness and blunders by the government and the officers who commanded the East India Company's army, who had often shown themselves insensitive to the religious feelings and customs of the sepoys. There had also been an almost wilful purblindness in the months before the first uprising at Meerut, which was summed up by Lord Dalhousie, who wrote dismissively in June 1857, 'The Indian public, civil and military, is much given to panics so that floating rumour deserves little attention.'

'Floating rumour' could not be ignored after the events of 1857- 8. The gossip which alleged that pork- and cow-fat had been used to grease the cartridges for the new Enfield rifles, and that pig- and beef-bones had been added to flour to defile Muslims and break the Hindu's caste, might have been dismissed by officers, but they left the sepoys fearful. Likewise, arrogant attempts to foist Christianity on the soldiers helped to create an unsettled atmosphere in the cantonments. During the years after the mutiny when the Indian Army was reconstituted, great care was taken to make sure that its British officers were well tutored in the background, customs and faith of their soldiers. In their memoirs, many former Indian Army officers revealed an arcane and intricate knowledge of the communities from which their men were recruited. All officers were expected to speak their soldiers' language, look to senior native NCOs for guidance and advice, and always be willing to listen to the grievances of the other ranks.

Another lasting lesson of the mutiny was the knowledge that it had been unexpected. That it might happen again was a fear which quickly came to the forefront of the official and military mind whenever restlessness broke the surface. The presence in India of many survivors, some living well into the second decade of the twentieth century (one contributed to a fund for General Dyer after the Amritsar shooting) was a constant reminder of what had happened. Veterans who had fought in the campaign to put down the mutiny still hung around barracks in the 1900s when Frank Richards, like other greenhorn soldiers, heard their lurid tales. What Richards and his comrades heard were not just old tales to frighten the novice, for there were extremist nationalists who looked to 1857 as a source of example and inspiration. During the upheavals in the Punjab in 1919, Colonel Morgan of the 124th

Baluchis was alarmed when 'my own subadar-major brought me a letter from the rebels saying that the time had come to murder all British officers'.[2] Another officer who was present during these troubles recollected that the army was not infected with nationalist propaganda, but others took the possibility seriously.[3] Dyer and his many champions, at all civilian and military levels, argued that his severity had forestalled another Indian Mutiny. Much later, in 1939, John Masters remembered coming across terrorist propaganda leaflets crammed with grisly details of the fate of white women and children when 'the day' came.

Whether or not such threats were made later, what mattered was that in 1857 the sepoys had shown disloyalty and turned on their officers and their wives and families. This fact could not be erased and indeed it soon burnt itself deeply into the consciousness of many British soldiers and administrators in India and elsewhere. One immediate consequence was the massive and vindictive terror which followed the Morant Bay uprising in Jamaica in 1865. Psychologically the mutiny created a rift between the British and all their colonial subjects, and made the former over-vigilant and ready to interpret the slightest sign of unrest as the prelude to savage rebellion. This attitude, prevalent in India as elsewhere, was summed up by Major-General Sir George Younghusband, whose service in India and with the Indian Army extended from the Afghan War of 1878 to the campaigns in Mesopotamia in the First World War.[4]

It is never wise to stand studied impertinence, or even the semblance of it, from any Oriental. Politeness and courtesy, by all means, and even camaraderie, as long as these are reciprocated, and all is fair, and square, and above board. But the moment there is a sign of revolt, mutiny, or treachery, of which the symptoms not unusually are a swollen head, and a tendency to incivility, it is wise to hit the Oriental straight between the eyes, and to keep on hitting him thus, till he appreciates exactly what he is, and who is who.

This kind of bluff, no-nonsense approach lasted as long as the Raj and permeated all ranks of the British Army.

Alongside this common belief that in India the white man had to stay firmly in the saddle, there existed much warmth and affection towards the Indian people, and especially the Indian soldier. Generations of officers who served after the Mutiny and, indeed,

211

many who served before it, had come to love the men they commanded. Close bonds of mutual understanding, respect and admiration were established which went far beyond the everyday relationship between officers and other ranks. The memoirs of the officers are a testament to this and one incident, which occurred during the First World War, may speak for many.[5]

> Nathu Ram had been my orderly for a number of years and was devoted to me. When he found me lying wounded, he flopped down beside me. He had been very badly wounded himself. He said, 'Sahib, I am dying.' I said, 'Nathu, so am I. Let us die together.' I held his hand and we lay there expecting death until picked up and carried away by some Highlander.

As in the British Army, Indian regiments developed a sense of corporate pride and honour. An official seal of approval was given to the restored harmony within the Indian Army nearly fifty years after the Mutiny, when Indian troops were issued with the magazine Lee-Enfield rifle, which had been the main arm of British soldiers for some years. This policy continued during the First and Second World Wars when Indian forces were equipped like their British counterparts.

One sequel of the Mutiny had been the rebuilding of the Indian Army into an efficient and reliable force. With memories of the uprising still fresh in 1858, it had been decided that in the future there would always be a garrison of British troops in India so that for every two or three Indian battalions, there would be one British, and that major arsenals would be guarded by British soldiers. This precaution remained official policy until 1939-45, but in emergencies the guidelines had to be ignored. The demands for Indian troops during the First World War meant that the strength of the Indian Army rose from 150,000 in 1914 to about a million in 1918. After the war, the Indian Army was reduced to 118 battalions with a British garrison of 45 battalions, both forces being paid for by the Indian Treasury until 1933. High costs and commitments elsewhere led to the steady reduction of British troops from 57,000 in 1925 to 51,000 in 1938. By this date, nearly two-thirds of the British battalions were dissipated into small detachments, scattered around the country, to support the local police. Yet, with the exception of the expedition to Tibet in 1903-4, active service units always contained at least one-third British troops, even if, as in the North-West Frontier campaigns of 1919-20, it necessitated the deployment of untried British soldiers.

Security on the North-West Frontier was one of the principal duties of the Indian Army. During the surge of imperial expansion in the last quarter of the nineteenth century, Indian troops were deployed in Egypt, the Sudan, Somaliland, East Africa, Malaya and China, sometimes, as in China, as permanent garrisons. The First World War saw Indian troops in action in France (until 1915), Mesopotamia and East Africa. Two and a half million Indians volunteered for the forces between 1939 and 1945, when an Indian navy and air force were created. In the ninety years between the Mutiny and the end of the Raj, the Indian Army had become indispensable to Britain in the maintenance of her role as an imperial global power.

But for what was the Indian Army fighting? The handsome medals given to the soldiers showed the features of the Queen Empress, then her son, grandson and great-grandson, each with the title 'Kaisar-i-Hind'. This was appropriate since the Indian fighting man swore his oath to the King Emperor, obeyed his officers and took his wages. In the eyes of at least one Indian soldier – a prisoner taken by the Japanese in 1942 who later joined the Japanese-sponsored Indian National Army – he was no more than a mercenary hired by men who wished to keep India in subjection. This was a crude view and a minority one. As those Indian officers who tried to dissuade men from service with the INA argued, the soldiers had taken an oath to George VI which was binding and could not be lightly thrown aside. After the war, Indian officers destined to serve in the new Indian Army refused to have former INA men working with them, and their protests about what they considered a dishonour were heeded by Nehru. Loyalty to King Emperor and his officers and their regiment was the mainspring of the Indian soldier's motivation. His British officers liked to talk about the 'warrior classes' of India, those communities and races which, by tradition, had been soldiers and who adhered to ancient martial codes of honour and obedience. The East India Company had found such men compliant and gallant soldiers, and employed them, as did its successor, the Viceregal government. Much earnest stuff was written about the 'warrior races', based on observation, experience and a certain amount of romantic fancy. Lieutenant-General Sir George MacMunn, who had served with the Indian Army from 1892, observed with housemasterly certainty (he in fact

213

turned headmaster on retirement) that 'the mass of the people of India have neither martial aptitude nor physical courage'. He continued, in an analysis called *The Martial Races of India* (1933), to explain this shortcoming as the consequence of 'prolonged years of varying religion ... of early marriage, of premature brides, and juvenile eroticism' combined with hookworm and malaria.[6] At the same time, a subaltern of the 15th Punjabis noted that his battalion needed sturdy, honest men of farming stock. 'The bazaar corner boy who was regarded as corrupt and sly, weaned away from the pure traditions of the deep Indian countryside and its inherent integrity' was definitely not wanted.[7]

Within the villages, there often persisted a long tradition of sending men for service with the army. When his service ended, the returning soldier received a pension, and the progress of his career was a matter of local pride. In Paul Scott's *A Division of the Spoils*, it is recognised that news that some of the men of the Pankot Rifles, due to return to their homes after the war, would bring nothing to distress and shame their communities, for they had been suborned by the Germans into the 'Freies Indien' Army. During the prolonged reading of the death sentences on the mutineers from the 5th Light Infantry at Singapore in 1915, the dishonour of several of the men was highlighted. It was recounted that they came from villages and families which had long traditions of sending young men to the King Emperor's army, and their actions had brought discredit to their communities and kin.

The best fighting men were generally thought to be Sikhs, Rajputs, Gurkhas and Punjabi Muslims, although the subject was often debated among the respective commanders of each group. Certainly, the traditions of the Gurkhas and the Sikhs, who, through their own system of land tenure, produced a large number of landless young men in search of employment, tended towards military service. This obsession with 'natural' warrior races led, in the 1930s, to the choice of men from these races as potential commissioned officers under the scheme of 'Indianisation' of the Army. It was not an entire success and, in the view of one officer who witnessed the development of the scheme, 'other despised tribes did very well'. His own regiment, the Bengal Sappers, was drawn from all religions, castes and communities, and did not suffer in either courage or efficiency.[8]

The concentration of men from a particular caste, community or religion in one battalion had been frowned on since the reforms after the Mutiny. This was not a hard-and-fast rule, for, in certain cases, men of a single race or religion were concentrated in one regiment. In the 1930s, the 15th Punjabis was still formed along traditional lines, with a company of Sikhs, one of Punjabi Muslims, a half company of Muslim Pathans and another of Hindu Dogras. Problems could arise from religious differences; in 1934 a Hindu sentry at Razmak shot dead two Muslims who were ostentatiously slaughtering cattle in his view. Above all, his commanders hoped that the Indian soldier stood above local and national politics. 'The warrior classes respect soldiers more than agitators,' thought Major-General Willcocks who hoped that the Army would keep aloof from the nationalist unrest of India during the 1920s.[9] The bonds of regimental pride, the enjoyment of sport, and loyalty to just, fair-dealing officers were thought to be stronger influences than the patter of the urban nationalist. It was indeed sometimes so. Philip Mason recalled conversations with a former Garhwali subahdar-major who was astonished that the Imperial government in Delhi had surrendered some of its powers to the 'bad characters' of the Congress Party. After Mason had explained to him the coming to power of the Labour Party in Britain, the old soldier was even more bewildered. He imagined that Ramsay MacDonald and Ernest Bevin were no more than 'coolies'; for him and many other Indian soldiers there existed a natural order of command and obedience in the relations between men.

WE KNOW REAL FEELINGS

On 15 February 1915, four companies of the 5th (Native) Light Infantry, a Muslim regiment stationed at Singapore, mutinied. The mutineers murdered seven of their officers and then randomly killed any European they came across. Some hurried to a nearby camp and tried to enlist the help of German internees and POWs, but without success. The uprising was suppressed by a scratch local force, which included Russian and Japanese sailors, and 422 of the miscreants were rounded up during the following days. They were tried by courts martial and thirty-seven were publicly executed. The incident caused much disquiet, and news of it was deliberately withheld from other Indian forces. Much of the blame was placed on local Muslim subversives and their Turco-German propaganda. Behind all these local influences was perceived the hand of German intelligence. Later accounts of the mutiny have played down its ideological dimension and have laid emphasis on the mundane military grievances of the mutineers. Yet it is hard to explain away the violent antipathy towards Europeans as merely the consequence of petty regimental intrigue, squabbles about promotion, and backbiting amongst British officers.[11]

For over twenty years before the Singapore mutiny, the administrations in London and Delhi had been particularly careful not to offend the religious sensibilities of Muslim soldiers. Precautions were taken to ensure that Muslim troops were never placed in a situation where they might have to choose between their faith and loyalty to the King Emperor. The reason for this official sensitivity lay in the recent history of Islam in the Middle East and Asia. For over a century, Britain, France and Russia had extended control over Muslim states and communities in North Africa, West Africa, the Middle East, Central Asia and India. As Islam retreated in the face of colonial conquest, alarm and apprehension were bred amongst all Muslims, even though their new rulers made no attempt to interfere directly with their religion. Islam seemed to be in peril and it was the duty of all Muslims to brace themselves spiritually so as to be ready to stand up to the adversaries of their faith. The successes and failures of one Muslim community were the concern of all; in 1897 news of Turkish victories over the Greeks spread to the Pathan tribesmen of the North-West Frontier and did much to stimulate their resistance to the encroachments by British forces. The focus of opposition to imperial columns and their 'forward policy' were local religious leaders, the mullahs and faqirs whose zeal often earned them the title 'mad'. However unstable such figures appeared to the British, the government in Delhi was unwilling to expose Muslim soldiers to their influence, and none fought in the Frontier wars of 1897-8. Neither could Indian Muslim forces be deployed in Egypt or the Sudan in the event of a Turkish invasion and local uprising.[12] Behind this caution was an uncertainty as to how Muslims would react when ordered to fight their co-religionists who were waging war for Islam. When, in the spring of 1918, the Turkish commander, Enver Pasha, declared that his advance from the Caucasus into Central Asia was a *jihad*, a holy war for Islam, the War Office feared repercussions in India. 'None but white troops' could be trusted to defend India if and when

216

Turkish forces menaced its borders, or so argued one staff officer.[13]

Militarily, it was sensible to avoid any clash of loyalties which could have been provoked by Muslim soldiers having to face an Islamic army fighting under the banners of the faith and urged on by holy men. The outbreak of the First World War made the problem of the loyalty of Muslim soldiers even more difficult. Since 1898, when the Kaiser had publicly announced that Germany was the friend of the world's Muslims, the German and Turkish empires had moved closer together. Both the German and Turkish governments recognised the potential for disruption which could be exploited by religious appeals to Muslims living under British, French or Russian rule or serving in their armies. On 12 November 1914 the first blow was struck in the war for men's minds when the Turkish Sultan, Mehmed V, speaking in his role of caliph and religious leader of Islam, declared a *jihad* against the Allies. In pronouncing a holy war, the Turkish government also announced that the Kaiser himself had been converted to Islam and had undertaken a pilgrimage to Mecca. The message of the *jihad* was conveyed by agents to Egypt, East Africa, and India where there were 66 million Muslims, a fifth of the sub-continent's population. Within a few weeks there was a recrudescence of raiding and attacks on British posts on the North-West Frontier where the Pathans were swift to respond to the caliph's call.

The ordinary Muslim soldier faced a dilemma. On one hand there was the caliph's appeal which called upon him to fight for his faith, and on the other there was that of the Aga Khan, the leader of India's Muslims, who required that his followers stayed loyal to the King Emperor. Something of the crisis of conscience faced by many was reflected in the remarks of Risaldar Major Mur Dad Khan, a cavalryman and father of Ayub Khan. In conversation with a holy man, just after the war, he commented, 'Maulvi Sahib, my only desire is to die under the flag of Islam, but where is that flag? There is no Muslim country today which is free. They are only dominated by colonial powers.'

Turco-German intelligence and its agents were anxious to turn such sentiments to their advantage. The East Intelligence bureau in Berlin and its operatives in India and the Far East were keen to foment any kind of religious unrest, especially in India. This task was assisted by the co-operation of Indian dissidents who, immediately the war began, looked to Germany for encouragement and money to buy arms. The director of the bureau, a former

217

consular official and archaeologist, Max von Oppenheim, and his successors drew into their net both Bengali nationalists – who had been waging a terrorist war against the British for several years – and Sikh Ghadrites. The Ghadr movement had grown up in the 1900s and had collected a large body of activists and sympathisers from among the expatriate Sikh communities in California and British Columbia. The movement had as its aim the creation of a free Punjabi state from which the British would be violently expelled. The Ghadrites hoped for a mutiny among Indian soldiers, like that in 1857, and their propaganda was therefore specially directed towards fellow Sikhs in the Indian Army.

News of the outbreak of war with Germany in August 1914 triggered an exodus of Ghadrites from the United States and Canada towards Hong Kong, Singapore and the Punjab. Their supporters in the United States quickly established contact with German officials there who promised them arms which would be secretly shipped to India and Siam, where both Bengali terrorists and Ghadrites had established bases. In the United States, Franz von Papen, then a consular official, paid for 10,000 rifles and 250 Mauser automatics which were to be shipped to Karachi where the Ghadr leader, Ram Chandra, predicted that thousands of revolutionaries would be waiting to take them. This scheme was bungled and, like its two successors, came to nothing, thanks to the vigilance of British intelligence, the assistance of the American government and the incompetence of the Germans and the Ghadrites.

Inside the Punjab, and unaware of the hitches encountered by their American backers, the Ghadrites proceeded to plan their revolution. The first stage was a series of dacoities and acts of sabotage together with secret canvassing of Sikhs stationed at various garrison towns. In military terms, the British seemed to be at a temporary disadvantage, for the demands of the war in Europe and the Middle East had led to the withdrawal of the bulk of British troops and their replacement by Territorial battalions from Britain. The subversion of the Sikh soldiers was in the hands of an American, N.C. Pringle, and Rash Bihari Bose, the leader of a group which had tried to murder the Viceroy, Lord Hardinge, in 1912. Together with other Ghadrites, they obtained pledges of support from the Sikh squadrons of the 23rd Cavalry at Lahore, the Sikh squadrons of the 12th Cavalry at Meerut, the 28th Pioneers at Meerut and the 26th Punjabis at Ferozepur, all centres of the intended uprising. The Ghadrite network had already been penetrated by police intelligence and at least one agent had been captured, who, under interrogation, revealed details of the timing of the insurrection.

The rebellion and mutinies had been planned for 19 February 1915, but the authorities, forewarned and under the formidable direction of the Lieutenant-Governor of the Punjab, Sir Michael O'Dwyer, moved quickly. The Ghadrite leadership was arrested and the regiments infected by their propaganda were disarmed. With its leaders either in custody or in flight, the revolution was stillborn, and the subsequent Defence of India Act gave the administration powers to detain without trial suspected Ghadrites and Bengali revolutionaries. Schemes for invasion from Siam also came to nothing. In the aftermath of the Ghadrite plot, would-be mutineers from the 12th and 23rd Cavalry, the 26th Punjabis and the 28th Pioneers, were arrested and tried. Some were executed, including a number from the 23rd Cavalry, who had been found in possession of bombs. It would be impossible to say what the results of the uprising and mutinies would have been and there is no evidence to suggest that the Ghadrite movement had much deep, popular support among the Sikhs in the Punjab. Given that Sikhs comprised only one and a half squadrons of the two cavalry regiments, it is hard to say whether they would have been successful, in spite of their bombs, in enlisting their fellow *sowars* who were Muslims and Hindus.

The forestalling of the mutinies in the Punjab had been the result of good intelligence work by the police. In Singapore, local intelligence was less than effective in its efforts to isolate and handle local subversion and, more importantly, anticipate its consequences. Ghadrite agitators had been active since the autumn of 1914 and may well have played a part in encouraging restlessness among Sikhs of the Malay States Guides. The regiment had been founded in 1873, from which time its duties kept it in the Malay states as a garrison. Prior to the war, the Guides had volunteered for service in China during the Boxer Rebellion, but their offers had been refused. In November 1914, they had been asked if they wished to serve abroad and appeared, on the surface, to be willing, but in December they had changed their minds. According to the Governor of the Straits Settlements, the Guides' turnabout was the consequence of their apprehensions about 'reports of casualties at

219

the front'. The Sikhs' terms of enlistment gave them the legal right to refuse service outside Malaya, but there were fears that their attitude was a reflection of disloyalty. 'It is undesirable to maintain troops, who having volunteered for active service, subsequently change their minds,' wrote Sir Bertram Cubitt, the Assistant Secretary at the War Office, and, on his advice, all but one company of the Guides were transferred to Penang. The regiment's mood changed, for by September 1915 it had agreed to service in Aden, but by this time the War Office, still suspicious of the men's demeanour, had agreed to its reduction in strength.

Accounts of the heavy losses during the first months of the fighting in 1914 had perturbed other Indian troops. Mahsuds and Mohmands from the North-West Frontier deserted from the 129th Baluchis since, as their colonel noted, they were lacking 'sentiments of patriotism' with which to sustain morale in the face of casualty lists from France.[14] Such behaviour was exceptional, but news of the great battles in Europe was causing concern to the Muslim sepoys of the 5th Light Infantry in Singapore. 'We receive letters and we know real feelings,' recalled one mutineer, although, in his evidence, he was not clear whether the correspondence came from friends in India or from Ghadrites in the United States who were in the habit of sending propaganda by post to Indian troops. There were, however, those in Singapore who were willing to play on the soldiers' feelings. Kassim Ismail Mansur, a Turkish sympathiser and coffee house proprietor, had made contacts with fellow Muslims in the 5th Light Infantry and with Sikhs from the Guides. He visited soldiers in their lines and entertained them in his coffee house, where he encouraged them to resist service abroad. Kassim Ismail also attempted to make contact by letter with the Turkish consul in Rangoon, whom he asked to send a warship to Singapore to assist a Muslim uprising there. Kassim's activities came to the attention of the local police and he was arrested on 23 January. He was found guilty of treason and executed at the end of May. The coming of a warship, a German one, was one theme used in the anti-British sermons of Nur Alam Shah, who preached at the Kampong Java mosque. Warrant officers from the 5th Light Infantry were among his congregation, and after the mutiny he assisted at least one of them when he was a fugitive. Speculation about enemy warships probably had its roots in reports of the activities of the German cruiser *Emden* which had lately been at large in the Bay of Bengal and, on 28 October 1914, had engaged and sunk a Russian cruiser and a French destroyer in the Penang roads. The *Emden* had itself been sunk soon after, but its destructive cruise had tarnished local British prestige.

Sermons in the mosque on Fridays may well have increased the anxieties of many Muslims in the 5th Light Infantry. One mutineer later confessed that 'the *Maulvi* [a Muslim holy man attached to the regiment] had told them that although it is true that they had fought against Moslems previously, the present war is on a different footing as it entails fighting against the head of their religion, i.e. the Sultan at Stamboul.' It was a disappointment to this man's interrogators that he had no knowledge of the appeal to Muslims by the Aga Khan. There were hints that soldiers on guard duty at the dock were approached by Ghadrite agitators, but local intelligence was never able to pinpoint the precise nature of their involvement in the mutiny. Nevertheless, soon after the mutiny, the local officer commanding, Colonel Ridout, turned down offers of reinforcements from the 25th and 26th Punjabis, both of which had recently been the subject of Ghadrite attentions.

Direct German involvement in the Singapore mutiny is impossible to trace. In August 1915, a German agent, George Kraft, was arrested in Singapore and, when questioned, revealed his government's plans for making mischief in the Far East. Described by Colonel Ridout as having 'coarse ugly features', Kraft had been born in Dutch Sumatra, and until a few months before had been serving in the trenches. It was there that he had heard of the Singapore mutiny, which he later considered to have been promoted by local German intrigue, not by the government in Berlin. His own brief, which he disclosed to Ridout, was to assist the subversion of Indian troops in Burma, and a raid on the Andaman Islands penal settlement to release political dissidents. He admitted to the existence of an 'extensive organisation of secret service for stirring up revolution in the East' backed by Germany and with its centre in Bangkok. The Siamese, still brooding after the loss of territory in northern Malaya to Britain, were willing partners in this enterprise. Subversion in Malaya had, he asserted, been hindered by the prompt suppression of the mutiny in February. Whether or not this was so, it was clear from Kraft's extensive confession that the mutiny had taken the Germans, like the British, unawares. His mission was a belated attempt to seek out some advantage in what appeared a suitable area.

The mutiny also encouraged local Muslim and Sikh groups. A

letter from M.R. Sarma, a resident in Sumatra, was intercepted by the Singapore police on its way to the vice-president of the local Muslim League.[15] It contained 500 guilders, collected by Sumatran Muslims and Sikhs, and asked when the expected Malayan revolution was about to begin. The swift repression of the mutiny within a matter of days had given the mutineers no chance to test local sympathy towards them. There were 300,000 Indians throughout Malaya who might possibly have been willing to make common cause with the mutineers, and a few did help individual fugitives. Yet if the mutiny had been intended as a call for an uprising by Muslims and Sikhs against British rule in Singapore, the ground had been very poorly prepared by local anti-British elements.

The full and exact extent to which the mutineers of the 5th Light Infantry had been swayed by Pan-Islamic and Ghadrite propaganda cannot be judged. The troops had certainly been exposed to agitators, and the casual murders of Europeans in the streets was just the kind of slaughter advocated by the Ghadrites and had formed part of the scenario for their revolt in the Punjab. Three of the NCOs who formed the leadership of the mutineers were members of the congregation of the Kampong Java mosque. One of them, Jemadar Chiste Khan, had busied himself with spreading anti-British propaganda among the sepoys whom he also encouraged in malingering to avoid parades. It was perhaps natural that men who nursed resentments against the army system were also likely to extend their grumbling to embrace wider, anti-British sentiments.

Chiste Khan, Colour-Havildar Imtiaz Khan, and Subadar Dunde Khan were all Rajputs and at loggerheads with other NCOs of different regional and racial backgrounds. Their mood had been particularly sullen for a few weeks before the mutiny after Imtiaz Khan had been slighted in a matter of promotion after Pathans had objected to his advancement to the rank of subadar. This source of grumbling was of course small beer and no cause for anything more than backbiting in the mess, although Imtiaz Khan and his cronies were able to spread their message amongst their men. They played on fears about posting overseas, perhaps to the killing grounds of France, and may well have sowed deep doubts about the cause for which they might soon have to fight.

The sepoys' misgivings were given considerable credibility

during the regiment's departure parade on 15 February 1915. All the men were inspected by the local officer commanding, Colonel Ridout. At the end of the inspection, he addressed the men, and his speech was rendered into Hindustani in such a way that many of his audience were left with the impression that they were about to join the Indian Expeditionary Force in France, rather than Hong Kong which was in fact their destination. This misunderstanding immediately caused bewilderment and alarm. There were shouts of protest from the men of A, B, C and D Companies as they marched off. For the next seven hours the rumour that these men were soon to be shipped to France worked as a catalyst for mutiny. Working behind the scenes were Imtiaz Khan, Chiste Khan and Dunde Khan, but the precise tenor of their arguments to their men is not known. They were sufficiently convincing to persuade over four hundred men from the four companies to join the conspiracy and risk a rebellion.

The plotting in the regimental lines was hurried. The regimental troopship, SS *Fiji*, was already lying in the Singapore roads, and that afternoon the regiment's stock of ammunition, over 30,000 rounds, was being loaded onto lorries for transport to the local ordnance depot. This ammunition was the mutineers' first target. At a signal from a sentry who fired into the fatigue party, other men from A and B Companies opened fire. One of the loaders was wounded and the rest scattered. Under the direction of Imtiaz Khan, Chiste Khan and Dunde Khan, the mutineers broke open the boxes and distributed the cartridges. Their next objective was the Tanglin Barracks compound where there were 295 POWs from the *Emden*. About a hundred mutineers under a havildar set off from the Alexandra Barracks, and attacked and overwhelmed the camp guard, which was drawn from local volunteer forces. Fifteen were killed in the exchange of fire, including an officer who was 'fiendishly bayoneted' and a POW who was hit by a stray bullet. The POWs were unco-operative; they refused to take rifles and ammunition from the mutineers, and instead did what they could for the wounded in the hospital. Eleven did use the confusion as a cover for an escape, and eight of them eventually got back to Germany.

The disinclination of the Germans to take any part in the uprising was a blow to the mutineers. A further blow came when a party under Dunde Khan went to the quarters of the one company of the Malay State Guides which had been left behind in Singapore.

Here they shot dead a British officer, but found the Sikhs lukewarm to their enterprise although some joined when coerced. Other parties, which had set out from Alexandra Barracks for Singapore City and Keppel Harbour, also faced setbacks. On their way they accosted Europeans and murdered several, killing for which the only motive must have been racial – local Chinese were spared. Inept attempts to enter police stations and murder British police officers also failed, and by the early evening most of the mutineers appear to have withdrawn to their barracks. In the course of just over two hours, they had shot dead fourteen civilians, including a woman and a Malay chauffeur, and over twenty British officers and local volunteers. Yet in spite of the element of surprise which they had had at the start of the mutiny, the mutineers had gained no outside support or any strategic points.

Most importantly, the mutineers had been unable to prevent the local civilian and military authorities from taking counter-measures once they had woken up to what was happening. The first reactions of the officers of the 5th Light Infantry had been fumbling. Rifle-fire from the mutineers quickly convinced junior officers that any attempt to talk the men back to their obedience would have been foolhardy and fruitless. Colonel Martin, who was having a nap when the mutiny began, collected some officers and NCOs together and retired with them to his bungalow, which he placed in a state of siege. He received offers of help from the men from the four loyal companies, but on the advice of a native NCO, he did not issue them with ammunition. Fired on by the mutineers and lacking a lead from the officers, the loyal men had little choice but to scatter, although some later obtained cartridges from the mutineers and returned to assist Colonel Martin. Disbelief and muddle marked the first reaction of the police and army authorities in Singapore. It was an official holiday to celebrate Chinese New Year and much of the shooting was at first thought to be firecrackers. As telephone calls and eyewitness accounts of the murders piled up, the local authorities soon realised what was going on and began to take hurried precautionary measures. Individual initiative, so lacking at the Alexandra Barracks, was more commonplace in Singapore. An ex-sergeant-major at HQ had the good sense to alert the commander of the sloop *Cadmus*, then at anchor in the harbour, who immediately sent an armed party of bluejackets ashore. Major Dewar, after seeing a murder from the verandah of his bungalow, took command of a detachment of Sikh police and engaged a group of mutineers who quickly made off. The sailors from *Cadmus* also discovered the mutineers' reluctance to fight after a few exchanges of fire in the streets.

Martial law was declared at 7.30, and European women and children were evacuated to ships in the harbour. The energetic Colonel Brownlow of the garrison artillery was placed in command and at his HQ at the Central Police Station began to enlist a force of volunteers. It embraced Methodist ministers, who had been attending a conference in Singapore, and a sizeable number of local Japanese. A watch was kept throughout the city, and at 3.00 a.m. Colonel Brownlow led 176 volunteers, armed with mid-Victorian rifles and a Gatling gun (oddly, since there were six Maxims in Singapore) amongst other weapons, to relieve Colonel Martin. The mutineers put up a feeble resistance and then melted away. The whole affair had a *Boy's Own Paper* stamp about it and a bravado which contrasted with the pusillanimity of Colonel Martin and other officers of the 5th Light Infantry. The official inquiry later castigated them for their tergiversation.

> The time-honoured maxim of 'l'audace, toujours l'audace' when dealing with Orientals was apparently lost sight of. We believe that resolute action by a formed body of Europeans would, even at this stage of the outbreak, have exercised a marked effect upon the course of the mutiny.

This call for boldness owed much to hindsight. After the first outbreak, the mutineers had soon lost heart and offered no more than a timid resistance to armed police and sailors. Even before Brownlow's sally, there were indications that the mutineers were seized by a sense of helplessness. Many had already run for the jungle, tried to swim for the mainland or sought refuge and anonymity in local mosques, coffee houses and railwaymen's huts. Here and there they were sympathetically received by Sikh watchmen and the poorer class of Arab, but many other local residents were tempted by the offer of a reward of a hundred Malay dollars for any information which led to the arrest of a mutineer.

More and more sailors and soldiers were pouring into Singapore to assist in the hunting of the fugitives. Troops were sent by the Sultan of Johore who joined forces with sailors from Japanese, Russian and French warships which had been summoned by wireless. These men were split into small detachments which patrolled in search of fugitives. Occasionally, small groups of

225

mutineers put up some resistance when discovered, but the only casualties amongst the hunters were two Russian seamen who were wounded. By 31 March, fifty-one mutineers were thought to be still at large. Those who had been rounded up were vetted by officers and loyal NCOs and 202 suspects were weeded out for trial by court martial. Of these, forty-seven were sentenced to death and the rest to varying terms of imprisonment.

The first executions began on 23 February when Chiste Khan and Dunde Khan were publicly shot in front of the Outram Road gaol. Soon after, a further twenty-one were shot in the presence of large crowds. The firing squad of over a hundred men was drawn from local detachments which had suffered casualties during the fighting. It was a grotesque spectacle since the name and sentence of each man was read aloud in three languages, a ritual which unnerved the condemned men. One cried out in strain, others followed and soon all were 'swaying, praying and shouting', in the words of Police Cadet Dickinson who was standing nearby and taking photographs. The firing squad lost patience and fired an ill-aimed volley which left several mutineers wounded. They were shot with revolvers by prison officers.

An official inquiry followed. The members regretted the backbiting amongst officers of the 5th Light Infantry and censured all but three for a 'lamentable want of initiative' in the time which followed the outbreak of the mutiny. Colonel Martin was regarded as too relaxed in matters of discipline by some of his officers, whose obstreperousness and cliquishness was considered 'improper and subversive of discipline'. The four companies which had mutinied were known to have had an unwholesome record for indiscipline, and had clearly come under the sway of discontented NCOs. The three NCOs who led the mutiny had intimate connections with the local network of pro-German and Turkish sympathisers and agents. They were also covertly encouraging their men to resist foreign service and propagated religious doubts about the war.

There was nothing about the mutiny which suggested long-term planning. Men already disturbed were pushed into an uprising by what they thought they had heard on the parade ground on the morning of the 15th. The circumstances seemed in the men's favour; the Regular British battalion on garrison duty had been recalled to France, and the day before the mutiny the French cruiser *Montcalm* had sailed away. Many of the credulous may have believed that they would be helped by the German POWs and even a German man-o'-war. No such aid was forthcoming, and at the first sign of determined resistance, the mutiny crumbled and became a mass desertion.

The compilers of Turco-German, Pan-Islamic propaganda quickly took over the mutiny and used it as an example of Muslims fighting back against the infidels. Singapore gossip in the days after the mutiny was full of tales about mutineers found in possession of large sums of German cash, which in fact was money plundered from regimental funds. German subversion, together with obvious domestic problems inside the regiment appeared, in both Singapore and London, to be the explanation for the mutiny. Yet one captured mutineer admitted to having 'real feelings' – what were they? Perhaps under the influence of Muslim preachers, the reports of the slaughter in France and fears that they might soon be drawn into that war, some of the men of the 5th Light Infantry had begun to ask questions about themselves. For whose advantage were they fighting? The men were also troubled by racial tensions which exploded in the killing of British civilians and officers, many of whom had been in no position to resist them. Memories of these killings came to surface in 1934 when the Malayan Europeans were disturbed by the news that an Indian regiment was to replace a Burmese one in Malaya.

Whatever their true feelings, four hundred or so men of the 5th Light Infantry suddenly decided that they were no longer going to serve compliantly in a war which many did not believe in. The Singapore mutiny was a backward-looking event; it was an explosion of anger born of religious misgivings and rumour very much like the mutiny of 1857. The mutineers possessed no ideology nor any very clear grievances and the uprising soon disintegrated. The regiment survived and, reconstituted around the loyal men, was sent for service in the Cameroons a few months later. The problem of purely religious loyalty did not reappear during the First World War which saw no further serious unrest among Indian forces.

In the months after the war there was much Muslim agitation throughout India in the wake of the dismemberment of the Turkish Empire and the removal of the Sultan. This unrest had its most serious repercussions on the North-West Frontier where, during the 1919 Afghan War, many hundreds of tribal militiamen mutinied and deserted to the Afghan or Wazir insurgents.

ASIA FOR ASIANS

The Singapore mutiny of 1915 had been an isolated precursor of a broader and more formidable challenge to British and indeed European supremacy in Asia which emerged between the wars. In its widest sense, this challenge took two forms. The first was the expansion of popular movements, inspired and led by educated elites, which clamoured for responsible government, and the second was the growing and vigorous power of Japan. These two affronts to European paramountcy in Asia were linked, for Japan's victory over Russia in 1904 had awakened many Asians to the possibility that their European rulers were not invincible in war. As Japan pushed towards economic, political and military dominance in the Far East, her successes were applauded by Asian nationalists who saw them as examples of what Asians could do unaided. When, in 1941-42, Japan made her spectacular bid for primacy in the Far East, her rulers could utilise the slogan 'Asia for the Asians' and cultivate local nationalists.

The Western reaction to the new forces in Asia was fumbling and dismissive. The independence movement in India was countered by a mixture of concession and moderate repression, while the Japanese were disregarded on the grounds that as Asians they were mentally, industrially and militarily incapable of shaking the foundations of European hegemony in Asia. Britain and the United States were woefully misinformed about the skill and efficiency of the Japanese, who remained, in Churchill's phrase, 'little yellow men'. This contempt permeated the minds of politicians, administrators and naval and military men at all levels and took many forms. One of the more absurd was the official reaction to the Japanese bombing and strafing of Hong Kong in December 1941, where it was assumed that, whilst the aircraft showed Japanese markings, the pilots must have been German for they were so accurate. Yet, as Duff Cooper concluded in a report compiled in the same year, 'We are now faced by vast populations of industrious, intelligent and brave Asians who are unwilling to acknowledge the superiority of Europeans or their right to special privileges in Asia.'[16]

Yet, in order to throw back the Japanese, Britain had to mobilise just over two and a half million Indians alone. They were fighting in what both Britain and the United States officially and

228

unofficially considered as a race war. The adversary was the 'Jap' – a word of racial scorn – against whom there were deep feelings of revulsion, caused in part by the mistreatment and humiliation of European prisoners in Japanese camps. Coloured fighting men found such sentiments less easy to accept. One black American soldier suggested that his epitaph might read: 'Here lies a black man, killed fighting a yellow man for the protection of a white man'. In South Africa, General Smuts had heard natives argue, 'Why fight against Japan? We are oppressed by the whites and we will not fare worse under the Japanese.'[17] From the standpoint of some Indian nationalists, the prospect of a Japanese victory in Asia offered the chance to secure self-government. This argument, often backed by intimidation, persuaded 20,000 Indian soldiers held by the Japanese to volunteer for the Indian National Army and fight against the Allies in Burma.

However credulous some of these men may have been, many of them believed that they were fighting for India, whereas their opponents were waging a war to reinstate the old order of European paramountcy. The same thought troubled many Americans who asked whether they were at war with Japan just to restore the European colonies in the East. Moreover, were the war aims laid down in the Atlantic Charter of 1941 compatible with Imperial government as practised in Malaya, Indochina or the Dutch East Indies? Whereas in the European theatre of the war, the ideological battle lines were clear, in Asia they were blurred and, for the non-European soldier, often bewildering.

Two mutinies were the outcome of this mental confusion. One, by a handful of Sinhalese artillerymen stationed on the Cocos-Keeling Islands, was a small affair, although it shed much light on the crisis of loyalty faced by Asians during this war. The other, in February 1946, involved large numbers of sailors from the Royal Indian Navy and was a violent side-product of the political agitation for self-government. Both mutinies reflected the transformation of attitudes which had taken place within India over the past thirty years. Each, in its way, also showed that a limit had been set on British power in Asia.

The Cocos-Keeling mutiny occurred on the night of 8-9 May 1942 in the middle of a bleak period in which British prestige in Asia was at its lowest. Since Japan had declared war in December 1941, her land, sea and air forces had overrun Hong Kong, Malaya and Burma. In February 1942 the vaunted base at Singapore had

229

surrendered after a desultory defence, and soon after the Americans had been forced to pull out of the Philippines. At the beginning of April, Britain suffered a further blow when a Japanese fleet crossed the Bay of Bengal and carrier-borne aircraft attacked Colombo and Trincomalee as Royal Navy units prepared to withdraw westwards to the sanctuary of the East African coast. North-east India waited for a Japanese invasion and so too did Australia, which suffered Japanese air raids.

The Cocos-Keeling Islands, hitherto a backwater of the war, was now in the front line. A U-shaped scattering of coral islands, the Cocos-Keelings were an imperial oddity since they had been more or less the private estates of the Clunies-Ross family for just over a hundred years. They did possess an RAF base, established in 1941, and an important wireless station. Lying in the Indian Ocean, 2,000 miles south-east of Ceylon and just under 1,000 miles north-west of the Australian mainland, the islands assumed considerable strategic importance in 1942. Part of the small force stationed there was No. 11 Battery of the 1st Coast Regiment of the Ceylon Coast Artillery.

This detachment, commanded by a British captain, was entirely Sinhalese and had shown no indications of restlessness or dissatisfaction with their remote posting in the midst of what was, for a brief time, a Japanese lake. One of them, later sentenced to death for his part in the mutiny, afterwards claimed that he joined the Army freely and he enjoyed the life there. Another, also under sentence of death, offered no other explanation for his behaviour than simple folly. He had no grievances against the Army, and was unable to explain why he had fired on an officer.

The mutiny's ringleader, a bombardier, possessed many grievances and expressed them forcefully, before and after the uprising. As an NCO he had some authority and he appears, for at least four weeks before the mutiny, to have wielded considerable influence over the ten men who joined him. Yet, while he seems to have been able to compel rather gullible comrades to share in his enterprise, his own state of mind was confused. Whilst in custody, he chatted to his guards who were anxious to know his motives. He told one that sometime before he had had anti-British feelings. He said that the black man was always trodden down, and why could they not be equal?

The Bombardier also claimed that his anti-British feelings had taken root in his mind when he had lived in Kelantan in Malaya. This seems quite plausible, since the Malayan white 'plantocracy' had become a byword for racial arrogance. Shortly before the fall of Singapore, planters' wives had protested when commissioned Indian officers had been allowed to use club swimming pools. Such people were not chastened by their misfortunes, for in the summer of 1945 British soldiers were irritated by the disdainful manner in which they were treated by the local European women, especially planters' wives.

Whatever slights the Bombardier had suffered at the hands of the *tuans*, they had left him with a bitter resentment. He was anti-European rather than anti-British, believed firmly in Asia for the Asiatics and wished to do some thing to further the Japanese war aims. Personal setbacks in Ceylon, including a failed love affair, made him volunteer for services in the Cocos-Keeling Islands.

The Bombardier's political ideals were the mainspring for his mutiny which he planned as a *coup* which would deliver the islands into Japanese hands. Not all who listened to him took his schemes seriously – one, who later played a peripheral part in the uprising, thought that he would never act as he planned. In his conversations, the Bombardier explained how he intended to disarm the guard, get the sentry to murder the officer on duty and then take over the battery. He then thought that he would lure the detachment from Direction Island to the battery, kill them and then destroy the wireless station. Some listeners were puzzled and they told him not to be mad. On another occasion, the Bombardier contemplated seizing some boats belonging to the islands' owner and taking them to Christmas Island, 550 miles to the east.

None of those drawn, closely or loosely, into this conspiracy were told when it would take place, so the uprising was a surprise to them. Just before midnight on the night of 8-9 May, the Bombardier, who was NCO of the guard, and two confederates who were part of the guard, locked up their comrades. The duty officer was roused, found the guards locked up, and was informed that someone had got into the artillery store. He was fired on by one of the mutineers and wounded. He then heard the Bombardier calling out for him. Thereafter everything was pandemonium with wild shooting in the dark. The Bombardier had got hold of a Tommy gun, but, unable to fix the magazine, he abandoned it for a bren gun. He placed his followers in the gun battery and opened a wild fire which he kept up for two hours. His fire was directed at the gate to his detachment's quarters, his intention being to hit the men as they crowded in, and he also hoped to kill his commanding officer 'because he was white'. In the confusion, one man was killed and another, a mutineer, was wounded. Another mutineer ran off when he heard the machine-gunfire, while the commanding officer gathered twenty-one loyal men together.

In the darkness and disorder, it was impossible for loyal men and mutineers to tell each other apart. The Bombardier, realising that there was no chance of success, surrendered. Three days later, he and ten others were tried by a court martial. The evidence against them was overwhelming and seven were sentenced to death. When the convicted men were shipped to Colombo, the Viceory confirmed three of the sentences. The Bombardier was hanged in Colombo gaol on 5 July, and two other mutineers, one who had tried to murder an officer and another who shot dead a fellow gunner, were executed on the following two days. In mitigation of his actions, the Bombardier pleaded that the events of that night were the result of jealousies and resentments which had been smouldering for years.

The Cocos-Keeling mutiny was the expression of one man's rage created by a sense of injustice and humiliation, real or imaginary, and a feeling that he was fighting against his own peoples' interests for the wrong side. Seen from the perspective of the wider war in the Pacific and Asia, the affair on the Cocos-Keeling Islands was, like the islands themselves, of very slight significance. Yet one man's pent-up fury and its eruption were representative of wider sentiments felt by many Asians.

WHAT IT MEANS TO BE FREE

Over 3,700,000 Indians served with the Allied forces during the Second World War. It was a splendid response which seemed to affirm the old soldiers' faith that the warrior classes of Indian society had been untouched by twenty years of nationalist agitation. Yet even Churchill, whose faith in the essential soundness of the warrior classes was as firm as any, was troubled by fears of political agitation which could turn Indian soldiers against Britain.[18] His anxieties proved groundless, for in spite of efforts by nationalists to subvert troops, there were no outbreaks of disloyalty.*

There were signs of restlessness amongst Sikhs, as although they took pride of place as members of the warrior classes, the growth of nationalism, and fears that the Punjab might eventually pass to either Hindu or Muslim rule, had made many Sikhs anxious. Early in 1940, the Sikh squadron of the Central India Horse mutinied at Bombay and refused to embark for the Middle East. This unit contained *sowars* who were sympathetic to the *Kirti Lehar* movement, which was Communist-inspired and drew support from Punjabi peasants. The squadron, on arrival at Bombay, had been forced to wait in a railway siding for thirty-six hours, and the disgruntled men were ripe for the arguments of their *Kirti Lehar* comrades. The men involved were tried and sentenced to transportation to the penal colony on the Andaman Islands, from where they were rescued when the Japanese took them in 1942. Other Sikhs were ashamed and the Sikh squadron from the 19th Lancers volunteered to take the mutineers' place on foreign service.

In the Punjab, there was much anxiety about the region's future when India received independence, and this led to some resistance to recruiting. A more serious, openly pro-Japanese mutiny occurred amongst the men of a small detachment of Indians of the Hong Kong and Singapore Artillery. The unit of thirty-three (including one British officer and four NCOs) was stationed on Christmas Island, which came under Japanese bombardment on 4 March 1942. With no hope of relief, the detachment hoisted the white flag, and, on the morning of the 11th, the Indians mutinied and murdered the British officer and NCOs in the hope that they would gain some favour from the Japanese who were about to land. After the war, they were discovered in Java and transferred to Singapore, where they were tried. Of the seven who were tried in December 1946, one was sentenced to hang (this was commuted to penal servitude for life) and five others were given long prison

---

* Sriram, one the central figures in R.K. Narayan's *Waiting for Mahatma* (1954), breaks into an army cantonment and pastes up bills calling for the soldiers to mutiny: blood from a cut suffered whilst getting through the barbed wire was imagined by him to have been shed in the cause of Indian freedom.

sentences. An eighth man was detected and tried in June 1948, sentenced to death, and then given a life sentence.

India had declared war on Germany in 1939, at the sole insistence of the Viceroy, Lord Linlithgow, much to the vexation of nationalists who saw the gesture as a token that India was still dependent upon Britain, without a political will of its own. The Congress Party's attitude to the war was one of disobliging neutrality, but the Muslim League, anxious to secure British approval for partition and the creation of a Muslim Pakistan, backed the war effort. Political agitation by Congress intensified during 1942 with the 'Quit India' campaign, but the wave of disorders which reached their climax during August were contained by British and Indian forces. After, it was clear that independence would not be achieved during the war, in spite of Nehru's suggestion to Roosevelt that a free India would actually offer more in the way of manpower to the Allied war effort. Yet it was also clear that independence would come, the only question being when and in what form.

Military service heightened the political consciousness of many Indian soldiers, especially those who served abroad. They could not help but be infected by Allied propaganda which claimed that they were fighting for ideals of personal and political freedom throughout the world. Just as British soldiers expected the termination of the war to herald a better and more just ordering of life at home, Indian soldiers came to see victory as having fruits for their own country. This feeling was expressed by an Indian naval rating involved in the 1946 mutiny at Bombay. 'We have been in a few countries which have recently been liberated from the fascists, we have seen in the people a new life, a new spirit. Thus we have learned what it means to be free.'[19] Such sentiments help to explain why the mutineers demanded that Indian troops were to be removed from the Dutch East Indies where they were serving in operations to restore Dutch colonial government. The war in Asia had not been waged to deliver Asians from Japanese Imperial rule to Dutch, or, for that matter, British or French.

The individual experiences of some Indians heightened their sense of nationalism. One Indian, who served during the seaborne landings on the Burma coast during 1945, recalled that he and his comrades were always placed at the bottom of the pile when it came to shipboard accommodation, rations or evacuation from beaches. The mindless racism of some European soldiers ('Hi,

Black Bastard!') was wounding and fostered nationalism.[20] The Germans and, later, the Japanese were both keen to take advantage of the seemingly irreconcilable position of Indian soldiers in British service and hoped to encourage defectors. The first architect of these schemes was the fanatic nationalist, Subhas Chandra Bose, who believed that India would be freed from British rule only by an armed struggle. He had flirted with Nazi Germany before the war, but found that Hitler had a deep respect for the British Raj in India. The war altered Hitler's attitude, and in 1942 the fugitive Bose was more warmly received in Berlin, where plans were made for the creation of the 'Freies Indien' corps, which was to be manned by Indian POWs in Germany. The unit's principal value was as a propaganda exercise and its military duties were limited to coastal defence.

Japan, not burdened with Germany's racial theories, took the matter of the formation of an Indian army of liberation more seriously. The Japanese of course had a better opportunity, in the shape of the 60,000 Indian prisoners who had fallen into their hands during the Malayan campaign of 1941-2. The first stages of the operation were managed by Captain Mohan Singh, a Sikh enlisted man who had been commissioned and was a nationalist. Later, the Indian National Army was run by Bose, who set up the Azad Hind (Free Indian Government) in October 1943 after he had been shipped by U-boat and Japanese submarine from Germany to Malaya. The Indian National Army grew to be over 20,000 strong, with a large Sikh contingent. The motives of the men who joined were various. When captured, many Indian soldiers were demoralised and disillusioned by the moral and physical disintegration of British authority in Malaya. The shameful *sauve qui peut* attitude of many Europeans and a few officers, together with the bungling which permitted the collapse of resistance, destroyed the reputation of Britain in the eyes of many Indians. Many were therefore susceptible to Japanese propaganda, and to Indian propagandists who held out for them the chance to fight for the liberation of India. Where nationalist persuasion failed, coercion, accompanied by brutality, was used and there were some recruits who tagged along to get better treatment from the Japanese. The defection of thousands of Indians was not a mutiny, although many loyal officers and men tried to dissuade the renegades and suffered accordingly. Fear, bewilderment and a feeling that they might be striking a blow to help their fellow countrymen were the motives which drew men into the INA, but they were not the moral cement which created an effective fighting force. In battle, the INA proved a mixed blessing to its Japanese masters; during the Imphal campaign over 2,500 surrendered or deserted back to the British and a further 3,000 gave themselves up during the British advance to Rangoon in 1944-5.

The fate of the men who had joined the INA posed a dilemma for the British. In sorting through the flotsam of the army, it was found that at least three out of five men had been duped by propaganda and deserved no retribution. Among the rest was a minority which had condoned and committed murder and torture, and Delhi was determined that these men should answer for their crimes just like civilian collaborators elsewhere in British Asia. Indian nationalists did not regard these men as traitors, and therefore reacted angrily at the decision to try three ex-officers – a Sikh, a Hindu and a Muslim – at the Red Fort in Delhi. The INA trials quickly became a focus for all Indian nationalists, and for a short time allowed Hindus and Muslims to cease their bickering about partition. Nehru, the Congress Party leader, espoused the accused men's cause, and a bevy of India's best lawyers was called in to defend them. Serious riots broke out in many cities during the trials in December 1945. The three men were found guilty and given prison sentences, which the Viceroy, Lord Wavell, confirmed in spite of the pleas for pardon from Nehru and other nationalist leaders. Popular support for the INA men continued, and, on 7 March 1946, Indian soldiers who took part in the victory parade through Delhi were hooted by the mob. Political pressure was kept up, and while Nehru later changed his attitude, demands for a pardon were repeatedly set before Wavell and his successor, Lord Mountbatten. In the end, the attitude of the loyal Indian Army was decisive. Former commissioned officers who had served with the British throughout the war steadfastly refused to have any truck with former INA men. Since these men were to be the officers of the new Indian and Pakistani armies, their views prevailed, as did the code of honour which they represented.

The fuss about the INA trials came at an awkward time for the British authorities, and also for the leadership of Congress and the Muslim League. Churchill had been defeated in the British general election in 1945, and his departure marked the removal of a major stumbling block to Indian independence – at the end of August he had written to Wavell and pleaded with him to 'Keep a bit of

India', and after independence in 1947 he told Mountbatten that he had delivered him a blow akin to being struck with a riding crop![21] Yet whilst the new Labour government was sympathetic to Indian independence, no one was clear as to the form of the new state or states and the timetable for self-government. It was, however, clear that the days of the Raj were numbered, but the nationalist leadership was anxious about how the transition to the new government would take place. In particular they wished to avoid violence.

Since 1919 and under Gandhi's tutelage, the Indian national movement had attempted to secure its goal peacefully. This had proved impossible, since the nature of the nationalist message, and the temperament of many who heard it, frequently triggered off riots. At the end of 1945, Wavell was fearful that more disorders were on the way and, he warned London, 'It would not be wise to try the Indian Army too highly in the suppression of their own people.' There had been similar caution about the deployment of Indian forces against disturbances stirred up by Burman nationalists. As to British troops, they were few on the ground and many were anxious to be demobilised. A year before, in October 1944, Wavell had judged that 'the British people will not consent to be associated with a policy of repression, nor will world opinion approve it, nor will British soldiers wish to stay here in large numbers after the war to hold the country down'. The onus for keeping order rested on the Indian Army.

The test for that loyalty came, unexpectedly, on 18 February 1946 with the start of a widespread mutiny amongst Indian sailors of the Royal Indian Navy.[22] The RIN had expanded considerably during the war and at the time of the mutiny its numbers stood at 28,000. The hurried expansion of the Indian Navy had created a number of problems, the greatest being in finding suitable officers. Many were unfitted, and a British officer later commented, 'I doubt if many of these European officers would have been officer material in their own countries.' They included former planters from Ceylon and Malaya, South Africans and Indians, but here the navy had to compete for men of high quality with the army 'and the air force, and may have suffered in its intake. The European officers included some whose high-handedness and offensiveness angered the Indian ratings. Terms such as 'black bastards', 'sons of coolies', 'junglies', jarred and created racial tension. Service abroad brought the Indians face to face with the entrenched European attitudes of

Durban, Trincomalee and Singapore, and mixing with white sailors, they discovered irritating contrasts between their own pay and conditions and those of Europeans.

A purely service grievance started the mutiny at HMIS *Talwar*, a signals training school at Bombay. As one mutineer remembered, 'Somebody suggested, let us refuse to eat breakfast. If all of us refused to eat breakfast, that will be mutiny and once mutiny happens we can take over the navy.' The food was indeed poor, but the act of defiance was more than just a protest against rations, it was a touchstone for what became a nationalist insurrection. Shouts of 'The food is rotten, give it up, we won't eat!' left the officers, Indian and British, dumbfounded and scared. The sailors, realising their collective strength, went wild and began to chant, 'British must go!' News of the incident was swiftly leaked to the clandestine, nationalist All India Radio, which broadcast it across the sub-continent. The mutineers also utilised their own wireless transmitters to contact other shore establishments and ships with such messages as 'We are on strike', 'We have started our struggle, you must join.'

The wireless messages spread the mutiny. On the next day, 19 February, 10,000 ratings, from eleven shore establishments and fifty-six ships, were in rebellion. Officers were expelled from their ships, many of which hoisted red flags or the colours of the Muslim League or Indian National Congress. The Bombay mutiny had spread from the *Talwar* men to ratings in other shore stations and Fort Barracks and Castle Barracks, which together housed over 3,000 sailors. A mass meeting was held ashore which turned into a slogan-shouting nationalist demonstration which the local police could not control. Bands of mutineers paraded with fire-axes and hockey sticks, burned the American flag outside the US Information Office, and opened negotiations with local trade unionists and Communists, who quickly began to mobilise dockyard and industrial workers. At the same time, a committee of ratings gathered on board *Talwar* and drew up a list of grievances which embraced racial insults, discrimination in canteens, equal pay with RN sailors, and speedier demobilisation. Talks with the Flag Officer Commanding in Bombay, Admiral Rattray, broke off after he refused to agree to a policy of no arrests.

From Delhi, the position appeared grim. There was the possibility that the mutinies were the prelude to a wider, nationalist uprising. Wavell and General Auchinleck, the Commander-in-Chief of the Indian Army, both agreed to take a firm line with the mutineers.

British and Indian troops were called to stand by in Bombay and Karachi, the major centres of the mutiny. The disobedient ships and shore stations were placed in a quarantine, but this did not halt the disaffection which spread to new ships on the 19th and 20th. Efforts were made to subvert Mahratta soldiers on piquet duty in Bombay, who were asked, 'You are Indian, so are we. Why do you want to shoot us?' What followed is disputed. Nationalist sources suggest that some at least of the Mahrattas made common cause with the mutineers and went so far as to get hold of rifles and machine-guns and engage British troops near the Castle Barracks. Another version, from a British officer, suggests that the Mahrattas went on with their work of clearing the streets of gangs of mutineers and keeping others from coming ashore. On the same day, 21 February, it was clear that the British authorities were ready and willing to deploy force. A flight of Mosquitoes flew over Bombay, and on 24 February British men-o'-war, including the light cruiser *Glasgow*, anchored in the bay with guns trained on the mutinous warships.

This implacability was approved by the official nationalist leadership, which regarded the mutiny and the riots it was spawning with horror. Gandhi, Nehru and Jinnah knew that they were soon to receive power from the British, and on the day of the first outbreak in Bombay they had been informed that a Cabinet Commission was to be sent from London to negotiate the final transfer of government. None of the moderate leadership wanted violence; this could provoke a British backlash, and it might undermine their own leadership of the national movement. In Bombay the common cause between local Communists and the mutineers offered an additional threat to the Congress and Muslim League. So nationalist spokesmen did what they could to turn the heads of the mutineers and persuade them to surrender. Faced with overwhelming firepower, and all but disowned by the popular nationalist parties, the mutineers threw in the towel on 26 February.

The Indian naval mutiny provoked a series of strikes by men serving in the Royal Indian Air Force, although these were peaceable and ended without the authorities having to take forceful action. Lieutenant-General Tuker blamed some of the trouble on the poor example of the RAF, some of whose men had staged a number of strikes during January 1946 at various bases in India. He also noted disapprovingly that the Indian Air Force may have

239

taken rather too many of its personnel from the Indian universities. 'There is no more unbalanced and indisciplined body than the student class of the Indian universities,' he observed, and their 'permeation with political propaganda' made 'many of these boys unsuitable members of the fighting service'.

The mutinies by sailors and airmen during February 1946 were the most formidable experienced in British forces since the naval mutinies at the end of the eighteenth century. Their suppression was a bloody affair which showed that even in its final days, the Raj was determined to rule unchallenged. Perhaps also the events in Bombay and Karachi raised the ghost of 1857. There have been allegations that in both these ports Indian troops were unwilling to fire on the mutineers or their supporters, leaving the task of repression to British troops alone. What was essentially a nationalist propaganda line was denied by the British government. There was plenty of fighting; on 23 February infantry, supported by bren-gun carriers and tanks, handled the riots by mutineers and their sympathisers who had called a general strike. The death toll may have been more than two hundred during the day's skirmishing. On 20 February, mutineers aboard the corvette *Hindustan* had opened fire on British troops with an Oerliken cannon and the ship's main armament, a 4-inch gun. During the night, 75-mm guns and mortars were set up on the quayside, hidden among bales of cotton and sacks of grain. At nine on the morning of the 21st, the *Hindustan* was bombarded, and after nearly two hours of shell- and small-arms fire, the mutineers surrendered. They had lost six dead and twenty-five wounded.

Unexpected, the naval mutiny of 1946 had started as a protest against mistreatment, but it had quickly become a nationalist uprising which was exploited by local Marxists who found a chance for a revolution on their doorsteps. The Communists who hoped to take over the mutiny were disappointed, thanks in large part to the intransigence of the local British military authorities who were willing to use overwhelming force to restore order. The Indian sailors did not have time to develop any political programme beyond calls for the expulsion of the British. This was inevitable anyway, and had been made possible by a civilian leadership whose public renunciation of force, and pacific methods, were approved by most Indians. A mutiny was unnecessary to secure Indian independence. This was understood by many nationalist officers and men in the Indian Army, some of whom actually assisted in the suppression of the mutiny. Less than eighteen months after the mutiny, India received its independence, and those mutineers still in detention were released. They were disappointed by their treatment, for the new government preferred to forget them and their mutiny. From the orthodox nationalist standpoint which was upheld and developed by the Congress Party, the naval mutiny of 1946 was an abberration which ought not to have happened. The sailors' precipitate violence endangered India's peaceful progress towards self-government and was to be deplored as a rejection of Gandhi's principles – which was tantamount to a fall from grace.

GALLANT BLACKS FROM TOGOLAND

> This work of yours is second only in importance to that
> performed by my sailors and soldiers who are bearing the
> brunt of the battle. But you also form part of my great
> Armies which are fighting for the liberty and freedom of
> my subjects of all races and creeds throughout my
> Empire.
>
> George V, addressing the South African Native
> Labour Corps, Abbeville, 10 July 1917

WILD MEN FROM THE WOODS: THE BLACK SOLDIER

Black men had served in the British Army since the eighteenth
century, when their value was first appreciated as garrison soldiers
in tropical regions, such as the West Indies and the west coast of
Africa, where there had hitherto been a high wastage of white
troops through disease. The expansion of Britain's empire in Africa
after 1880 increased the demand for black troops. West Indian
battalions were stationed in West Africa, where they were
frequently used for punitive expeditions, and the companies which
had been empowered by the British government to run private
enterprise colonies in Nigeria and Central and East Africa soon had
sizeable black armies on their payrolls. British political control over
Egypt placed Egyptian, and later Sudanese, troops under British
officers.

Old and new black armies were always commanded by
European officers, usually young careerists attracted by the higher
rates of pay and the chance to build a reputation on imperial

battlefields. The 'insatiable desire to get brevets, DSOs and medals' guided the junior officers who had attached themselves to Macdonald's expeditionary force in Uganda in 1897, and similar motives were found elsewhere on the Empire's frontiers.[1] Kitchener, Wingate, Lugard and Trenchard all advanced their careers commanding black troops. There was occasionally another type of officer in the tropics, the regimental misfit who had been sent abroad as a result of debt, scandal or sexual misbehaviour.[2] Yet, whether keen for promotion, on the lookout for profit, or in disgrace, the British officer in charge of black soldiers carried with him methods of training and command which had been proved on European soldiers. His overriding object was to instil into black men the qualities of self-respect, discipline and obedience to orders which were the hallmarks of the British Regular. Black men were drilled and trained as if they were British recruits. When they performed well, the highest accolade which could be awarded to them was favourable comparison with white troops. A black junior officer in the Oil Rivers Protectorate *gendarmerie* showed that he was 'as plucky as any white man', according to his commanding officer in the 1897 Benin campaign, and in the same year native soldiers serving with the Royal Niger Company were praised for their steadiness, which so impressed their officers that they imagined themselves in command of British troops.[3] The same soldierly qualities were shown by men from the 1st Battalion of the West Indies Regiment in Palestine during August 1918 when, according to their divisional general, they displayed 'great steadiness under fire and dash in the attack'.[4]

Such creditable behaviour was a vindication of British methods of drill and training as well as of the leadership of British officers. The raw material was not always thought to be very promising. Lieutenant-Colonel Burroughs, who commanded a battalion of the Sierra Leone Regiment during the Ashanti campaign of 1900, summed up his soldiers as, 'wild men of the woods, but a very cheery lot and very childish', which meant that, 'they want a tight hand over them'.[5] Firmness was essential for the command of black troops, but conventional military wisdom also insisted that the white officer treated his men with fairness. Contemporary opinion considered the black man a childlike fellow, rash and wilful, prone to sulkiness or laughter, yet capable of devotion and gallantry. British discipline imposed by just and honest officers could suppress the worst habits of the black man and bring out the best, or so it was thought.

As in India, British officers believed that they could detect latent qualities of soldierliness in certain 'warrior' tribes: in West Africa the Hausa were highly regarded, in East Africa the Sudanese and, later, the Somalis. By teaching such men to be soldiers, the imperial governments of Britain, France and Germany thought that they might eventually create loyal élites within their colonies. In 1917 a British intelligence officer in East Africa, Captain Phillips, thought that it would be a good idea to build up the African military élite to counterbalance the emerging élite of mission-educated Africans whose thinking was inspired by European and American ideas which made them question the basis of colonial government.[6] For many blacks, soldiering was an attractive and rewarding career. During a recruitment drive in the Gold Coast (Ghana) in 1916, the local authorities cautioned the Army to set their wages below those offered on the cocoa farms and in the mines for fear of a mass exodus of workers.[7] Askaris recruited in Nyasaland (Malawi) during the First World War were paid 21s 4d a month, three times the average local wage. The men who took this pay were not just pushed into soldiering by the cash rewards. 'We joined because we were men,' one veteran remembered proudly.[8] Like their European counterparts, black soldiers quickly came to feel pride in their calling and an attachment to their units. In April 1918, hints that the British West Indies Regiment and the 2nd West India Regiment were about to be merged provoked an angry reaction from the men in both. The mere suggestion 'is found to be so repugnant to the former unit ... [that] ... serious trouble would result,' reported General van Deventer, the local commander in East Africa.[9] Such sentiments indicated how British methods had influenced the men.

Before 1914, Britain's black soldiers' duties were confined to colonial peace-keeping. France, on the other hand, had long exploited her black forces, which had been deployed in the Crimea and during the Franco-Prussian War. Then, and later, Arab, Senegalese and Indochinese troops were a makeweight for France's regular army, whose recruitment suffered from a birthrate which was outstripped by that of Germany. France's tropical empire was later described as *un immense réservoir d'hommes, prêt à défendre la patrie*. When France was imperilled between 1914 and 1918, her military planners raised 450,000 soldiers from her colonies, one-third of them from Africa, and a further 135,000 factory workers who came to France to fill the places left by Frenchmen who had gone to the front.[10] Britain, by contrast, had always been nervous about using black troops against Europeans. During the Napoleonic Wars black forces were kept in the Caribbean, and when, in 1855, a shortfall in enlistment meant a shortage of men for the Crimea, the War Office dug up the expedient of the eighteenth century and tried to raise a legion of Swiss and Germans. Disraeli broke with the tradition in 1877 when he ordered Indian units to Malta when a war with Russia seemed likely. (Russia had no inhibitions about 'white men's wars' and had used Asiatic cavalry during the 1812 campaign.)

What unease there was about the use of black troops, armed with modern weaponry, against white men was stifled by the War Office in 1914. In the next four years, 50,000 African soldiers were recruited, and about a million porters and labourers. The askaris and the volunteers from the British West Indies were, however, confined to the battlefields of the Middle East and West and East Africa. Only by chance did they find themselves fighting European troops (in Palestine and East Africa) although hundreds of thousands of Africans, Egyptians and Chinese were recruited to serve as labourers in France. Like India, Britain's African and West Indian colonies played a crucial part in Britain's war effort by providing the manpower for a global war. Their strategic value was again recognised in the Second World War: between 1940 and 1945, 500,000 men were raised from Britain's African colonies. Some were used for garrisons in Africa and others for combat in North Africa and the Far East. Recruiting methods were sometimes unusual: in the Gold Coast chiefs just picked out young men at random.[11]

Two world wars transformed the role of Britain's black soldiers from that of imperial policemen to front-line fighting men who were engaged in a struggle for the survival of Britain and her empire. The experience of these two conflicts gave many black soldiers a new view of the world and brought them into contact with new ideas and values. Undercurrents of the thoughts which fighting a world war had inspired were detected in East Africa by military intelligence as early as 1917. Returned soldiers carried with them stories of a destructive war in which white men killed each other in great numbers. War experience helped to expose myths of white supremacy, for black men had been trained to fight as Europeans and handle modern European weapons as well as white men – in the 1890s only European soldiers were allowed to fire machine-guns. Pan-Islamic propaganda, and the message of black

Christian clergy, often trained in America, encouraged the spread of 'Africa for the Africans' sentiments.[12] By drawing black soldiers into their wars, the imperial powers had inadvertently contributed to profound changes. The horizons of black men had been widened, they were given a new view of the world and were prompted to ask questions about their place in it. The mutinies of black soldiers in British service reflect these changing attitudes. The mutinies in Uganda in 1898 and the Gold Coast in1900 were parochial affairs, even though the first provoked a short war, concerned only with conditions of service. The mutinies by West Indians in 1918, and by imported Chinese and Egyptian labourers, embraced wider political and racial issues.

UNFIT FOR COMMAND OF HIS REGIMENT

It was axiomatic that the black soldier trusted his British officer and that the British officer knew something of the minds of the men he commanded. In Uganda and the Gold Coast, black soldiers believed that their officers had broken faith with them, and in consequence deserted. Attempts, natural enough, to forestall these mass desertions led to resistance and mutiny. The Sudanese askaris who garrisoned the Uganda Protectorate were mercenaries, not unlike the kind who operated in Renaissance Europe. They had once formed part of the Egyptian army which held down the Sudan and, in the face of the Mahdist revolt of the 1880s, had moved southwards under their commander, Emin Pasha. They were Muslims and were followed by their wives and families who settled with them when they took British service in Uganda.

In the middle of 1897, these Sudanese soldiers were called upon to act the part of pawns in an African chess game. The players were based in London and Paris from where the moves were made. Monsieur Hanotaux, the French Foreign Minister, wanted a French empire which stretched across the Sahara to the Nile, and the Marquess of Salisbury, Britain's Prime Minister, wanted his country to control the White Nile, which meant the occupation of the Sudan. Both players moved their big pieces first: Major Marchand set off from West Africa for the Nile and, far to the north, General Kitchener marched out of Egypt to do battle with the Khalifah Abdullah, who ruled the Madhist empire in the Sudan. The next move was made by Salisbury who, in August 1897, ordered Major MacDonald, an officer of Engineers, to lead an expedition of Sudanese troops northwards from Uganda along the Nile. It was a secret mission, and so MacDonald told his men that their purpose was no more than exploration.

The Sudanese may well not have believed MacDonald, a fair but hard officer whom many disliked.[13] As he was mustering his men and gathering transport at Ngare, they asked his permission to bring their wives and families with them which, given the fact that they were about to embark on a scientific and geographical expedition, seemed quite reasonable. MacDonald refused. He did, however, allow each soldier to have one member of his family with him, and suggested that since they would be moving into unknown and uncontrolled territory, the rest of the families could follow later. More complaints followed about overwork, unpaid wages and the fact that men left behind in garrisons with their families were clearly better off. MacDonald temporised and promised everyone an easy time on the expedition, even though he knew that at some future date his forces might have to fight the Khalifah's dervishes.

Unconvinced by MacDonald's assurances, two companies of Sudanese deserted on 22-23 September, led by a junior officer, Mabruq Effendi, who had played an important part in laying the men's grievances before MacDonald. The men were determined, and threatened their pursuers with rifles. They were soon overtaken by Captain Kirkpatrick and a loyal company. Kirkpatrick set up a Maxim machine-gun 200 yards from the mutineers' camp and deployed half a company around them. He pleaded with the men to return to obedience, but they were swayed by Mabruq and their NCOs. Then Kirkpatrick tried force, and opened fire with the Maxim, which promptly jammed, whilst his Sudanese deliberately fired high. Kirkpatrick retired, and Masai runners were sent on to warn other British officers of what had happened.

At this stage the mutiny spread with an alarming quickness. The garrison at Nandi mutinied under a junior officer, Jadeen Effendi, who took over the fort. On 16 October the garrison at Lubwas mutinied and seized the fort which overlooked Lake Victoria. They were joined by a hundred pensioners who were living nearby, and the original mutineers, moving westwards towards the lake, were augmented by Sudanese civilians who had settled at Mumias. The Lubwas mutiny was the most serious of all, since the mutineers had gained possession of a Maxim and a steam launch. Three officers who had been taken prisoner were shot. One, Major Thruston, warned his executioners of the fate which awaited them:

> If you are going to shoot me, do so at once, but I warn you that many of my countrymen will come up, and that if you do this thing, you will have reason to regret it.

The mutineers may not have been convinced. Captain Austin, who took part in the campaign, discovered that most of the mutineers thought themselves safe from any retribution. They were certain that Britain had very few troops beyond those in Uganda. This ignorance of the British Empire was perhaps excusable, since the only other non-Sudanese forces in Uganda consisted of 300 Sikhs in Mombasa and some companies of Swahili askaris.

The overall objective of the mutineers seems to have been to escape from the Army and from British jurisdiction. They hoped, it seemed, to make their way along the Upper Nile and settle somewhere, and there was some talk of founding an Islamic state. Their actions, which had temporarily knocked away the props of British government, gave the chance for Mwanga, the Kabaka of Buganda, to throw off British tutelage, and he raised men to make common cause with the mutineers. While he got ready to enter the fray, the mutineers set up Lubwas as their base, digging trenches and shelters against the possibility of artillery bombardment. There were well over 600 of them, drawn from the men who had first deserted at Ngare and the mutineers from the forts, and a great many were accompanied by their families.

The mutiny forced MacDonald to abandon all plans for his Nile expedition. His first thoughts were to take measures to preserve British rule elsewhere in the Protectorate and to blockade the mutineers in Lubwas. He moved first to Kampala, which he secured on 21 November, while his junior, Captain Woodward, began to besiege Lubwas. The forces available were just adequate for his task and included 350 Swahilis, over 1,500 local Waganda tribesmen who had hastily enlisted, a small detachment of Sikhs, and several machine-guns. A further 150 Sikhs were also on hand, having been rushed up from Mombasa, and the 27th Baluchis were due to arrive from India at the beginning of March 1898.

The reinforcements were not needed. MacDonald's loyal forces were sufficient both to crush the mutiny and fend off the threat from Mwanga. Mwanga, with 2,000 men, including Sudanese from the Buddu garrison who had mutinied on 18 December at his suggestion, was beaten on 14 January 1898. The siege of Lubwas, which had started on 5 December, lasted until 1 January. There were several attempts to take the fort by frontal attack in which the Waganda tribesmen, armed with spears, took a prominent part. Their losses were heavy since the fort's Maxim gun was well manned by a mutineer sergeant. On 1 January the mutineers and their families escaped by water in the commandeered launch and a dhow. They landed and proceeded north along the banks of the Nile towards Lake Albert under harassment from loyal forces. The skirmishes lasted until March, by which time the bulk of the mutineers had disappeared in the bush, been taken, or been killed. The war had been a hateful business according to Captain Austin, who noted women and children from the mutineers' families among the casualties after one engagement. Two sergeants, including the man who had manned the Maxim gun at Lubwas, and six privates were tried for mutiny, found guilty and shot at Kampala on 20 April.[14] The mutiny had cost the lives of eight European officers and 853 of the government's forces, including over 500 Waganda tribesmen.

The Uganda mutiny had started as a mass desertion by men who no longer trusted their commander and who were dissatisfied with the terms they were offered. Much the same reasons lay behind the mutiny by the Sierra Leone Regiment in March 1901.[15] On their departure from Sierra Leone, in June 1900, the regiment had been seen off by the Governor, Sir Frederic Cardew, with the words, 'I shall see you back in three or four months, covered with glory.' The men were part of a scratch force which was assembling to relieve Kumasi in the Gold Coast after it had been besieged by Ashanti tribesmen. The town was relieved and Ashanti resistance broken only at the end of the year, by which time the Sierra Leone Regiment had experienced much hard fighting.

The end of the Ashanti campaign saw the departure of other troops from West Africa, but the Sierra Leone Regiment was ordered to remain in Kumasi as a deterrent against future unrest. The men were weary of garrison duties and wanted to get back to their wives and families. They showed their feelings, and their commander, Lieutenant-Colonel Burroughs, passed them on to Governor Cardew. He wrote, on 14 January 1901, 'The men are not discontented but I am often asked with an anxious look if I know the date they are to return to their houses.' The new Governor of the Gold Coast, Major Nathan, was also pressed about a date for the regiment's return when he visited Kumasi during March. Nathan was not concerned about this matter, since his main interest was local security and the building of new forts. Burroughs also seems to have cared little about his men's future, for he announced his departure on leave to them when they paraded on the morning of 18 March. His words – 'I am leaving tomorrow on the usual six months' leave that all officers of the regiment obtain on completion of a year's service on the West Coast' – suggest a degree of indifference towards their welfare.

Burroughs does not appear to have earned himself much affection during his twelve months in command of the Sierra Leone Regiment. 'He punish too much and flog plenty,' was the observation of one NCO, which was well supported by the regimental punishment book. Between October 1900 and May 1901 there were 35 floggings for offences, which together suggest a growing discontent amongst the men. Private Governor Boy received 25 lashes for leaving a piquet and getting drunk, and Private English Boy received 14 for disobeying an order. More serious was the arrest of six men on 4 February for threatening to shoot an officer. By this time, the regiment was in a parlous state. Men were still wearing the blue uniforms they had worn when they left Sierra Leone, many were in huts with leaky roofs, rations were poor and no pay had been given for several months. This was bad enough, but it was made worse by the news that Burroughs was going back to England, careless of what became of the men. There were also rumours that he was to be replaced by a severe officer, Captain Charrier, who was widely feared.

During the hours after Burroughs' announcement of his departure, 178 men, nearly half the regiment's strength, deserted and set out along the road to the coast. Their absence from the evening's parade was not a cause for undue worry, and when the Governor was informed the next morning, he was told that such behaviour was not out of the ordinary. Nathan, whatever he may have felt by the oddness of Burroughs' ideas about regimental parades, was alarmed and sent an officer and senior NCO after the men. In all, 244 men and a number of porters had gone missing and were moving along the tracks through the bush in the direction of Cape Coast. They were pursued by loyal men and officers, including Charrier, who warned them that they would be shot for mutiny and promised that the regiment would stay in the Gold

251

Coast for another six years.

By 27 March, the mutineers had been rounded up and were placed in a school at Cape Coast. Burroughs addressed then for thirty minutes, during which time he demonstrated the gravity of their crime, assured them that they would each lost £8 10s in pay, and commanded them to surrender their arms. His speech concluded, Burroughs retired to his quarters on board a steamer anchored off the shore. The men argued amongst themselves what was to be done, and set about one loyal man, Sergeant Brown, hitting him with sticks and sword-bayonets before he was rescued. The crisis came on 30 March after the mutineers, determined to get back to Sierra Leone, tried to commandeer some boats on the shore. Private Mandingo, who had been identified as a ringleader, attacked an officer with his sword-bayonet and was arrested after a scuffle. The loyal men had been drawn up into two lines with two officers between them, and the mutineers broke ranks and loaded their rifles once Mandingo was arrested. There were calls to shoot Charrier, but the officers were able to calm the men, whose temper was improved by the Governor, who offered each a £5 advance on his wages. Mandingo was tried, sentenced to death and executed the same day by a firing squad drawn from the local police. His death 'had an excellent effect' on his comrades who began to surrender. They were taken, along with the loyal men, by the government steamer *Sherbro* to Freetown.

When the regiment was mustered at Freetown, it was found that 128 men, all mutineers, had gone missing. Of those who remained, thirteen were tried and two of them, both sergeants, were sentenced to death. Lord Roberts, the Commander-in-Chief, commuted the death sentences to imprisonment for life and reduced the other prison terms. A report on the incident had been made, following a local investigation, and Roberts and Field-Marshal Sir Evelyn Wood were distressed by what they read in it. They recommended that Burroughs was to be placed on the retired list with the rank of major and the appropriate pension. He was judged 'unfit to command' a regiment in which he had shown scant interest, and whose men he had treated cruelly and shamefully.

HURLING YOUR SPEARS AT THE ENEMY

On 10 July 1917, George V, accompanied by General Haig, inspected the men of the South African Native Labour Corps at Abbeville. After the parade, he explained to them the value of their work.[16]

> Without munitions of War my armies cannot fight; without food they cannot live. You are helping to send those things to them each day, and in so doing you are hurling your spears at the enemy.

It was a nice conceit; mass armies needed arms, ammunition and food, and these had to be unloaded from ships and carried to trains and lorries, which, in turn, needed tracks and roads. When the King reviewed the South African blacks, there were already 220,000 men in France, many drawn from parts of his Empire into a huge corps of labourers. Most had arrived during the past six months, and they had taken the place of Europeans at the great depots and marshalling yards around the Channel Ports and Marseilles.

The men for this workforce had been recruited in China, Egypt, Africa and the West Indies, where they had signed contracts which set the length of their service and rates of pay. When they arrived in France, the labourers were organised along military lines into companies, with gangers who took the rank of NCOs, and were placed under the command of British officers. They were subject to military discipline which ruled out strikes, although when disagreements arose over conditions of service, the British authorities were prepared to bargain with the men so long as their behaviour was not threatening. The labourers were placed in hutted or tented encampments which were surrounded by barbed wire and patrolled by armed guards. The explanation for the camps was the official wish to avoid rowdiness, easy access to drink and affrays with British personnel and the local population. Leave to enjoy the pleasures of French towns was permitted, but it was strictly rationed. Another reason put forward for the camps in which South African blacks were housed was the need to keep them at a safe distance from their fellow workmen in the British penal battalions whose 'slackness' would set ' the 'Kaffirs' a bad example.[17] The camps were joyless places (one was called 'Cinder City') and their inmates faced a life of hard work in an unaccustomed climate broken by only occasional recreation.

When they had signed for service with the British forces, many of the labourers had been far from clear about the exact terms of their contracts. In many cases, particularly among Chinese and Egyptian labourers, there were many men who believed that they had been or were being cheated. Local newspapers in Wei-Hai-Wei, a British island off the North China coast, had warned would-be recruits that they might find themselves in war zones, although their contracts stated that they would not be placed in danger from enemy action. The Egyptians, whose country had been bulldozed into the war by the British government, had a long tradition of resentment against the British administration of their country, and their mood was made more bitter by the high-handed and brutal treatment commonly given to them by British and Dominion troops.[18] Working under British military discipline meant that miscreants were liable for trial by summary courts martial, which were empowered to have serious offenders flogged. Disobedience and theft by Egyptians, Arabs and Indians serving in war zones was regularly corrected by beatings; there were five beatings in three months among the Arabs and Indians serving in a penal battalion in Mesopotamia during 1918.[19] Severe discipline, coupled with differences over the precise nature of their duties and terms of their contracts, caused a series of mutinies amongst Egyptian and Chinese labourers in 1917-18.

The gravest involved Egyptian and Chinese labourers who were employed on the docks at the French Channel Ports. During the late summer and early autumn of 1917, there had been an intensification of German air raids against targets on British lines of communication. Heavy aerial bombardment was still a novelty of war, although men in the front line had learned to live with it and its artillery equivalent, as far as that was possible. The labourers had not and, anyway, they repeatedly claimed that their contracts excluded them from areas where their lives were imperilled. During a raid on Dunkirk on 4 September, Chinese labourers working on the docks suffered fifteen dead and twenty-one wounded. They panicked and scattered, following the 'bad example' set by Belgian labourers. On the next morning they were reported 'wandering about ... doing a great deal of damage, and breaking into houses, and beginning to misbehave generally'. Some were found disconsolate among the sand dunes near Dunkirk, where they insisted on staying, rather than return to the docks and the risks of more air raids.[20] Four companies of European troops were ordered to stand by, although they were not needed since the Chinese were eventually pacified and persuaded to go back to work. The mood of restlessness had not been entirely dissipated, for, on 7 September, Chinese labourers broke out of their camp at Vendroux near Calais.[21]

By now the trouble had spread to the Egyptians. At nine on the morning of 5 September, two companies of the Egyptian Labour Corps at Boulogne went on strike. They claimed that their six-month term of service had expired, arguing that it began the day they had left their villages, and that they were wet and cold and had been frightened by the air raids. Colonel Coutts, who commanded the Second Labour Group, was called from Abbeville and he met and talked to the Egyptians. By six in the afternoon he had made no headway, for they refused to shift their ground, and so he returned to HQ at Abbeville, promising to resume negotiations the next morning. That morning, 6 September, the Egyptians tried to get out of their camp and were fired on by the garrison battalion, who killed twenty-three and wounded twenty-four.[22] The Egyptians went back to work.

More trouble followed at Calais where 74 Company of the Egyptian Labour Corps went on strike on 10 September. They were still adamant the next day when reinforcements were called in. Again there was shooting, in which five were killed and fifteen wounded. There were twenty-eight arrests, and twenty-five of the Egyptians were sentenced to terms of imprisonment by a court martial held at Dieppe the following day.[23] A further mutiny by Egyptians occurred at Marseilles on 16 September after a quarrel in which the Egyptians insisted that their term of duty was up. Later they alleged that they had been told that if there was any more of this kind of trouble they were to be held in France permanently and that they would be flogged. About 500 ran off from an evening parade, and about 150 returned armed with sticks and led by a mutineer who had got himself a rifle. This mob attacked a junior officer, who was knocked down by the ringleader, and there were threats to kill all officers and NCOs. The ringleader was overpowered by some Egyptian NCOs, arrested and tried for mutiny. He had already been flogged for insubordination and stirring up a riot and was executed, having been found guilty of mutiny, on 10 October.[24]

What is surprising, perhaps alarming, about these incidents was the readiness with which the local army commanders ordered their men to fire into the mutinous crowds. This response, however dreadful it may appear, was unavoidable. In the first place the only forces available to handle the disturbances were soldiers armed with rifles whose presence had clearly not intimidated the mutineers. Without any other resources with which to contain the disorder, the officers had little choice but to order their men to fire. Other considerations affected this decision. First, the strikes held up the movement of supplies to the front line during the vital offensive known as the battle of Passchendaele, and it was of overriding importance that the flow of material was maintained. Secondly, the apparent spread of mutinies from 4 September onwards had to be checked even by the most condign means. The alternative was disruption along the lines of communication, which might possibly lead to difficulties with the German POWs whose camps were close by those of the Labour Corps. The disturbance among the Chinese at their camp at Audruicq in February 1918 gave the opportunity for four German POWs to escape from their prison camp nearby.[25] The policy of firing into crowds was not confined to non-European rioters. Two Austrian or German POWs were shot dead by their guards after a disorder at Loniga in Italy on 31 December 1918, in which Italian soldiers had thrown bread at the prisoners; whether out of compassion or antipathy is not known.[26]

Chinese and Egyptian labourers continued to fight for what they saw as their rights. A 'serious disturbance' took place at Fontinettes, near Calais, on 16 December 1917 and the guards were forced to open fire, killing four. A Canadian private in the ASC was also killed, hit by a stray shot. There was a further riot amongst the Chinese at Audruicq on 25 February 1918, in which two were wounded. A few days later it was alleged that the Chinese had murdered a Frenchwoman at Calais and stolen 25,000 francs from her, so the entire labour force was confined to its camps for four days until it was discovered that none of them was responsible for the crime.[27] In the Middle East, a strike occurred at Yeghal, where the Egyptian labourers insisted that they had been deceived about the length of their service. Mounted police and 200 Sikh Pioneers were called in on 5 January 1918 and clashed with the mutineers, who were subdued without loss of life.[28]

At the beginning of 1917, the massive expansion of foreign labour had seemed a good answer to the logistical problems of Britain's army in the trenches. Yet the men from Africa and Asia who came to man the supply lines found themselves in an invidious position. They were treated as soldiers and sometimes found themselves running the same risks as soldiers. The officers who commanded the labour corps were also uncomfortably placed, for they had the responsibility for order behind the lines and for the uninterrupted flow of supplies to the front. From the often taciturn official accounts of the unrest, it was clear that many of the Egyptians and Chinese chafed against the restraints imposed on them and believed that they had been defrauded by the Army. When unrest of this sort occurred, its details were often glossed in official war diaries. Press criticism in the form of an article in the Liberal *Daily News* of 14 September 1917, which asked for an inquiry into the treatment of the Chinese, was fended off by the Army. An official statement asserted that: 'No armed force has ever been used to make men work', which was untrue.[29] The matter was a politically sensitive one, since there had been much public disquiet a few years before about the import of Chinese 'coolies' to South Africa to work the mines. The scandal which followed was fresh in the minds of the Army which wanted to keep the business of what was happening to the Chinese in France as quiet as possible.

No details survive of the strikes of South African native labourers. One old soldier recalled that soon after the Armistice in 1918, his battalion had been called in to handle a strike by blacks, presumably South Africans. The colonel confronted the strike leader, then called a soldier who knocked the striker over with his rifle butt. The strike ended and the soldier concerned got quick demobilisation.[30] Such rough and ready methods may well have been used elsewhere. The long-term effect on those at the receiving end of such treatment may only be guessed, although the sullen resentment of many of the men who had worked with the Egyptian Labour Corps was a factor in the outbreak of anti-British, nationalist disorders in Egypt in March 1919. The foreign labour corps may well not have been faultless and no doubt included shirkers, but they also contained men who were not prepared to lie down and take whatever was handed out to them by the authorities.

THE KNOWLEDGE OF ARMS
AND DISCIPLINE

In 1916, a party of West Indian soldiers, in high patriotic mood, approached the YMCA hut at Gabbari Camp in Egypt singing 'Rule Britannia'. They met a dusty reception from the British soldiers who were there. 'Who gave you niggers authority to sing that? Clear out of this building, only British troops admitted here!'[31] It was a hurtful piece of loutishness which still rankled three years later, when a British Honduran soldier told it to a commission of inquiry. Like many others who had joined the ten battalions of the West Indies Regiment, this man had been moved by a sense of duty and affection for Britain. He returned, like many others, bruised by slights delivered by British soldiers and the general crassness of the Army authorities. The mistreatment suffered by West Indians contributed to a mutiny of several thousands at Taranto at the beginning of December 1918, more unrest which broke into disorders in Jamaica, Trinidad and Jamaica in the following year, and, in the long term, the growth of local movements for self-government. The commonly unhappy experiences of many men in the war proved the foundation of West Indian nationalism and the parallel growth of black consciousness.

The various official reports which followed the mutiny and the disturbances in the Caribbean contained details of the ways in which the West Indian servicemen had been abused. Able Seaman Henry complained in March 1918 that whilst on a transport ship he had been bullied by officers who kept 'calling us black bastard'. In anger he struck one and got two years in gaol.[32] Other incidents like this added to the West Indians' sense of indignation. In Egypt, they were ordered into stinking railway trucks which Australians had just refused to travelled in. When coloured troops recuperating at the Belmont Road Military Hospital brawled with Military Policemen, about fifty other black troops joined in to help them, and the Military Policemen needed aid from several hundred British convalescents. This Breughelesque fracas in which crutches and walking sticks were used as cudgels so shocked one nurse that she died of a heart attack. A colonial office official who read the report was also shocked, but for another reason, since he added the minute, 'I only hope white nurses have nothing to do with them' – that is, the black wounded.[33]

Everywhere they were abused as 'niggers', and their distress was so deep that many were reported to be moving away from Christianity towards agnosticism and theosophy.[34] It is interesting to note that close contact with Europeans in the war led many African Christians to turn away from what they came to see as 'white man's religion' towards Islam.[35] What pained the West Indians was that they had hitherto regarded themselves as on some kind of par with Europeans, for, as one man from British Honduras complained, 'we were put in wards with Africans and Asiatics, who were ignorant of the English language and Western culture'.[36] Such treatment was all the more unpleasant since many men clearly expected better, perhaps as the result of their education, the benevolent paternalism of colonial government, and the affection for Empire instilled in local churches.

The gulf between them and white soldiers and their handling by the Army contributed to the resentful feelings which first led to the mutiny at Taranto and then troubles in the West Indies during 1919. Taranto Camp was a place to be feared, where conditions were 'very severe' and the mood of the men there was made more sour by the news that they had been excluded from the Army pay rises lately given to British troops. Added to this, soldiers who were proud of being 'fighting men' found themselves again relegated to labouring chores. On 6 December 1918 a mutiny began, led by men of the 9th Battalion who attacked officers and NCOs. The upheaval lasted for four days, in which a black NCO of the 4th Battalion was forced to shoot dead a mutineer in self-defence. Another was executed for murder after British troops had been called in. Order was finally restored and sixty men were tried for mutiny and given prison sentences, some of which were served in West Indian gaols.

This violent protest was followed by one more sober and constructive. On 17 December, sixty or more NCOs gathered at the sergeants' mess of the 10th Battalion to discuss ways in which they could promote an association for the advancement of black rights in the Caribbean. The Army had brought together many men from different islands and the links which had been made were to be continued after the war through an association which would work for a closer bond between the islands. A second meeting was held three days later in which it became clear that the sullen mood of the mutiny was still present amongst the men. In the chair was Sergeant Baxter, who had just been superseded by a white NCO, and much of the meeting was taken up with backbiting about the system which placed white NCOs over black troops. 'The black man should have freedom and govern himself in the West Indies,' demanded one sergeant who added, 'that force must be used, and if necessary bloodshed to attain that object'. His words were applauded, but at this meeting and others, there were loyal men who were prepared to give an account of what passed to their commanding officers. Official disapproval worried older and more conservative men, and the Company Sergeant-Major who chaired a meeting on 2 January called for circumspection in language and behaviour. 'Remember,' he argued, 'that the West Indian cannot stand up against the British Tommy and it was the British Tommy who beat the German.'[36]

The continued grievances of the West Indians soon posed a problem for the Colonial Office and the local administrations in the Caribbean, which had shortly to face the return of several thousand sulky and potentially disruptive ex-soldiers. 'The knowledge of arms and discipline which had been acquired by men of the Regiment' made them a danger to the peace of their home islands, warned one official. In Jamaica, the position was very uncertain since the island's labour market, already glutted, was to be swollen by 7,500 jobless men. Trouble of some kind was anticipated, and, since the War Office could not spare a British battalion for garrison duties, cruisers of the West Indies Station were ordered to be in readiness to sail to Kingston.

The official diagnosis was correct. In Jamaica, Trinidad and British Honduras, there was a sequence of disorders during 1919, and in each former soldiers took a prominent part. Feelings of anger were intensified by newspaper reports of the racial riots in Cardiff and Liverpool where local black men were attacked by white mobs. The assaults on sailors from the cruiser *Constant* and on over twenty Europeans in Kingston on 18 July 1919 were thought to have been in retaliation for similar outrages in Britain. 'Gangs of toughs' and the 'hooligan element' were blamed, but it was noticed that the marauders included ex-servicemen. Their participation may have been the result of the recent arrival of forty military prisoners who had to finish their sentences in local gaols. Further disturbances followed at the end of July and beginning of August, when there were attacks on British sailors whose ship, the *Cambrian*, had just disembarked a large body of West Indian seamen ... 'the most impudent, surly and unruly type of men', who presumably had been discharged from British service.[37] Armed parties of bluejackets patrolled the streets on both occasions.

Major Maxwell-Smith, who had commanded the 8th Battalion of the British West Indies Regiment at Taranto, was now serving in the Trinidad police. He feared a repetition of the Jamaican troubles, and sensed a conspiracy to turn the local peace parade into an uprising. Nothing more occurred than jeering from ex-soldiers who had placed themselves behind the saluting platform. They were angry about pay they were owed, outstanding gratuities, and the knowledge that sixteen or the Taranto mutineers were still locked up in the local prison. Before they had been discharged from the Army, all had been searched for arms and Mills bombs and it was thought wise not to issue the men on the parade with rifles, since many were feared still to possess cartridges. During November and December 1919, Trinidad was facing a series of strikes and it had been thought judicious not to raise an armed force from former soldiers whose sympathies were thought to be with the strikers. Even the loyalty of the local volunteers was open to question, since 'these men were feeling the pinch like anyone else, and no doubt had friends or relatives amongst the strikers'.[38]

The riots in Belize on 22-23 July 1919 involved over a hundred men from the British West Indies Regiment, one of whom put his training to some use, for a witness noted that he 'blew his whistle and ordered, "Halt, smash!" ' outside shops singled out for looting. Whites were attacked on the streets and in their houses, and order was restored only on the morning of 24 July when a landing party with machine-guns was put ashore from the cruiser *Constant* which had been summoned by wireless.[39] Wartime price rises which had run ahead of wages were blamed for the riots, but the evidence given a subsequent inquiry included a catalogue of racial slights suffered by former soldiers.

Of course, the Scotsman, Welshman and Irishman in the armed forces was prone to having his nationality attached to coarse abuse, and white soldiers were as foul-tongued to each other as they were to black men. Yet, what the bewildered black found was that there

261

existed a gulf between him and the British which was as wide as that which separated the American white from the American black. This was more distressful for the West Indian than for the American Negro, who had been born and bred to contempt and intolerance. The West Indian saw himself differently, for he was a Christian and the subject of the King just like white men who spoke the same language. The response to finding himself in a hostile world was a mutiny, and later, in the Caribbean, mindless violence against whites and property. The reaction of the NCOs at Taranto was to express aspirations towards self-government and towards taking themselves and their islands away from what they had discovered was a white man's empire. One development of that movement was a revival of trade unionism in Trinidad, in which ex-soldiers took leading parts, and the formation of the Soldiers' and Sailors' Union under a former officer, Captain A.A. Cipriani. (Commissions were sparingly given to native West Indians and, when they were on offer, the War Office liked the recipients to be 'slightly coloured' rather than Negro.)[40]

SHOOT DOWN WITHOUT MERCY

The experience of the First World War had taught many West Indians to see themselves as black men and to question a system which predestined them to lowly positions. The better educated and more intelligent began to wonder whether their own and their countrymen's future really lay within the British Empire with all its contradictions and inequalities. It was hard to be loyal to an institution whose practices were so at odds with what black men had been told about the Christian religion and freedom. The path trodden by some West Indian soldiers had already been taken by many officers within the Egyptian Army.

In 1881, the educated officers of the Egyptian Army had revolted against the domination of their country by a commission of Europeans who ruled solely to satisfy rapacious bondholders in Paris and London. Colonel Arabi's national movement had been checked a year later, when British forces invaded Egypt, ostensibly to restore order, but in fact to occupy the Suez Canal. As a consequence, the administration of Egypt passed into British hands, and its army was placed under British officers. The purpose of this exercise was to create a biddable force which, in time, became the instrument of Britain's conquest of the Sudan. Under British officers and drillmasters, it was hoped that the new army would acquire efficiency, and that resentment against alien and infidel rule would be expunged.

From 1896 onwards, as more and more of the Sudan passed into British hands, Sudanese blacks were drawn into the Army, for British officers recognised 'natural' soldiers amongst their former adversaries. G.W. Steevens, *Daily Mail* journalist and Imperial panegyrist, explained the process:[41]

> The black is liable to be enlisted wherever he is found, as such, in virtue of his race; and he is enlisted for life. Such a law would be a terrible tyranny for the fellah Egyptian peasant farmer; in the estimation of the black it gives only comfort and security in the natural vocation of every man worth calling such – war.

Steevens noted, approvingly, the training of such men:

> Every morning I had seen them on the range at Halfa – the British sergeant-instructor teaching the ex-Dervish to shoot. When the recruit made a bull – which he did surprisingly often – the white sergeant, standing behind him with a paper, cried, '*Quaiss kitir*' – 'Very good'. When he made a fool of himself, the black sergeant trod on him as he lay flat on his belly; he accepted praise and reproof with equal satisfaction, as part of his new game of disciplined war. The black is a perennial schoolboy, without the schooling.

Like the contemporary public-schoolmaster, who always claimed to be able to penetrate his pupils' minds, the British officers who trained and led the black soldiers boasted an ability to see into the minds of their men. Invariably this arcane knowledge led to such conclusions that the infallible remedy for signs of restlessness was condign punishment, a treatment which the patient would always respond to. What were called 'elementary factors' dictated the relationship between the British officer and the black soldier, but in the Egyptian and Sudanese Armies these were complicated by the presence of Egyptian junior officers. Their influence was often underestimated, as they were themselves, but as Major-General Sir Charles Gwynn noted after the 1924 Khartoum mutiny, 'When men are in a state of excitement, racial feelings come into play which at other times are masked.' In other words, when the black soldier was at odds with his British officer, he looked to officers of the same race, background and religion.

Twice, in 1900 and 1924, Sudanese troops mutinied against their British officers, and on each occasion they received covert encouragement and support from their Egyptian officers. One reason was the persistent attachment of many officers to the cause of Egyptian nationalism which, during this period, was inevitably characterised by hostility to British overlordship. The accession of the young Khedive, Abbas-Hilmi, in 1893, animated the nationalist movement to which he gave his blessing and support. Amongst the nationalist groups which he patronised, in defiance of Lord Cromer, the British Consul-General and political puppet-master, were those of young army officers.

The nationalist sympathisers among the officers in Khartoum were delighted by the news of British reverses in the Boer War, and openly celebrated the news of the defeats in Natal during December 1900.[42] Rumours spread through the junior officers' messes that:

> The British were being defeated at the Cape, whole regiments taken prisoners, the whole British Army is now at the Cape, and there are no troops available to send to Egypt in cases of disturbances, that Russia was advancing on India, and France preparing to move against England by sea.

The circumstances seemed right for a challenge to British paramountcy, and several officers broadcast the news to their men, according to one of their colleagues who informed the Sirdar (Governor-General and Army Commander), General Wingate, 'These boys are full of talk and get the Dervish black to listen to them.'

How far the Sudanese were influenced by such information is not known for certain. They were part of an army of occupation in a country which had been just, and only just, pacified in the previous year and the British authorities were still jumpy about a Mahdist revival. What Wingate described as the 'very unfriendly spirit towards the English' shown by the Egyptian officer corps may well have encouraged him to order the Sudanese 14th Battalion to hand in their ammunition on 22 January 1900. The order created alarm and the cartridges were handed over resentfully. Many soldiers asked, 'Who will defend us in case of any attempt against us?' and it was thought wise to call in the 11th Battalion to supervise the surrender of the ammunition. Since this battalion possessed no ammunition, it could not prevent a disturbance the following day. Soldiers from the 14th tried to get their cartridges back and there were scuffles around the storehouse when men of the 11th became involved. The soldiers' wives, armed with sticks and knives, joined in to help their husbands. A compromise was eventually arranged to forestall any further friction and each battalion was permitted to keep 500 rounds for emergency use. It was soon discovered that many men had kept ammunition and it was not until March that it was all recovered.

Egyptian officers had watched the rumpus with approval. One congratulated his colleagues, 'Bravo, you have done well in the 11th, we in the 9th are old women and, Inshallah, the British will now be turned out of the country.' Men like this had, in the view of Wingate and Cromer, to be purged from the Army, and the Khedive's knuckles had to be rapped for giving them secret support. Cromer, aware of the delicate military and political situation in the Sudan, counselled Wingate to temporise at first and then, when loyal men and British forces were on hand, to 'shoot down without mercy anyone who shows the least hesitation or reluctance to obey you'.[43] Such measures were not required. Several officers of the 11th and 14th were dismissed and sent to Cairo. There, at Cromer's insistence, they were seen by the Khedive, who was forced to castigate their behaviour and have their medals (presumably earned during the 1896-98 campaign) taken from them. The humiliation was rounded off by a statement by the Khedive in support of Wingate which was published by the Egyptian press.

The disturbances in Khartoum in 1900 were repeated in 1924 when Egyptian officers again began to spread the nationalist message amongst their soldiers. After disorders in 1919 and mounting local pressure, the British government ended its protectorate over Egypt in 1922, although a garrison, which now included RAF squadrons, was retained. The Wafdist nationalist movement was not satisfied,

265

for the new Anglo-Egyptian agreement contained clauses which severely restricted Egypt's freedom of political action. A further focus for nationalist fervour was the Sudan, which Egyptians had long regarded as their province. It stayed under Anglo-Egyptian control with Britain as the dominant partner in the administration.

In support of the Egyptian government's demands for the Sudan, the White Flag Society was formed with adherents in both Egypt and the Sudan. Its membership included Egyptian officers in the Sudanese Army, and during June and July it masterminded a series of pro-Egyptian demonstrations in Khartoum. Support was strong among cadets at the Khartoum Military College, and the nervous Sirdar, Sir Lee Stack, thought it safest to disarm the young officers.[44] Such precautions were dictated by memories of the events of 1900 and were soon vindicated by a mutiny of the Egyptian Railway Battalion at Atbara. This was checked by troops from the Leicester Regiment, which formed the permanent British garrison in Khartoum, and from a Sudanese battalion. The arrest and detention of the mutineers was resisted, and several were shot. The incident incensed nationalists and drew a protest from the Egyptian government which insisted that its rights in the Sudan were being trampled on. Ramsay MacDonald's government in Britain was not, however, willing to acknowledge these rights and sent a battalion of the Argyll and Sutherland Highlanders to reinforce the Khartoum garrison.

The deportation of nationalist officers and the trials of the mutineers did not reduce the tension. On 12 September 1924 there was a mutiny by the 12th Sudanese at Malakal, which had been instigated by Egyptian officers. The prompt despatch of a small British force ended the trouble, which was merely the prelude for more formidable mutinies in November. On 19 November, Sir Lee Stack was assassinated in Cairo by a nationalist. The British believed that the murder was the consequence of prolonged nationalist agitation and that some responsibility rested with the Egyptian government. Lord Allenby, the British High Commissioner, demanded compensation and insisted that, among other concessions, the Egyptian government withdrew all its officers and troops from the Sudan, which was tantamount to a public refutation of Egypt's claims to the province. Zaghul Pasha, the Egyptian Prime Minister, refused to sign such an order so Allenby instructed Major-General Huddleston, Stack's successor, to expel the Egyptians. It was a provocative gesture which led to a showdown with the local pro-Egyptian movement.

The expulsions had to be supervised by two British battalions, for it was rightly feared that many Sudanese soldiers were infected with pro-Egyptian sentiments and might be reluctant to fire on brother Muslims. One Egyptian battalion acquiesced, but the 3rd Egyptian Infantry and the artillery brigade in Khartoum demanded to see the orders, and their obstinacy led to a British officer flying to Cairo where he secured the necessary papers signed by King Fuad. Meanwhile, the 11th Sudanese had mutinied in Khartoum, and the 10th at Talodi in the south. Here, under the guidance of their Egyptian officers, they had seized British officers and locked them in the local gaol. Immediately a column set off from Khartoum with eight armoured cars, 500 camelry, and machine-gunners from the Leicesters, which, when it arrived, was sufficient to overawe the Sudanese, who surrendered.

The difficulties in Khartoum were less easily overcome. After their barracks had been surrounded by the Leicesters with Vickers and Lewis guns, the Egyptian infantry gave up, acknowledged their orders and entrained for Egypt. The artillerymen were more stubborn. They trained their guns on the British barracks, secured two heavy machine-guns and attempted to take over the military hospital after an exchange of fire with a patrol of the Argylls. Their entry into the hospital was blocked by a British medical officer, who was murdered along with a British NCO and two Syrian doctors. The gunners were joined by more mutineers, Sudanese from the musketry school, and the combined forces took refuge from British patrols in the Egyptian Officers' Mess, which they defended against attacks by British infantry with well-aimed rifle and machine-gun fire. After a number of unsuccessful assaults by the Argylls, a 4.5-inch howitzer was brought over from Khartoum fort. It was placed 150 yards from the mess and opened fire.

The mutineers were shelled and machine-gunned for about seven hours and, to one onlooker, 'it seemed impossible that any living thing could have survived the holocaust'. A white rag eventually appeared, firing stopped and the Argylls advanced into the smoking ruins. Thirty wounded men were found and taken to the hospital. The number of the dead is not known. Major-General Gwynn thought that it was high and claimed that there were no survivors, although it seems that many had escaped, perhaps during the night of 27-28 November before the shelling started. Two Sudanese officers were amongst the wounded, and once they were nursed back to health, they were tried for mutiny, found guilty, and shot. The other ranks who survived were pardoned. The Egyptian forces having been evacuated, the British stayed in control of the Sudan, and future security, both from Mahdism and mutiny, was underwritten by the building of airfields and the permanent posting of an RAF squadron at Khartoum.

The mutinies at Khartoum in 1900 and 1924 were part of a longer story which stretched back to Arabi's *coup* in 1881 and looked forward to that by General Neguib and Colonel Nasser, in 1952, which overthrew the Egyptian monarchy. Army officers were the backbone of the Egyptian nationalist movement; they were educated men who, under British rule, suffered from a promotion structure which reserved senior posts for British officers. The nationalist tradition was a powerful one and the experience of the Egyptian Army was repeated elsewhere in Africa and Asia, where the armies of newly independent states were closely entangled in internal politics. What is also interesting is that, for all the commonplace British boasting of winning the hearts of Egyptian soldiers through training and example, a wide gulf separated the leaders from the led. It was understood by Lord Cromer who commented, 'There is no getting over the fact that we are not Mahommedans, that we neither eat, drink nor intermarry with them.' Yet, by a strange irony, the army which the British so carefully created as the instrument of their own empire building and policing, kept alive the national spirit which Cromer, Wingate and their like wished to destroy.

ENVOI:

Mutiny Past and Present

The general story of mankind will evince, that lawful and settled authority is very seldom resisted when it is well employed. Gross corruption, or evident imbecility, is necessary to the suppression of that reverence with which the majority of mankind look upon their governors, and on those whom they see surrounded by splendour, and fortified by power. For though men are drawn by their passions into forgetfulness of invisible rewards and punishments, yet they are easily kept obedient to those who have temporal dominion in their hands, till their veneration is dissipated by such wickedness and folly as can neither be defended or concealed.

Dr Johnson, *The Rambler*

In the widest political terms, none of the mutinies which occurred after 1797 did any lasting damage to the state. This had not always been the case. The mutiny of English soldiers at Portsmouth in January 1450 and their subsequent murder of one of Henry VI's ministers, and the mutiny, a few months later, by baronial retinues who had no wish to join the suppression of Cade's rebellion, both helped to weaken the government. At the end of the Wars of the Roses, the defection of the Stanley contingent and the refusal to serve of Northumberland's retinue sealed the fate of Richard III. In each case the soldiers were reflecting a popular opinion which was turning against discredited and shaky governments. At the end of the Civil War, what amounted to a mutiny by a large number of

269

units of the New Model Army forced its commanders and Parliament into postures and decisions which they might have not otherwise have taken. In 1688, the more or less wholesale desertion of James II's army ensured his deposition and exile and the relatively smooth accession of William and Mary.

The Glorious Revolution of 1688-9 was the last occasion when the Army involved itself directly in British political life. Thereafter, restlessness in the Army and Navy was solely concerned with matters which directly concerned soldiers and sailors. This did not exclude a political element from mutinies, indeed it was present in nearly all of the larger ones. The sailors who mutinied between 1797 and 1800 knew something of the libertarian ideas which were circulating in Britain, and were able to apply some of those principles to their own conditions. Most were civilians, and it had been noted that many militiamen spent time reading 'little books' which contained a radical message. The advantages secured by trade unionists in the second half of the nineteenth century made sailors envious and anxious for some of these rights for themselves. Whilst it was possible in peace time to cut soldiers and sailors off from those currents of political and social thought which questioned the moral basis for the established order, mass enlistment made this impossible, both in the 1790s and in 1914.

The political dimension of mutinies did not mean that they were guided or led by men armed with chapter and verse of a particular political ideology, although such characters existed. What was common was the presence in the ranks of men who were acquainted with general principles. After 1918 such men were said to be 'bolshie'. An official assessment of morale, made in 1942, noted that 'bolshie' sentiments were found in the letters of men who were 'browned off', or annoyed by a 'stand-offish' officer.[1] Such men might easily express approval for Soviet Russia, with little understanding of what went on there beyond the assumption that 'they' were not in charge. In the same way, the mutineers either hoisted a Red Flag or sang the song of the same name. The banner and the lyric were a form of defiance of authority which carried with it a reminder of the power of the underdog. In myth at least, Soviet Russia became the embodiment of a world where the working man might get his rightful deserts and was not the slave of an authority based on a traditional social hierarchy. In 1945-6 the man awaiting demobilisation believed, with some justification, that he was to return to a country where the government planned to take care of his and his family's interests. His predecessor in 1918-19 had no such assurance, which may, in part, explain why the demobilisation after the Second World War was such a comparatively harmonious business.

Mutiny also involved deeper political instincts. The upheavals of the seventeenth century and the patriotic propaganda of the eighteenth created the stereotype of John Bull, the free-born, independent Englishman who was pushed around by no one. No man was born booted and spurred with a right to ride others, who existed just to obey his orders and serve his interests. This assumption, not always boldly stated, lay behind much of the unrest in the Navy in the 1790s and reappeared during the clashes between soldiers and the military authorities in the First World War.

Those who ruled knew this and acted accordingly. Lord Bingham cautioned the tyrannical Colonel Keane of the 7th Hussars, after a minor mutiny by men of the regiment in October 1832, with the advice that the troopers 'should know that you *will* be Master, but they should also feel you interest yourself about their comforts and are kind to them'.[2] This patrician's appeal for the moral economy between ruler and ruled was backed up by an appropriate tag from Virgil. Army and naval officers of the nineteenth and early twentieth centuries were not noted Latinists, but most understood the good sense of such counsel and tried to act on it. It was not easy, given that many of the men who served under them were knaves and rogues. It was perhaps over-exposure to what was often considered the 'riff-raff' which led to an over-emphasis on tough discipline as the only way to create efficient soldiers.

The men who were wedded to the philosophies of late-Victorian soldiering misapplied them in many instances during the First World War. There had been a natural tendency to look back to the soldiers of the past as real models of soldierliness; the Duke of Cambridge lamented the 'new' ideas which, in his opinion, led to the early misfortunes of the Zulu War, not least the reliance on short-service men who lacked the stamina and experience of the old twenty-one-year men he had fought alongside in the Crimea. Naval officers in the twentieth century likewise regretted the new type of men who were joining and who seemed less willing to accept the old forms of discipline. Old war horses and their sea-going equivalents passed on and were replaced by younger men, more in tune with

271

new harmonies. In January 1942 the engineers on board the transport HMS *Helvig* went on strike after the senior engineer had been refused leave to visit his family. The captain justified his action on the grounds that he was repeatedly badgered by such requests. The Admiralty supported the engineers – who, it was admitted, were all former Merchant Service men and therefore unfamiliar with naval discipline – and censured the captain, who, it was thought, had been too high-handed.[3] Such an official view would have been unthinkable even a dozen years before, but it seemed that the Admiralty had learned something from its past experience with civilians turned sailors, and was willing to compromise it traditions.

The *Helvig* mutiny was a trivial affair, even if the attitudes taken suggested a turnabout by those who controlled the Navy. Most mutinies were of this kind, for sailors and soldiers, like the rest of mankind, need food, clothing, shelter and the wherewithal to supply comforts for themselves and their families. In return for obedience, the fighting man expects to be sustained by his country and, when he is not, may demand his rights. This had always been so; English soldiers had mutinied over pay, lodgings and rations in Ostend in 1588 and in Ireland soon after. It seemed inexplicable to Colonel de Montmorency that British soldiers always showed an attachment to generals who cared for their welfare even though, as commanders, they squandered their lives. The cases in question were Buller in Natal in 1899, and others, unnamed, in the First World War.

Whilst mutiny had much to do with what went on behind lines, it was absent from the front. There, the soldier or sailor was concerned with keeping alive, killing or being killed, considerations which left little room for mutiny. Indeed on the battlefield, mutiny, like panic or cowardice, would have endangered the mutineer and the men who fought at his side. Only in North Russia and the Baltic in 1919 did British servicemen state that they did not want to fight, and then in peculiar circumstances, when the men involved found themselves victims of decisions taken by politicians, like Churchill, out of touch with reality and prisoners of their own rhetoric.

The Russian mutinies, like those earlier in 1919, had spread quickly from unit to unit. Copycat mutinies stemmed, in part, from one group having seen another get away with indiscipline, and making up its mind to do likewise. During the 1790s the rowdy militiamen from South Lincolnshire, whose officers turned a blind eye to their misdeeds, mocked their Cambridgeshire colleagues for their docility. The upshot was that the Cambridgeshire men's discipline quickly deteriorated.[5] Something of this sort may well have encouraged the sustained disobedience of the troops at Etaples, where those who did not wish to join in the evening sprees may have been ridiculed as staid and timid.

Kicking over the traces was all the more fun when former restraints had been strict. The last large-scale mutiny – by paratroopers in Malaya in 1946 – contained an element of daring. Today, what has been called social restraint is said to be disappearing, although the historical perspective which leads to this conclusion is seriously flawed; over the past century the British have not always been a moderate and well-behaved people. All the same, the apparent increase in rowdiness, especially amongst the young, has led to the belief that service discipline, as handed out during National Service, would correct youthful excess. Lord Slim's riposte to this suggestion, delivered in 1951, is still unanswerable. It was, he suggested, impossible for the Army to inculcate in eighteen months what parents and schools had failed to teach in eighteen years.[6]

The services still maintain a discipline and cohesion which wins admiration from outside. What is significant is that this is achieved without the coercive machinery which was once considered necessary to produce efficient fighting men. What is different, perhaps, is that today's discipline tends to resemble the harmony achieved by an orchestra, rather than the slavish submission secured by the martinet. Still, to the outsider, service discipline can appear strange. A doctor, whilst training for the Royal Marines, remembered that he and his kind were considered to be 'soft' and needed instruction on how to deal firmly with the malingerer. 'There were good servicemen and bad servicemen, not good servicemen and ill servicemen,' he discovered.[7]

> The bad marine is immediately recognisable because he is dirty and his trousers aren't creased, his boots don't shine and he's always in the sick queue. Chaps repeatedly come with alcohol-related problems and we were encouraged not to encourage psycho-therapy or the social worker approach ...

This seemed hard, but it made practical sense, as the same officer discovered:

273

It wasn't till I got to Northern Ireland that I actually understood what it was all about, why it was so important that these bad ones were weeded out and the others would do what they were told.

Someone says, 'Corporal, cross that bridge in two minutes.' The chap says, 'What me? Go across there?' You're terribly frightened and so is everyone else. You can't start having to justify every order on Christian name terms. It wouldn't work.

It would not have worked at Badajos or Trafalgar either.

Mutiny, or the possibility of it, has not been forgotten. It 'wasn't something that happened on the *Bounty* and hasn't happened since,' this same officer recalled being told. It could happen, and you had to take care that 'you didn't make the situation worse or precipitate anything either by your own stupidity or being lax'.

The possibility of mutiny still existed with black forces under British command, although the numbers of these diminished rapidly with the dismantlement of the Empire in the 1960s. There were echoes of the past in November 1953, when a small but bloody mutiny occurred among the Trucial Oman levies. A squadron, lately recruited in Aden and in training at the Buraimi Oasis, showed signs of restlessness and were under justifiable suspicion of selling ammunition to local Arabs.[8] The men included 'unsatisfactory characters', according to the British Resident in Bahrain, and had, on reaching Buraimi, required vigorous measures to get them to settle down. Matters came to a head on 4 November after a man had been shot whilst trying to leave Hamasa, and the unit's commander decided to have an autopsy performed on the body. The NCO in charge of the post, which had claimed for over 100 rounds fired during the incident, was placed under arrest. The men at Buraimi refused to parade on 6 November and demanded the release of the NCO, which was conceded. The ringleaders were sent back to Sharjah, but when a party went to fetch an NCO who was implicated, three officers were killed and two were wounded before he was overpowered. 'In newly-formed Arab units of raw peasants or tribesmen occasional outbreaks of this nature are not unusual,' concluded the British Resident. The ways of native troops were always strange and the incident carried echoes of former Imperial wars on other frontiers.

Elsewhere in Asia and Africa, mutiny has become commonplace. The armies of the new republics soon took on themselves a role in

274

political life akin to that of the Praetorian Guard in first-century Rome or the legions in later centuries. They 'made' and 'unmade' governments and a service career often became a high road towards political posts for many officers. During the time in which this book was written, mutinies by troops in the Sudan and the Philippines have ensured the overthrow of two regimes. In each case, the soldiers defied orders from their political masters and instead threw in their lot with popular demonstrations. Soldiers, in a sense, became civilians, and exercised the political rights of civilians. Other military *coups*, particularly in South America, are solely the response of individual officers to governments they find distasteful, although once in power, military administrations tend to offer themselves as 'saviours' of national honour.

Mutiny for ideological causes still occurs, and did during the United States war in South-East Asia, when in the late 1960s many drafted men protested against being sent into action. The mutinies did not affect government action, but the soldiers added some weight to the civilian mass movement which demanded an end to the war. Very recently, Colonel Gadaffi of Libya has called on black soldiers in the United States services to mutiny against their officers and government; so far there is no evidence of any positive response.[9]

So, today, mutiny is something which occurs in foreign countries. It would however be rash to say that in Britain sizeable mutinies by servicemen are a thing of the past. Whenever they have occurred, they were always unpredicted and unexpected. The welfare of soldiers, sailors and airmen is more carefully attended to than in the past and this, coupled with the high professionalism of the fighting services as a whole, means that morale is very good. What one junior officer, recently trained at Sandhurst, described as the 'glib principles of leadership' were touched on during his instruction. He learned much more once he took charge of men. Still, 'leadership', which was once recognised but seldom analysed, is now taught in some institutions in much the same way as geography or economics. Those who aspire to learn leadership might profit from a study of mutiny, but the lessons they would learn have long been common knowledge. They were understood a hundred and fifty years ago by the poet John Clare, by birth one of those destined to be led.

The 'people' as they are called were a year or two back as harmless as flies – they did not seem even to be susceptible of injustice but when insult began to be tried upon them by the unreasonable & the proud their blood boiled into a volcano & the irruption is as certain as death if no remedy can be found to relieve them.

SOURCES AND BIBLIOGRAPHY

Public Record Office, London

Admiralty: ADM 1, ADM 2, ADM 3, ADM 36, ADM 51, ADM 53, ADM 116, ADM 137
Cabinet: CAB 24
Colonial Office: CO 123, CO 137, CO 884
Foreign Office: FO 371
War Office: WO 32, WO 71, WO 80, WO 86, WO 90, WO 92, WO 95, WO 106, WO 158

Published and Private Sources

> *: Unpublished papers
> IWM: Imperial War Museum
> NAM: National Army Museum

Ahrenfeldt, R.H., *Psychiatry in the British Army in the Second World War*, 1957.
Allison, W., and Fairley, J., *The Monocled Mutineer*, 1978.
Andrew, C.M., and Kanya-Foutier, A.S., 'France, Africa and the First World War', *Journal of African History*, 19, 1978.
* Anon. 'Experiences of a Recruit', *c.* 1890 (NAM).
Ashmore, E.B., *Air Defence*, 1929.
Austin, H.H., *With MacDonald in Uganda*, reprinted 1973.
Babington, A., *For the Sake of Example*, 1985 ed.
Bartlet, T., 'An end to moral economy: the Irish militia disturbances of 1793', *Past and Present*, 99, 1983.
* Beavan, W.M., Papers (NAM).
Beckett, I.F.W., 'The Singapore Mutiny of 1915', *Journal for Army History Research*, 1985.
*Brown, E.A., MS Account of the Singapore Mutiny, 1924 (IWM).
Bruce-Lockhart, R., *Memoirs of a Secret Agent*, 1954.
Brugger, S., *Australians in Egypt, 1914-1919*, Melbourne, 1980.
Burn, W.L., *The Age of Equipoise*, 1964.

Cantlie, N., 'Mutiny in Khartum', *Army Quarterly*, 81, 1960-1.

Carew, A., *The Lower Deck of the Royal Navy, 1900-1939*, Manchester, 1981.

Cathcart, W., Letters, *Navy Records Society Mischellanea*, I, 1902.

Carsten, F.L., *War Against War*, 1982.

Chandos, Lord, *The Memoirs of Lord Chandos*, 1962.

Childs, W., *Episodes and Reflections*, 1930.

Churchill, W.S., *The World Crisis*, V, 1929.

Clowes, W.L., *History of the Royal Navy*, IV, 1899.

Corbett, J.S. (ed.), *Spenser Papers*, Navy Records Society, 1914.

Costello, E., *The Peninsular and Waterloo Campaigns*, ed. A. Brett-James, 1967.

Cromer, Lord, *Modern Egypt*, 2 volumes, 1908.

Dewey, P.E., 'Military Recruiting and the British Labour Force during the First World War', *Historical Journal*, 27, 1984.

*Dickinson, A.H.D., Papers (IWM).

Dugan, J., *The Great Mutiny*, 1966.

Dobson, C., and Miller, J., *The Day We Almost Bombed Moscow*, 1986

Elkins, W.F., 'A source of black nationalism in the Caribbean: the revolt of the British West Indies Regiment at Taranto, Italy, in 1918', *Science and Society*, 1970.

Ellis, J., *The Sharp End of War*, 1982 ed.

Elliot, M., *Partners in Revolution: the United Irishmen and France*, New York, 1982.

Elmsley, C., *British Society and the French Wars, 1793-1815*, 1979.

Englander, D., and Osbourne, J.J., 'Jack, Tommy, Henry Dubb: the Armed Forces and the Working Class', *Historical Journal*, 21, 1978.

Firm: the journal of the Worcestershire Regiment, April 1934.

Fraser, T.G., 'Germany and the Indian Revolution, 1914-1918', *Journal of Contemporary History*, 12, 1977.

Frith, C.H. (ed.), *Naval Songs and Ballads*, Naval Records Society, 1908.

*Gibb, I.S., 'A Walk in the Forest' (IWM).

Gilbert, M., *Winston S. Churchill*, IV, 1916-1922 and companion volumes I and II, 1975.

Gill, D., and Dallas, G., 'Mutiny at Etaples Base in 1917', *Past and Present*, 69, 1975.

———, *The Unknown Army*, 1985.

* Goodall, Sergeant E., Letters and Papers (NAM).

Griffiths, P., *To Guard My People*, 1971.

Gwynn, C.W., *Imperial Policing*, 1936.

Gwynn, D., *The Life and Death of Roger Casement*, 1930.

Hansard's Parliamentary History, 33, 3 March 1797-30 November 1798.

Hyde, D., *I Believed*, 1951.

Ironside, E., *Archangel, 1919*, 1953.

James, L.E., *The Savage Wars*, 1985.

James, W., *Old Oak: John Jervis, Earl of St Vincent*, 1950.

* Jowett, R., Diary (IWM).

* Keane, Letters and Papers (NAM).

Keyes Papers, II, ed. P.G. Helpern, Navy Records Society, 1979.

Killick, A., *Mutiny!*, Militant pamphlet, 1976.

Killingray, D., 'World War I in the Gold Coast', *Journal of African History*, 19, 1978.

——, 'Recruitment in the Gold Coast', *Journal of African History*, 1984.

Kisch, R., *The Days of Good Soldiers*, 1980.

Lamb, D., *Mutinies, 1917-1920*, 1983.

Lammers, C.J. 'Strikes and Mutinies: a complementary study &c.', *Administrative Science Quarterly*, 14, 1969.

Lewin, R., *Slim, the Standardbearer*, 1976.

* Lewis, H.V., Letters and Papers (IWM).

MacLaine, I., *Ministry of Morale*, 1979.

Macmillan, H., *War Diaries, 1943-45*, 1984.

Manwaring, G.E., and Dobrée, D., *The Floating Republic*, 1935.

Marcus, G.J., *A Naval History of Britain*, 1971.

Marshall, J., *Royal Navy Biography: Supplements*, 1823 and 1827.

Maruchevsky, V.V., 'God na Seyer' in: von Lampe, A.A., *Beloye Delo, Letopis' Beloy bor'by*, Berlin, 1927.

Mason, P., *A Matter of Honour*, 1974.

Matthews, K., *Memoirs of a Mountain War*, 1972.

Maynard, C.C.M., *The Murmansk Venture*, 1928.

Middlebrook, M., *The Kaiser's Battle*, 1983.

Miller, B., 'The Adventures of Benjamin Miller', ed. M.R. Dacombe, *Journal for Army Historical Research*, 7, 1928.

Nastyface, J., *Nautical Economy, or Forecastle Recollections &c.*, 1836.

Page, M.E., 'The War of Thangala', *Journal of African History*, 19, 1978.

Patient, A., 'The Salerno Mutiny', *The Listener*, 25 February 1982.

Perrett, B., and Lord, A., *The Czar's British Squadron*, 1981.

Pollock, S., *Mutiny for the Cause*, 1969.

Pope, D., *The Black Ship*, 1963.

Prendergast, J., *Prender's Progress*, 1979.

Report from the Select Committee on the Army Act and the Air Force Act, 1953.

Richards, F., *Old Soldier Sahib*, 1965 ed.

* Roeber, C.T., Diary and Papers (IWM).

Rothstein, A., *The Soldiers' Strikes of 1919*, 1980.

*Rudd, R., Diary (IWM).

*Seventh Hussar Papers of Henry Paget, 1st Marquess of Anglesey (NAM).

Sherrill, R., *Military Justice is to Justice as Military Music is to Music*, New York, 1969.

Sinclair, K., *A Soldier's View of Empire*, 1982.

Somerville, A., *The Autobiography of a Working Man*, 1967 ed.

Soutar, A., *With Ironside in North Russia*, 1940.

Spector, R., 'The Royal Indian Navy Strike of 1946', *Armed Forces and Society*, VII, 1981.

Steevens, G.W., *With Kitchener to Khartoum*, 1898.

Stouffer, S.A., and others, *The American Soldier: adjustment to Army Life*, Princeton, 1949.

Summerfield, P., 'Education and Politics in the British Armed Forces in the Second World War', *International Review of Society*, 26, 1981.

Thomis, M.I., and Holt, P., *Threats of Revolution in Britain, 1789-1848*, Oxford, 1984.

* Thompson, A.E., Diary (IWM).

Thorne, C., *Allies of a Kind*, Oxford, 1979.

Townshend, C., *Political Violence in Ireland: Government and Resistance after 1848*, Oxford, 1984.

Tucker, J.S., *Memoirs of Admiral Earl St Vincent*, 2 vols, 1844.

Tuker, F., *While Memory Serves*, 1949.

Ward, S.R., 'Intelligence Surveillance of British ex-Servicemen, 1918-1920', *Historical Journal*, 16, 1973.

Warwick, P., ed., *The South African War*, 1980.

Wavell, Lord, *The Viceroy's Journal*, ed. P. Moon, Oxford, 1973.

Weller, K., *Don't be a Soldier*, 1985.

Western, J.R., *The English Militia in the Eighteenth Century*, 1965.

Wetherell, J., *The Adventures of John Wetherell*, ed. C.S. Forrester, 1953.

Willan, B.P., 'The South African Labour Corps', *Journal of African History*, 19, 1978.

Willcocks, J., *The Romance of Soldiering and Sport*, 1925.

Williams, J., *Byng of Vimy*, 1983.

Williamson, H.N.H., *Farewell to the Don*, ed. J. Harris, 1970.

* Wood, A., Letters (NAM).

Woolfe, S.H., 'The Bitter Road', *Tradition*, 65 and 68 (n.d.).

Woodward, L.D., 'Les Projets de déscente en Irlande sous la Convention', *Annales Historique de la Révolution Française*, 8, 1931.

Younghusband, G., *Forty Years a Soldier*, 1920.

BBC Broadcast: 'Indian Memories of the Raj', 19 May 1986.

SOURCE NOTES

1. ORDERS ARE ORDERS

1. Lloyd, 112.
2. WO 106/1412 GOC Straits Settlements to WO, 8 July 1915.
3. WO 32/5704.
4. Ahrenfeldt, 220.
5. Carew, 188.
6. Sherrill, 5-59.
7. Ibid., 223-4.
8. Edwards, 282; Carew, 163.
9. Gibb, 27.
10. WO 86/61; Care, 136.
11. WO 86/61 (21.7.01); WO 81/134B, 190-1.
12. Sherrill, 183-4.
13. I am indebted to Major E.A.D.C. Campbell for this point.
14. Stouffer &c., 70, Carew, xix.
15. Clowes, IV, 46-7; Edwards, 236-7.
16. Clowes, IV, 140-1; ADM 116/1022, 11-12.
17. WO 95/1334, 10-12 June 1919; Dallas and Gill, 167.
18. Englander and Osborne, 601.
19. Ellis, 256.
20. Miller, 38.
21. Edwards, 76.
22. Somerville, 131, 138-40.
23. Cowan, 68.
24. *See* p. 200.
25. *See* pp 229-32.
26. Spector, *passim.*
27. Mason, 451-3.
28. Somerville, 131.
29. 7th Hussars Punishment Book.
30. Wood.
31. Sinclair, 23-4.

32. ADM 116/1022 (Report of Committee of Inquiry and press cuttings).
33. 7th Hussars Punishment Book.
34. Cowan, 132.
35. Goodall; Anon.
36. Warwick.
37. Burn, 263.
38. Cowan, 72-3.
39. Willcocks, 51.
40. WO 90/1 f. 74.
41. Thorne, 153.
42. I am indebted to Captain John Metcalfe, RN for this comment; he was serving in a minesweeper squadron off the Malayan coast in 1946.
43. Wetherell, 7.
44. Montmorency, 249.
45. Cowan, 44.

2. WORM IN THE OAK

Courts martial are referred to by their date as there is no pagination in the Registers.

1. Manwaring and Dobrée, 10; ADM 1/5345, 1 June 1798.
2. Nastyface, i.
3. ADM 1/5339, 9 June 1797.
4. ADM 1/5360, 4 January 1802.
5. Tucker, I, 320.
6. ADM 1/5125.
7. Elliot, 101.
8. ADM 1/5345, 18 June 1798.
9. ADM 1/5360, 27 February 1802.
10. Manwaring and Dobrée, 59-60, 60-1.
11. ADM 1/5125.
12. Ibid.
13. ADM 1/5339, 20 June 1797.
14. Dugan, 375, 377.
15. Nastyface, 123.
16. ADM 1/5126.
17. Manwaring and Dobrée, 59-60.
18. ADM 51/1182.
19. Nastyface, 23.
20. ADM 51/1209.
21. Tucker, I, 320.
22. Emsley, 77.
23. ADM 1/5350, 19 June 1802.

284

24. Wetherell, 39-40.
25. Manwaring and Dobrée, 93.
26. Elliot, 144.
27. ADM 3/137, 4.
28. ADM 1/5125.
29. ADM 1/5353, 3 June 1800.
30. ADM 1/5350, 23 July 1799.
31. ADM 1/5375, 6 October 1806.
32. ADM 1/5125.
33. ADM 1/5351, 25 September 1799.
34. ADM 1/5345, 18 June 1798.
35. ADM 1/5345, 25 June 1798.
36. ADM 1/5126.
37. ADM 1/5345, 23 July 1798.
38. ADM 1/5346, 12 August 1798.
39. ADM 1/5346, 23 July 1798.
40. ADM 1/5339, 20 June 1797.
41. ADM 1/5346, 9 July 1798.
42. ADM 1/5346, 23 July 1798.
43. ADM 1/5345, 6 July 1798.
44. ADM 1/1352, 71-2.
45. Ibid. 72-3.
46. Ibid., 74.
47. Ibid., 76.
48. Ibid., 81, 83.
49. Tucker, I, 321.
50. ADM 1/6033, 218, 221.
51. *Hansard*, 33 (3 March 1797-30 November 1798), 478-9.
52. ADM 51/1352, 91.
53. ADM 51/1182.
54. Lloyd, 112.
55. ADM 1/5125.
56. Dugan, 395 *n*.1.
57. Cathcart, 269-70; ADM 1/396, 223 ff.; ADM 1/1352, 91.
58. ADM 1/396, 223.
59. Tucker, I, 325.
60. ADM 1/5339, 29 June 1797.
61. ADM 1/5345, 18 June 1798.
62. ADM 1/5345, 5 June 1798.
63. ADM 1/5348, 17 January 1799; Dugan, 404-5.
64. ADM 1/5350, 11 October 1799; Tucker, I, 324.
65. ADM 1/5348, 4 August 1799; ADM 1/5125.
66. ADM 1/5345, 14 July 1798.
67. Clowes, IV, 168, Manwaring and Dobrée, 9-10.
68. ADM 2/1119, 489-90; ADM 36/12266; ADM 51/1273.

69. Tucker, I, 438-9.
70. ADM 1/5345, 9 July 1798.
71. Pope, *passim*, for the account of the events on *Hermione*; the reaction of the Diligences from ADM 1/5343, 15 March 1798.
72. ADM 51/1637 (*Ferret*), ADM 51/1785 (*Crocodile*).
73. ADM 1/5375, 8 October 1806.
74. ADM 51/1776.
75. Pope, 268-70.
76. Nastyface, 106.
77. Ibid., 107.

3. A JUST CAUSE

1. Gilbert, IV, 31.
2. CAB 24/4, GT 173.
3. WO 106/401.
4. Childs, 139.
5. CAB 24/75, GT 6874.
6. Montmorency, 275.
7. Mottram, 323.
8. WO 106/401.
9. WO 32/5460, 2.
10. ·Babington, 59-60.
11. WO 32/5460. 2.
12. Childs, 139.
13. CAB 24/53, GT 4715.
14. Middleton, 188.
15. AB 24/53, GT 4715.
16. Gill and Dallas, 44-5.
17. WO 32/5460, 1.
18. Ibid., 2.
19. Childs, 137.
20. Babington, 113-5.
21. WO 90/50 f.108, WO 86/61 (14 July 1901), WO 92/8 (11 January 1901).
22. Childs, 170.
23. Babington, 247-8; Gill and Dallas, 38.
24. Babington, 248.
25. Childs, 144.
26. Chandos, 98.
27. Brugger, 34-5.
28. Ibid. 145.
29. WO 95/4725 (Monthly Reports October 1918, December 1918 and April 1919).

30. Read, 127.
31. Ibid. 125.
32. Englander and Osborne, 601.
33. CAB 24/75, GT 2052.
34. WO 95/4027 (Etaples Base Diary).
35. Gill and Dallas, 66.
36. WO 95/4027 (5 September 1917).
37. Ibid. (9 September 1917).
38. Gill and Dallas, 68.
39. Babington, 169-71.
40. Englander and Osborne, 596-7.
41. The claims for Toplis are made in Allison and Fairley; no sources are given.
42. Gill and Dallas, 73.
43. CAB 24/4, GT 173.
44. Carsten, 106.
45. Ibid., 108-9.
46. Englander and Osborne, 604-5.
47. CAB 24/75, GT 6874.
48. WO 95/4018 (24-28 July 1918).
49. CAB 24/75, GT 6874.
50. Private information from the Revd Richard Willcox; WO 95/4725 (Report November 1918).
51. Ibid.; Gill and Dallas, 123.
52. Childs, 178.
53. WO 95/465 App. C, Sect. 3.
54. FO 371/3950 and 488.
55. *Firm*, 37-8.
56. FO 371/3950, 273-4.
57. Ward, 184-5; Weller, 64.
58. Ward, *passim*.
59. CAB 24/79, GT 7218.
60. Ibid.
61. Gilbert, IV, 181.
62. Churchill, V, 161.
63. Ibid.
64. Lewin, 16.
65. Childs, 179.
66. WO 95/59 (Calais Base Diary, 26 December 1918).
67. Gill and Dallas, 95.
68. Ibid., 119.
69. WO 95/59 (22 December 1918).
70. Gill and Dallas, 95.
71. Gilbert, IV, 500-2, 503; Ibid., i, 192-3.
72. WO 95/1334 (10 June 1919).

73. Ashmore, 115.
74. Childs, 168-9.
75. For this account I am indebted to Elwyn Edwards, Sam Milligan and G.J. Parry.
76. Read, 126.

4. THIS ILL-CONCEIVED VENTURE

1. WO 158/714 (Staff assessments of situation in North Russia, August 1918-March 1919).
2. Ullman, 28-9; FO 371/3950, 1, 94, 476.
3. Churchill, V, 163.
4. Mr M. Lumb, Royal Scots.
5. Maynard, 165; WO 158/714.
6. Rudd, p.7; WO 158/714.
7. Ibid.
8. Livock.
9. Roeber, Diary, 13 October 1918.
10. Mr Lumb.
11. Gilbert, IV, 274; WO 95/5430 (Sadleir-Jackson's Brigade War Diary), 18 August 1919; Williamson, 155.
12. Mr Lumb, Royal Scots.
13. Soutar, 26.
14. WO 158/714.
15. Mr Lumb; Roeber, Diary, November 1918.
16. WO 32/5675; WO 158/714.
17. Ibid., and Mr Lumb.
18. WO 158/714.
19. WO 158/714.
20. Thompson.
21. FO 371/3950, 22; WO 95/5430 (Varga River Front), 5 July 1919.
22. FO 371/3950, 22.
23. Bruce-Lockhart, 331-2; Roeber, papers.
24. Maynard, 320.
25. Jowett, Diary, 24 July 1919.
26. Ironside, 58-9; FO 371/3950, 22.
27. Rudd.
28. Ironside, 112-3.
29. Gilbert, IV, 261.
30. Maruchevsky, 43-4.
31. Ironside, 114.
32. Ibid., 113.
33. Gilbert, IV, 274-5 and IV, i, 607-8.
34. Edwards, 52-3.

35. ADM 53/37796.
36. Cowan, 112; Gilbert, IV, i, 687.
37. Jowett, Diary, 24 July 1919.
38. Thompson, Diary, 17 July 1919.
39. Letter from Mr B. Wynne-Woodhouse, *Sunday Times*, 6 April 1986.
40. Dadd, 42-3.
41. WO 158/714; Thompson, 26 March 1919.
42. FO 371/3950, 3.
43. Soutar, 72.
44. Thompson.
45. WO 32/5704; Ironside, 28.
46. WO 158/714.
47. Williamson, 66-7.
48. Ironside, 46-7.
49. Ibid., 57.
50. Ibid., 68-70.
51. Thompson.
52. Maynard, 202-5; WO 95/5427 (Syren Force War Diary), April, App.1.
53. For the account of the Toulgas Mutiny: Ironside, 127; WO 95/5430 (RAMC, Royal Scots and 16th Canadian Artillery War Diaries).
54. WO 95/5430 (Varga River Front), 5 July 1919.
55. For the account of the Onega Mutiny: Ironside, 162-3; Thompson and Jowett.
56. WO 158/714.
57. For the account of the development of the SBL and the mutiny: Ironside, *passim* and 158-9; Soutar, 87-8, 137-9, 156-7; Beavan Papers; WO 32/9245 (Secret Report to WO from Ironside, 17 July 1919); WO 158/714; WO 95/5430 (RAMC War Diary).
58. WO 32/9245, Appendix.
59. Gilbert, IV, 316.
60. Ibid., IV, i, 752.

5. TO INVERGORDON AND BEYOND

1. For authoritative and detailed accounts, see Edwards and Cowan, on whom I have relied heavily.
2. Englander and Osborne, 615.
3. ADM 137/2000, 271.
4. Ibid., 277.
5. Rothstein, 52; Gilbert, IV, i, 502.
6. Edwards, 67.
7. ADM 137/1685, 11.

8. ADM 137/1672, 575; Gilbert IV, i, 726.
9. ADM 53/39616; Edwards, 61.
10. ADM 137/1685, 43, 45.
11. Edwards, 57-8.
12. Gilbert, IV, 687.
13. Cowan, 113; ADM 137/1685, 504.
14. Hyde, 42-3.
15. Edwards, 416.
16. Cowan, 128-9.
17. Hyde, 42-3.
18. Keyes, 303, 305; Edwards, 97-8, 101-3; Cowan, 213.
19. Edwards, 227, 230.
20. Cowan, 164-5.
21. I am indebted to Commander Rex Young for this point.
22. Cowan, 177-8.
23. Summerfield, 139.
24. MacLaine, 182.
25. Summerfield, 152-4.
26. Ibid., 133-4.
27. WO 32/15772, 74 A.
28. Ibid., 45A; Ellis, 322.
29. WO 32/15722, *passim.*
30. WO 32/15722, 106A
31. I am indebted to Mr A. Roberts for this account; for the rest of the details I have used Ellis, 257; Ahrenfeldt, 216-9; Patient, *Report of the Select Committee for the Army and Air Force Act* (1953), App. B; *Hansard,* 22 March 1982; *The Times,* 24 February 1982, and a letter from R.S. Merton (*Daily Telegraph,* 5 June 1961).
32. Ahrenfeldt, 219-20; Kirsch, 153 ff.
33. Ibid.; Tuker, 84-5.
34. WO 32/15772, 74A, 93A.
35. Tuker, 86.
36. Summerfield, 139.
37. ADM 116/5088 (General report and telegrams relating to Greek naval mutiny).
38. Macmillan, 545.
39. Matthews, 76.

6. RED COAT AND GREEN FLAG

1. The courts martial on the men involved are as follows: *Caesar* ADM 1/5346 (7 September 1798); *Defiance,* Ibid. (8 September 1798); *Captain,* ADM 1/5347 (5 December 1798); *Glory* (11 October 1798).

2. ADM 1/5351 (30 September 1799).
3. ADM 1/5348 (7 January 1799).
4. Elliot, 140-2.
5. Spencer, II, 119-20.
6. ADM 1/5348 (7 January 1799).
7. WO 92/2, f.125.
8. Pollock, 26.
9. For Casement's activities in Germany, Gwynn, 273 ff.
10. Pollock, *passim*.
10. Perret and Lord, 43.
11. For the Rangers mutiny see Pollock, *passim*.
12. Richards, 143.

7. SHADOW OF MEERUT

1. Willcocks, 282.
2. Morgan, *passim*.
3. I am indebted to the late General Sir Ouvry Roberts for this point.
4. Younghusband, 5.
5. Rawlinson, 49.
6. Mason, 348-9.
7. Prendergast, 56-7.
8. I am indebted to the late General Sir Ouvry Roberts for this observation.
9. Willcocks, xiii.
10. Mason, 406-7.
11. This account is based on Dickinson, Brown, Beckett, WO 32/9560 and WO 106/1413.
12. WO 106/401.
13. Ullman, I, 204.
14. Lewis.
15. WO 106/413 (3 September 1916).
16. Thorne, 157.
17. Ibid., 8-9.
18. Wavell, 23.
19. Spector, 281.
20. Indian Tales &c (BBC).
21. Thorne, 696*n*.
22. This account is taken from Spector; Kisch, 136-41; Tuker, 85-88.

8. GALLANT BLACKS FROM TOGOLAND

1. Austin, xvi.
2. L. James, 250.
3. Ibid.
4. CO 318/350.
5. WO 32/4349.
6. L. James, 253.
7. Killingray, 49.
8. Page, 88.
9. CO 318/347.
10. Andrew, *passim*.
11. Killingray in, *JAH*, 23, 89.
12. WO 106/259.
13. This account is based on Austin and official report (WO 32/8417).
14. WO 90/5 f.108.
15. This account is based on the official report (WO32/4349).
16. WO 95/83 (10 July 1917).
17. Ibid. (6 January 1917).
18. Brugger, *passim*.
19. WO 95/5008 (Disciplinary Military Labour Corps: 13 April 1918-26 July 1918).
20. WO 95/83 (4-5 September 1917).
21. WO 95/4018 (7 September 1917).
22. WO 95/83 (5 September 1917).
23. WO 95/4018 (10-12 September 1917).
24. Babington, 226-7.
25. WO 95/4018 (16 December 1917).
26. WO 95/4204 (DAD Labour: 31 December 1918).
27. WO 95/4018 (25-28 February 1918).
28. WO 95/4725 (Lines of Communication: Provost Marshal: 5 January 1918).
29. WO 95/83 (21 September 1917).
30. I am indebted to the Revd Richard Willcox for this detail which he heard from a parishioner in Rochdale.
31. CO 123/296, 65699, Appendix.
32. CO 318/347, 18447.
33. Ibid.
34. Ibid., 51686 (Letter from Roland Green, 25 October 1918).
35. Page, 98-9.
36. CO 123/296, 65699, Appendix.
37. CO 318/347, 12932.
38. CO 884/13, p. 18.

39. CO 123/296, 65699.
40. CO 318/347.
41. Steevens, 12-13.
42. WO 32/6383 (Report of Khartoum Mutiny).
43. Ibid.
44. C. Gwynn, Chapter 7; Cantlie, *passim*.

ENVOI: MUTINY PAST AND PRESENT

1. WO 32/15772.
2. Keane, letter of 23 November 1832.
3. ADM 1/12020.
4. Montmorency, 319.
5. Western, 427-8.
6. Lewin, 262.
7. I am indebted to Lieutenant-Commander Hallam for these and the subsequent points.
8. WO 32/15497.
9. *Observer*, 3 March 1986.

INDEX

Abbeville, 91, 93, 253, 255
Acasta, HMS, 35
Adamant, HMS, 52-3
Admiralty, 25*n*, 29, 31, 43, 52, 53, 54, 55-6, 57-65 *passim*, 70, 74, 156, 157, 160, 162, 163, 164, 166, 272
African troops, 20, 243-53, 257, 263-8
Albanaise, HMS, 44-5
Alexander, A.V., 162
Alexander, Gen. Sir H., 172
Alexandria, 179, 180, 182
Allenby, F-M Lord, 266-7
Apostolis, HHMS, 181
Archangel, N. Russia, 122-3, 126, 127, 128, 130, 132, 136, 137, 138, 139, 142-3, 144, 154
Army Bureau of Current Affairs, 168
Army Education Corps, 168
Army Ordnance Corps, 108-12
Army Psychiatry Unit, 170
Army Service Corps, *see* Royal Army Service Corps
Army Welfare Committees, 175
Articles of War, 35, 41, 51, 58, 74
Ashley, Thomas, 39
Ashmore, Maj.-Gen. E.B., 113-4
Askwith, Sir George, 113
Asquith, H.H., 199
Asser, Lt-Gen. Sir J., 91, 92, 98
Atbara, 266

Auchinleck, Gen. Sir C., 238
Audacious, HMS, 56
Audruicq, 256
Australian and New Zealand forces, 24, 30, 85-8, 89-90, 114
Averof, HHMS, 179
Aylmer, Capt., 195

Barr, Capt., 148-9
Barrington-Wells, Col., 148
Basset, Maj. Sam, 164-5
Bath, 14
Battenberg, Adm. Prince Louis, 29
Beatty, Adm. Lord, 159
Beavan, Capt., 149
Bellerophon, HMS, 56
Blake, John, 47
Blargies Military Prison, 84, 85, 118
Blatchford, Robert, 83
Boer War, 82, 85
Bombay, 233, 234, 238
Boulogne, 255
Bounty, HMS, 12, 13, 274
Brady, John, 194-5
Bridport, Adm. Lord, 53-5, 61, 63
British Honduras, riots in, 260-1
Brownlow, Col., 225
Bruce, Capt., 41
Buraimi oasis, 274
Burke, Edmund, 46
Burroughs, Lt-Col., 247, 250-2
Byng, Gen. Sir J., 111, 112

295

Fagg, AB Len, 161
Fenians, 197-9
Ferret, HMS, 13, 46, 71-3, 74
Feilding, Maj.-Gen. G.P.T., 105, 114
Fifth (Native) Light Infantry, 7, 20, 21, 215, 216, 219, 220-7, 228
Field punishments, 31, 82-4, 85, 86, 89, 98
Fleming, John, 46-7
Flogging, 25, 31, 42
French, F-M Lord, 202
French, Lt, 64
French Army, in Russia, 128, 135, 136
Frost, Lt, 64

Gadaffi, Col. Muammar, 275
Galloway, James, 39-40
Gardner, Adm. Sir Alan, 54-5
Ghadrite movement, 218-9, 221
Gilbert, William, 51-2
Glory, HMS, 41, 185, 191, 192, 194, 195
Gough, Brig.-Gen. Hubert, 200
Greece, 177-8
Greek army, 177, 179-81, 181-3
Greek navy, 177, 179-81
Grey, Thomas, 71-2
Grogan, Brig.-Gen. G.W. St G., 137, 148
Guinness, Capt., 90
Guthrie, William, 39-40
Gwynn, Maj.-Gen. Charles, 264, 267

Haig, F-M Lord, 14, 79, 80, 81-2, 85, 86, 97, 98-9, 110-13, 253
Hallifax, Capt. O.E., 162
Hanning, Lt-Gen., 168
Harwood, Adm. Sir Henry, 179-80, 181, 182
Haughty, HMS, 51-2, 66, 67
Hawes, Pte Joseph, 203

Hayes, John, 49
Healy, A.J., 90
Hephaistos, HHMS, 181
Herbert, Sidney, 29
Hermione, HMS, 13, 44, 45-6, 48, 49, 65, 67-70, 71, 73
Highland Division (51st), 171-3
Holford, Thomas, 48-9, 68
Home Counties, disturbances in, 103-6
Hong Kong and Singapore Artillery, 10, 233-4
Hopkins, John, 194
Horne, Gen. Sir Henry, 100
Horwood, Brig.-Gen. W.T.F., 92
Hoskyns, Lt-Cdr, 162
Hotham, Capt., 52
Howard, John, 194
Howe, Adm. Lord, 48, 53, 56-7, 61
Hussar, HMS, 30, 45
Hyde, Douglas, 161

Ierax, HHMS, 181
Impéteux, HMS, 63
Incitement to Disaffection Act, 17
Incitement to Mutiny Act, 17
Independent Labour Party, 96
Indian Army, 29, 209-37 *passim*, 240; subversion, 216-7
Indian National Army (INA), 213, 235-7
Indian nationalism, 228-41 *passim*
Inflexible, HMS, 47, 48
Invergordon, 9-10, 14, 21, 138, 155, 162, 163-6, 167, 175
Ireland, 19, 44, 186-202 *passim*
Irish nationalism, 65, 197-202 *passim*
Ironside, F-M Lord, 123, 125, 126, 127, 128, 129, 132, 133, 134-5, 136, 142, 146, 148, 150, 152

Jackal, HMS, 12
Jacobin agitation in Britain, 19,